HERE
WITH
YOU

A MEMOIR OF LOVE, FAMILY, AND ADDICTION

Douglas & McIntyre

HERE WITH YOU

KATHY WAGNER

Douglas & McIntyre (2013) Ltd.
P.O. Box 219, Madeira Park, BC, VON 2HO
www.douglas-mcintyre.com

Edited by Rachel Rose
Cover photo by Leigh-Anne Franklin
Cover and text design by Setareh Ashrafologhalai
Printed and bound in Canada

Printed on 100% recycled paper

Douglas & McIntyre acknowledges the support of the Canada Council
for the Arts, the Government of Canada, and the Province of British
Columbia through the BC Arts Council.

Library and Archives Canada Cataloguing in Publication

Title: Here with you : a memoir of love, family, and addiction /
Kathy Wagner.
Names: Wagner, Kathy (Writer on grief), author.
Identifiers: Canadiana (print) 20230441920 | Canadiana (ebook)
20230441939 | ISBN 9781771623667
     (softcover) | ISBN 9781771623674 (EPUB)
Subjects: LCSH: Kroeker, Tristan, died 2017—Drug use. | LCSH:
Wagner, Kathy (Writer on grief)—
     Family. | LCSH: Drug addicts—Family
relationships—Canada—Biography. | LCSH: Drug addicts—Canada—
     Biography. | LCSH: Mothers and sons—Canada—Biography. |
LCSH: Parents of drug addicts—Canada—
     Biography. | LCSH: Sons—Drug use—Canada—Biography. | LCSH:
Sons—Death—Psychological aspects. |
     LCSH: Parental grief—Psychological aspects. | LCSH: Cocaine
abuse. | LCGFT: Autobiographies. |
     LCGFT: Biographies.
Classification: LCC HV5805.K76 W34 2023 | DDC 362.29092—dc23

*To every parent who has been
challenged to let their child walk
their own path, however painful,
while finding meaning in their own.*

AUTHOR'S NOTE

I HAVE used the real names of my son, Tristan, my daughters, Jenn and Tanis, my son-in-law, Damyen, and my cousin, Kimiko. The martial arts instructors, Master Lee and Shifu Wang, also retain their real names. The names of all other people in this book, and the addiction treatment centres mentioned, have been changed.

I've tried to tell my story with as much honesty as possible, but we each see through a different lens and memory is faulty. This is nobody's story but my own.

I

FOR LOVE
OF TRISTAN

I

MY FEET nestled happily between a faux-fur throw blanket and my husband's thighs. On the small TV across the room, thousands of balloons were lifting an old curmudgeon and his house upwards toward his dreams, when my phone rang.

I paused the movie.

"Hello?"

The voice sounded young and innocent and scared. I didn't recognize it.

"Um . . . can you come get Tristan? He's not . . . okay."

In one breath I was standing, blanket tossed aside, heading for my coat.

"What happened?"

She told me they were drinking, and Tristan wasn't well. He was sick and couldn't stand up.

"Where are you?"

In the park a few minutes from my house, she said.

"I'm on my way," I told her, dropping the house phone onto the pile of backpacks and gym bags by the door.

"I'll drive you," my husband said, when I told him what happened.

Early Christmas lights felt out of place as we drove through the cold darkness, cheerful sparkles taunting me with cozy fires and hot chocolate. But not for us. Not tonight. Instead, I focused on the tail lights ahead and tried to calm my mind. Tristan was my youngest, fourteen years old, too moody to be labelled an easy child, but the easiest of my three at the time. He'd been the least of my problems. Until now.

Pulling into the park, I saw four teenagers huddled near the volleyball nets where the girl on the phone said they'd be. A body lay on the ground. I jumped from the truck and raced over, giving the teens a fleeting glance before kneeling beside Tristan. Wet grass soaked my jeans. He was shaking. *Was he having a seizure?* I saw froth at his mouth and panicked. Tragedy raced through my mind like certainty: brain damage, paralysis, death.

"Tristan!" I shouted, shaking his shoulder.

My husband, Scott, squatted beside me and, when Tristan didn't respond, carried him to the truck without a single snarky word about my wayward teen. I was grateful for that.

Resisting the urge to follow, I turned to the group of kids. "What drugs did he take?" I asked, trying to look non-judgemental, but serious. I needed them to tell me the truth, and quickly.

"Nothing, I swear," said a pimply boy in a bomber jacket. "I don't think so anyway. We were just drinking. We had some beer and some vodka. That's it."

"And we smoked a bit of weed," a girl with thick eyeliner piped in. She sounded like the voice on the phone. "Nothing bad."

They looked concerned and relatively sober. My gut said they were telling the truth, but I didn't know these kids.

"Thank you for calling me," I said to the girl, sincerely, and hurried to the truck.

Scott drove us to our local hospital, only ten minutes away. I sat in the back with Tristan, my hand on his shoulder. He remained semi-conscious, and I focused on taking deep breaths in, deep breaths out, trying to stay calm. *Needing* to be calm, so I could be ready. For whatever.

At the emergency department, two paramedics managed to load him into a wheelchair. I grabbed the chair's push handles while Scott held onto Tristan to keep him upright. As we were wheeling away, one of the paramedics laughed and said, almost under his breath, "Have a good life, buddy!"

I wasn't sure what I'd heard. Were they ridiculing my fourteen-year-old child? Fury flashed hot within me, but I didn't slow my pace. I tightened my grip on the wheelchair's handles and pushed Tristan inside.

Scott left us at the registration desk and returned a few minutes later.

"I just gave that paramedic no small piece of my mind," he told me. "I couldn't help myself, there's no excuse for that kind of comment. I told him if that's how he felt about the young patients he brought in, he should find another line of work. I'm sorry you had to hear that."

My tension eased, and I remembered why I loved Scott.

The ER doctors suspected Tristan had alcohol poisoning but ran a full drug screen to see if he'd taken anything else we needed to worry about. Need or not, worry had seeped into my body, churning my stomach to the point of nausea, but my mind remained calm and clear. I stood beside my son's bed and breathed deeply, ready and waiting for the next thing that had to be done, the next decision to be made. Scott sat on a chair, holding a coffee he wasn't drinking.

Eventually, Tristan began to come around. A nurse with a no-nonsense look gave him a firm shake.

"Hello, son." Her voice boomed as if she were addressing a deaf old man. "What's your name?"

"Tristan," he muttered.

"Mm-hmm. And what year is it, Tristan?"

"Two thousand and nine."

"That's right, it is. Do you know where you are, Tristan?"

He lifted his head and looked around, looked at me, and then back to the nurse. "Looks like a hospital," he said, then closed his eyes and flopped his head back down.

Such relief! If he was already this coherent, I knew he'd be fine. He was in a good hospital. He was getting the medical care he needed. He'd be okay, for now. What I didn't know was what this heralded for his future.

I stood by his bed, stroking his arm, needing to feel connected with him. I worried he was following in his oldest sister's footsteps, running into a world of parties and school-be-damned.

The nurse had stripped Tristan down to his boxers to make sure there were no injuries. He flailed and his boxers flapped open, leaving his private parts not so private anymore. I draped a blanket over him.

Finally, his test results came back: there was only alcohol in Tristan's system and a small amount of THC, the active ingredient in marijuana. No other drugs. And, while he was seriously drunk, he was nowhere near the point of alcohol poisoning.

"It's unusual to see that kind of physical reaction to the amount of alcohol he consumed," the doctor told me. "But," she paused, glancing over at Tristan, "some people are just more sensitive than others. We'll give him IV fluids until he's up and about—that might help with his hangover tomorrow—but he'll be absolutely fine."

Apparently, Tristan's body was as sensitive as his emotions. I remembered how, as a toddler, he'd crawl into my lap every evening for story time, soothing himself by stroking the skin under my chin— my dewlap, we called it. And how he'd give his sisters gifts when they were sad, wrapping his favourite toy car or dinosaur inside a sock patterned with stars or teddy bears or rainbows. Then he'd ask me to tie it with a ribbon so it would be a "proper" present. As a child, he gave and received love abundantly, but if anyone raised their voice to him, for any reason, he'd flop on the ground and scream like he'd been shot in the heart. As a teen, he'd developed some control over his expression of emotion. But only some.

In the wee hours of the morning, Scott and I took Tristan home. We drove past the park where we'd picked him up hours earlier, and my mind continued to wander. When I'd first separated from the kids' dad, I'd been thrilled to find subsidized housing across the street from this park. My children had grown up here: they'd played in the splash park on hot summer days, brought their favourite stuffed animals to the Teddy Bear Picnic in the spring, tried out new skateboards on the gentle slopes of the skate park—always safe with their helmets and knee pads securely in place. Those were hard days as a single mom with three young children, but I suddenly missed the innocence of those pre-teen years.

At home, I put Tristan to bed and left orange juice and Tylenol on his bedside table. *This is a young teen's mistake*, I told myself. He'd never done anything like this before and surely it wasn't something he'd want to repeat. I went to bed, lights off, feigning exhaustion as my mind reeled. I didn't want to see the look on Scott's face.

Our marriage had been limping along for some time. A month before, barely a year after we got married, we'd moved into separate homes and decided to only spend weekends together. Scott thought I let my three kids run wild and disrespect me. I thought he had no clue how to parent, and no sensitivity to the challenges of raising difficult teens. We both were right. Separating was our creative attempt to save a failing marriage. But I knew this late-night fiasco with Tristan would fan the flames of Scott's righteous indignation, so I turned over and held myself close, a single tear tracing its way to the pillow.

I had hoped this marriage would be different from my previous two: my first, a youthful mistake, and the second, a fifteen-year dance of blind love and self-sacrifice that gave me my kids. And it *was* different, in many ways. Scott was not abusive or obsessive. He was financially stable, though our finances were separate so that was no benefit to me. He had no trust issues, so I wasn't constantly fielding questions about where I was or who I was with. I was not scared of him. But I had wanted more from our marriage. I had hoped we could provide my kids with a relationship blueprint they could follow, an example of healthy love, strength and endurance.

In the end, it seemed, this marriage wasn't so very different from the others. I was still alone while my partner slept beside me, a million miles away.

THE NEXT evening, Scott came to visit, but he refused to talk to, or even acknowledge, Tristan.

"What's that all about?" I asked as Tristan retreated, grumbling, to his room.

"I told him I have no interest in speaking to him until he apologizes sincerely. He can't pull that kind of stunt and pretend it never happened."

"He isn't pretending," I said. "We've talked about it. He says he learned that alcohol doesn't agree with him, so that's a good thing. And of course he's sorry, and embarrassed. But he's barely fourteen and struggling with fitting in and making friends at high school. He's floundering. Don't you think he needs a strong relationship with you now, more than ever?"

"Unconditional love is your thing, not mine," Scott told me. "Someone needs to teach the kid there are consequences." He smoothed his goatee, kicked off his Blundstones and sat down on the couch.

I let the subject drop but wasn't happy with it. Or him.

After a while, Tristan walked into the living room where we were talking and, perhaps realizing that Scott was infinitely more stubborn than he was, mumbled, "Sorry."

"What's that?" Scott asked. "I didn't hear you."

Tristan turned, looking at a spot off to the side of Scott, and said again, louder this time, "I'm sorry. You wanted me to say sorry, so I am."

I watched them both, knowing this was a crucial moment. I saw what it cost Tristan to apologize. I saw his shame and his desperate hope for reparation warring with his fear of rejection. I was proud he'd made this effort and held my breath for Scott's response.

All Scott saw was belligerence.

"That's not good enough. I'm not feeling it," Scott said. "After what you put your mom through? After her having to see you with your balls hanging out, frothing at the mouth? Nope, I don't accept that apology." He stared at Tristan, looking disgusted.

"Fuck. Whatever, man. I tried." Tristan shot an icy glare at Scott and went back to his room to be alone with his hurt and shame.

"What the fuck, Scott?" I yelled. "He apologized! That was way out of line."

"No, I *drew* a line, Kathy. Your kids can't keep pulling these bullshit stunts, offer bogus apologies, and think everything is fine. It isn't. You shouldn't have had to see him like that."

"Scott, he's not Jenn. He hasn't messed up before. And it's not your place to decide what I should or shouldn't have to see from my kids. They're *my* kids!"

"Well, you don't seem capable of managing them and I'm not prepared to stand aside and let them trample all over you."

I paused to catch my breath and think carefully before saying something I couldn't take back. "Scott," I said, looking directly at him, "Tristan is having a difficult time right now and your hardnosed attitude is hurtful, not helpful. He needs a strong male role model, yes, but he also needs compassion and understanding. If you can't offer that to him, then you can't be around him."

We stared at each other, at a crossroads in our relationship, painfully aware of what was on the line.

Finally, Scott nodded. "Then I guess I won't be around him."

And that was that.

Over the next few days, Scott and I agreed that, for the most part, we'd only see each other when the kids were at their dad's. Knowing that my kids wouldn't miss Scott gave me some comfort. Jenn, my oldest, hated Scott even more than he disliked her. My middle child, Tanis, was polite but indifferent to him. And Tristan, who had once yearned for Scott's love and attention, had finally given up—as had I. We would never live up to Scott's expectations of the happy, functional family he wanted us to be. It would be easier without him.

But, easier, I knew, would not mean easy.

THE FOLLOWING weekend, I sat cross-legged on the couch, laptop on my legs, staring at a spreadsheet showing my projected income and expenses in neat little rows and columns. Could I afford to take a free ten-week program designed for people who wanted to start their own business? Or did I need to get a job—*any* job—now? Less than two months earlier, just weeks before Scott and I had moved apart, the recession had finally got up close and personal and I'd lost my job as a customer experience researcher at a major bank.

I set my laptop aside and scooped up our cat, Balloo, who consoled me with a meagre purr.

So many changes in the past couple of months. Within weeks of losing my job, and only days after moving apart from my husband, my fifteen-year-old daughter, Tanis, had been diagnosed with Type

1 diabetes. Despite my rocky marriage, despite moving into a rather rundown rental, and despite truly worrisome joblessness, Tanis's health was the only thing that concerned me for a full month after her diagnosis. I asked the kids' dad, Brad, to take Jenn and Tristan for a while so I could focus on caring for Tanis. He lived five minutes away and was happy to help. I learned how and when to prick Tanis's finger to test her blood sugar levels, how to give insulin and how much to give. I planned and cooked meals with specific amounts of carbohydrates, fibre, and sugar, and spent many nights hovering over my sleeping girl, endlessly awed by her cherubic face. I needed to be by her side in case she slipped into a diabetic coma. It worried me that she let me hover as much as she did: it was testimony to how sick she felt.

But not for long. Within a few weeks, she was talking with her healthcare team, rather than me, about insulin pumps and injections and food. She ditched my carefully balanced school lunches to grab her own favourites, as she had for years. She told me to stop coming into her room at night: it creeped her out. It was her body, she told me, and her responsibility. And she was right.

Jenn and Tristan came home and I got on with my life. I studied job listings every day, but there was nothing available in either customer experience or technical communications, which had been my previous career. Now was the perfect time to launch myself as a freelance consultant, but it would be a long road: my savings were sparse, and the cost of diabetic supplies was high. The numbers didn't look good.

I took a sip of tea. Dido's voice rose from my CD player and soothed me as I stared through the rain-smeared window to the darkness.

"Mom?" I turned to see Tristan poke his head tentatively through the doorway. "Is Scott here?"

I shook my head. "Nope, not tonight. He won't be around much anymore."

Tristan plopped himself on the couch beside me. "Is that my fault?" he asked. "Did I screw things up for you?"

"No, sweetie, Scott screwed things up for himself," I said, and gave him a quick pat on the leg. "You only did what many kids your age do. You fucked up, no doubt about it. Hopefully you learned something." I shot him a serious Mom glare. "But Scott doesn't deal very well with that stuff, so . . . he doesn't need to be part of it."

Tristan flashed a mischievous smile. "He does have a bit of a stick up his bum, doesn't he?"

"Tristan!" I said, landing somewhere between a scold and a laugh.

He picked up my laptop and set it on the coffee table. Laying his head in my lap, he placed my hands on his head and looked up, his big grin encouraging me.

I began massaging his head. His blond hair was cut short, buzzed in the back and sides. I loved running my fingers over the fuzziness of it and feeling my worries subside. Tristan was such a physical kid, so much snugglier than the girls. He and I had always connected through touch, and I felt my shoulders soften as I gently massaged his temples, then up through the crown and down to the nape of his neck. He made purring sounds like Balloo.

Then our peace shattered.

"Oh my god, Mom, you have to do something about your demon witch-child! She stole my new sweater . . . *again*!" Tanis yelled, a fuming ball of energy in the living room doorway. "Where is she? I'm going to kill that thieving, sneaking be-otch!"

At barely five feet tall, Tanis had a naturally soft voice. She looked as dangerous as an angry kitten, puffed up and hissing, but with her short fuse and strong temper, she required careful handling.

"Tanis, how do you know Jenn took it? Your room's a disaster, I'd be surprised if you could find anything." I continued to run my fingers in circles over Tristan's head.

"Mom, I know exactly where everything is, and where my sweater was, and where it isn't anymore. Why do you always take Jenn's side? I'm so tired of this." Tears filled her eyes.

I wanted to wrap my arms around her and tell her how much I cared, but I'd learned from experience she wasn't ready to hear that. I tapped Tristan's head to get him to sit up so I could give Tanis my full attention.

"I swear, Mom, if you don't punish Jenn this time, I'm going to go live with Dad. I won't stay in a house where Jenn can steal from me whenever she wants and get away with it."

"Well, she's not home right now. If she took your sweater, I'll get it back for you, I promise." Sometimes that worked to prevent Tanis from taking matters into her own hands, which usually ended in a physical fight and everything pulled out of closets and drawers before Jenn, inevitably, gave up the stolen goods.

"Geez Mom, you could ground her or something!"

I met Tanis's glare with my own, eyebrows raised and hands in the air, and just shook my head. No words came to me, but I hoped I conveyed a sense of *I know, you're right, and I wish there was something I could do about it, but there isn't, and you know that.* I never understood what parents could do with kids who wouldn't stay grounded. What power did I have to curb Jenn's behaviour when she wouldn't follow any rules I set? She was seventeen. I couldn't lock her in her room indefinitely.

Tanis roared a final burst of anger, stomped to her room and slammed her door.

I sat in the futility of the moment. My heart hurt. Tanis was right; I was inept. I couldn't control Jenn, and it wasn't fair to Tanis, or any of us. All I could do was minimize the damage Jenn caused until she grew out of her troublesome phase. It was a poor excuse for a plan, and I felt like a poor excuse for a parent.

Dido's voice broke through my melancholy and wrapped itself around me. She was singing about a good heart hidden behind tired eyes and a weary life. *I'm with you, Dido,* I thought, and reached for my chamomile tea. It was stone cold.

"Mom? You okay?" Tristan was still beside me on the couch. The concern in his eyes warmed me. "Here," he said, moving over and laying a cushion between us. "Put your head down."

I lay my head beside him and felt his strong fingers massage away the roughest edges of my stress. Relaxing into this simple connection with him, I listened for the front door to open, knowing I needed to hear Jenn's entrance before Tanis did.

2

THE NEXT eighteen months proved that Tristan's lapse of judgement was not a one-time affair. He had, indeed, learned that alcohol didn't agree with him. Instead, he turned to drugs.

Toward the end of Tristan's Grade 9 year, his principal called me into the office. After Jenn's final year of high school, the year before, we were on first-name terms.

"Kathy." He said my name like a sigh, as I sat on the blue plastic chair beside his desk, the same chair Jenn had sat on to do her schoolwork on so very many days.

"Hi, Derek. Is something going on with Tristan?" It wasn't the first time I'd been called in to talk about my son.

"Nothing new, no. But I gotta tell you, I spent so much time with Jenn last year trying to manage her truancy and get her through to graduation, I don't have the energy to do that again with another of your kids. Tristan's a good boy at heart, I see that. But between his skipping classes and smoking weed on school grounds, I just don't think he's heading in the right direction." He paused and shuffled some papers on his desk before looking up at me again. "I've decided that Tristan is not welcome back here next year. You're going to have to find a different place for him."

Tristan had shown no behaviours at school that Jenn had not, but his consequences were much more severe. I was disgusted by what I saw as gender inequity: a middle-aged man giving the benefit of the doubt to a pretty girl but cutting a troubled boy no slack.

I had no job to constrain me, so I decided to move six hours north to the small, close-knit community of 70 Mile House. I thought it might be better for Tristan and it was certainly more affordable for me. Tristan happily chopped wood and mended fences, and quickly made friends with the boys next door, who took him out on their ATVs and to practice target shooting. Even though Jenn had stayed back with her dad and Tanis grumbled about the endless chores associated with rural living, my heart was happy seeing Tristan thrive.

Then school started. Tristan met different boys. Before Christmas, I got a call from his new principal. Tristan had been found with cocaine and drug paraphernalia in his locker. He was expelled immediately.

With Tristan kicked out of school, and Tanis informing me she'd move to her dad's rather than stay in "this Hicksville, deep-freeze hellhole" through winter, I moved back to our old neighbourhood in town. Tristan lasted a bit longer at his next school—long enough for me to attend a parent-teacher interview and hear glowing accounts of his kindness and curiosity, to see perfect attendance and a string of As and Bs on his report card, to feel my heart swell with pride and hope again.

Then the call came.

Tristan had been selling weed to students in the park across from the school. I advocated strongly for him to remain at that school—where he was focused and interested and doing so well—to no avail. He was sent to an alternative school for at-risk youth. He wouldn't be kicked out again. There was nowhere they could kick him to.

I hated the label "at-risk youth." At risk of what? Not walking a perfectly straight line between middle school and a prestigious university? If he hadn't been at risk of that before, he certainly was now.

In my experience, teenagers used drugs. I was thirteen when I first smoked pot—my best friend Leigha and I discovered how hilarious it was to deliberately, repeatedly fall into bushes and pick ourselves up again. While I had limited myself to pot-smoking and beer, with the odd Southern Comfort fiasco thrown in, everyone else

I grew up with used harder drugs at one time or another. We all grew out of it. Tristan's biggest fault was in being so blatant about it.

At least that was what I thought until I saw him watch a TV show.

On a Saturday afternoon a few months after Tristan began going to the alternative school, Tanis turned the TV on to the show *Intervention*. She sat feet-up on the couch watching a family's tragedy unfold while she untangled her math problems for Monday. I was at the dining room table, on my laptop, working on a resumé for Jenn so she could get a second part-time job. Tristan, now fifteen, was draped sideways over an armchair, Balloo on his lap. He was far more interested in brushing the cat's fur than watching TV.

I was adding details about Jenn's most recent stint as a sales associate, when I was distracted by Tanis waving her arms to get my attention. As I glanced at her, questioning, she pointed at Tristan and silently mouthed the words, "What the ...?"

I looked over. No longer lounging in the chair, Tristan's feet were firmly planted on the ground, elbows on his knees, as he leaned forward, rapt, watching an emaciated man smoke heroin. On the screen, the man nodded off, then woke and ranted incoherently before falling over in a pile of filth. Tristan's eyes never wavered, never blinked; they were locked on the TV as if he were being walked through life's how-to manual and he didn't want to miss a thing. His face was alight, glowing, like he was watching porn, like he'd found his life's purpose. He exuded pure rapture.

I watched Tristan watch the TV until the drug scene ended and Tristan blinked, sat back, and seemed to physically deflate. He showed no interest in what happened next. Instead of sticking around for the intervention or rehab scenes, he wandered off to his room to do who knows what.

Tanis and I stared at each other, appalled, unable to form words to describe what we'd witnessed. My heart was beating like I'd run a mile and I felt sick to my stomach as I realized a world of worry was fast approaching.

So many things had gotten better in the past year and a half. Scott was around the kids less, and we had reconnected more as friends.

I was working as an independent consultant and earning enough money to pay the bills. Jenn was becoming more human every day and Tanis had installed a lock on her bedroom door. Tristan was struggling but nothing he had done, until now, had set my alarm bells ringing in such a critical way: not the fact that he was on his fourth school in less than two years, or the many nights he didn't come home, or the times he disappeared for a whole weekend. Not even his frequently dilated pupils, the smell of weed wafting around him like bad cologne, or him admitting he sometimes did cocaine and shrugging it off like it's what every fifteen-year-old did. I'd wanted to dismiss these things as a phase, as I had for Jenn. I'd wanted to believe he'd grow out of it, as so many people I knew had. I had told myself he was a sensitive boy who just needed more confidence, more self-esteem. He just needed to know he was loved. And he was *so* loved, he was sure to be fine.

Wasn't he?

After seeing him watch that show, I could no longer pretend he would be. I could no longer believe Tristan was a normal teenager who'd respond to drugs in a normal way. I saw his brain working differently and knew instantly, without doubt, that drugs could never be a passing phase for him. Drugs were his North Star and would lead him down a dark and tangled trail that ended nowhere—at least, nowhere good.

TRISTAN SOON stopped going to school altogether. He became angry or despondent much of the time. Having painfully accepted the reality of Tristan's dangerous relationship with drugs, I could not dismiss or deny the significance of this. I needed to do something to turn his life around while he still had a chance. But what?

I wondered about sending him to an addiction treatment centre. Was that an overreaction? It felt risky, so I decided to bounce the idea around with a few people.

"So, umm . . . I think I need to get Tristan into rehab," I blurted to my mom as I cut into my Shake-n-Bake pork chop. I had gone to her place for dinner specifically to have this conversation.

She looked a bit confused. "For drugs?"

I nodded. "He's destroying his life. I don't know how to get him to stop."

"But he's only fifteen," she said, passing me the sour cream for my potato. "How's that going to work? He needs to be in school."

I reminded her that he'd already stopped going to school.

"But rehab? Kathy, that's not something to do lightly. That will follow him through life. He's just a boy, not an addict. Maybe there's another way."

I knew that Mom was not averse to light drug use, on principle, any more than I was. Growing up, our home was designated party central, and beer and pot were the status quo on weekends through my early teenage years. She preferred to have my brothers and me, and our motley crew of friends, at home where we'd be safe and she could keep an eye on us. Nobody was drinking and driving. Everyone slept on the rec room floor, and we'd make a big brunch the next day.

Those times felt innocent, despite our lack of sobriety.

Yet my mom was not naïve. Two of her four siblings were alcoholics, one of them homeless. I also had a cousin in addiction, living on the street.

Other experiences had shaped me too. I'd chosen to live with my dad the year I was sixteen and had watched him stumble and slur his way through the evenings. I had to pretend not to notice, to show him the respect he deserved as an undisputedly brilliant cardiologist. My first love and first husband was an abusive nineteen-year-old alcoholic who was the son of an alcoholic mother. With him, I became a master of placation. The kids' dad, Brad, had grown up in a family ravaged by addiction: both parents alcoholics, one brother a cocaine addict and another a homeless heroin addict. He, along with one other brother, had wisely avoided drugs and alcohol, but the seeds of addiction still took hold: gambling in his brother's case, video games and overspending in Brad's.

I had seen firsthand that not all drug use was innocent, that addiction was volatile and devastating. My early experiences had given me an acceptance and tolerance of teenage drug use, but my later experiences had given me a ferocious fear of addiction.

"Have you talked to Brad about this? What does he think?" Mom asked, bringing me back to the present.

I told her that Tristan's dad didn't see treatment as a viable option: it hadn't worked for either of his brothers. "Honestly, Mom, Brad's just so exhausted with the whole thing. He doesn't agree with rehab but he doesn't have any better ideas either."

"And Scott? What does he think?"

I raised my eyebrows. "I haven't talked to him about it. He has no experience with this, and I don't need his oversimplified solutions." I told her I'd talked with my friend Leigha, and while she helped me to have a laugh, she didn't move me forward in a decision.

"Well," said Mom, "for what it's worth, I don't think it's a good idea. He's too young. He's already hanging around with the wrong crowd, and I don't think going to rehab will help him with that. Those places are full of drug addicts. Tristan will grow out of it, like Jenn. Our job is just to love him as much as we can."

I nodded but didn't agree. I was less concerned about Tristan going through life with the stigma of having attended a treatment centre than I was about where his unchecked drug use would take him. The school year was almost over and if Tristan wasn't attending classes, he wouldn't complete Grade 10 anyway. If he went to rehab over the summer, maybe he could catch up in the fall.

I went home that evening more determined than ever, a determination driven by a soul-deep knowing that defied reason. I just needed to do *something*.

I opened my laptop, searched for treatment centres and read reviews. The first thing I noticed was how different each centre seemed. Some were urban and community-based, others rural and surrounded by nature. Some seemed homey, others clinical, and some were boot camps. Some lasted a few weeks, others a few months. What they all had in common was a phenomenal price tag: tens of thousands of dollars, minimum. For some of them, you paid that price *each month*.

I didn't have that kind of money. I didn't have any money.

I had managed to set up my own business and land a good-paying contract a few months earlier, but I was still living paycheque to paycheque with no guarantee of future work. Still, money was a detail I could figure out later. I kept searching.

One place looked hopeful. Located in the Okanagan, in breathtakingly beautiful country only four hours away, it specialized in youth with addictions. Best of all, it had government-funded spots available.

The next day I phoned and asked to speak with an intake worker. I was transferred to a raspy-sounding woman who, without any preamble or greeting, began asking questions.

"What drugs does your son use, and how often?" she asked, sounding bored.

"Um, weed every day, all day," I said. "And cocaine when he can. I don't know how often. A few times a week, probably. And ecstasy. And anything else he can get his hands on. I don't think he has limits anymore."

"How long has he been using?"

"Since he turned fourteen, so a year and a half, but seriously for about eight months. That's when things started getting really bad."

"How has it negatively impacted his life?" She took a loud slurp of what I presumed to be coffee.

"Well, he's been kicked out of three different schools for using drugs. Now he's at an alternative school, where they can't kick him out, but he doesn't go to classes anymore. He barely goes through the motions in his taekwondo training, and that had been his life's passion. He disappears for days and is miserable when he's home. He doesn't seem to care about anything or anyone." I paused, thinking of how best to communicate how serious it was. "It's like my son's not here anymore, and there's a very scary and scared teenager in his place."

"Uh-huh. How does he feel about coming into treatment?"

"He doesn't want to. He doesn't think he has a problem."

"Oh," she said. "Well, we can't take him if he doesn't want to be here. Unless he chooses this, he won't connect with the program and do the work. It's just not worth our time when the beds can go to others who are more ready."

I paused to process her words. "But he needs help," I said. "He's only fifteen. A minor. He's clearly not thinking straight. He's not *able* to think straight. There must be something I can do. I'm his parent; he's my responsibility."

"Has he been arrested?" she asked in a monotone, as if a fifteen-year-old being arrested was no big deal.

"No!" I said. "He's not been in trouble. He's a good kid, except for the drugs."

"Has he had an overdose that required medical attention?" Another ho-hum, run-of-the mill question.

"No," I said quietly. "Well, maybe. When he was fourteen, I had to take him to the ER when he drank too much and couldn't stand up. He was shaking and frothing at the mouth. Does that count?"

"Did they pump his stomach or give him metadoxine?"

I had no idea what that was. "No. They gave him IV fluids and sent him home."

"Ma'am, kids overdrink all the time, that's not an overdose. Has he ever needed urgent medical care due to the use of other substances?"

"No." I realized it may have been better for him if he had.

The call wasn't going as I'd hoped. I stood from my desk and began pacing the cool linoleum of my kitchen floor. My mind raced, trying to find another angle that might produce a different result.

Her emotionless voice interrupted my thoughts. "If he had a police record or a history of overdose there are ways a parent can step in. If not, your son needs to agree to get treatment. I'm sorry, there's nothing I can do. You'll find it's the same everywhere."

I was livid. Tristan was a troubled kid, mentally ill from using drugs, and he got to make the call on his health care while I, a parent in her right mind, had no say? Did they *want* kids to get sick enough to overdose or break the law? For sure he was heading in that direction, but I thought the whole point was to avoid those things.

After I hung up, I phoned a dozen different treatment centres. Most of them didn't even take minors. I talked with two addiction support counsellors. They all had the same story: there was nothing I could do until Tristan wanted help. He needed to hit his goddamned, mystical rock bottom. *At fifteen*. Some people suggested kicking him out might expedite that process. Other, more compassionate souls wished me luck and suggested I try to look after myself.

Fuck them all. I needed to save my boy.

3

AT FIRST, I decided to challenge Tristan's drug use head-on. He would simply not be allowed to have, or do, drugs in my home. Period.

One afternoon when he was god knows where, I searched his room for evidence I could confiscate or accuse him with. On the shelf in his closet, beside his box of childhood photos, I discovered a bong and a pipe and a small metal can-like item with an embossed marijuana leaf on it. Inside an old backpack in the corner of his room was a sandwich-sized bag of weed. Scattered here and there, in the garbage can, under his bed, were tiny baggies. All empty, but some containing a residue of fine white powder. Used bus passes were rolled into narrow tubes.

I gathered the baggies with white residue and put them on the kitchen counter to confront him when he got home. I had a few glorious minutes watching the tight buds of weed swirl and disappear down the toilet into the sewer. I hoped they wouldn't harm some poor animal. I threw out the metal thing-a-ma-jiggy because it irritated me but I stopped short of trashing his bong and pipe. The bong looked expensive, and I knew it was important to Tristan. And the pipe? Well, I figured it might be good to show him I wasn't completely heartless. I'd tell him to take them to his dad's if he wanted to keep them.

Tristan did not appreciate my generosity.

"Holy fucking Christ, Mom, you fucking bitch!" he yelled, after seeing the empty bags on the counter. Then he ran to his room. I heard him crashing around and he came out a few minutes later, red-faced and puffing. "You went through my stuff, you cunt! You have no idea what you did. Where's my weed? So help me god, you better still have it!"

His language shocked me, but words were just words, I told myself. I'd been dodging the stinging blow of words my whole life and preferred Tristan's meaningless profanity to the clever, cutting cruelty my dad had hurled at my mom when I was young, before she left him. My dad's words held the power of a sharp, well-aimed stiletto to the heart—a bull's-eye every time—and I'd been pierced by them more than once. Tristan's were a rudimentary cudgel he brandished wildly, without thought or even reason. They were unpleasant, but easy to sidestep.

I looked him in the eye and shook my head. "Flushed," I said.

Looking like someone had punched him, he ran back to his room. More crashing and bashing and then he came out, his bong carefully wrapped in a towel and sticking up from his open backpack. His jacket was on.

"And you took my buster? What the fuck, Mom!" He looked at me like I was a disease-carrying cockroach. "I hate you. You can go die for all I care. The world would be better off without you."

The front door slammed behind him, and he was gone.

Good riddance, I thought, as I leaned against the kitchen counter, deflated. But my heart ached. I was acutely aware my boundary-setting hadn't gone as I'd hoped. I didn't believe for a split second that my raid on his bedroom would curtail his drug use, at home or anywhere else. It had just made him hate me.

I noticed Tanis standing in the hallway, looking at me, concerned.

I blinked back tears. "What's a buster?" I asked, my voice only a whisper.

"It's a bud buster, Mom," she said gently. "For breaking up weed."

I nodded my head as if I understood. But I didn't understand anything.

TRISTAN STAYED at his dad's for over a week and when he finally came home, he refused to speak with me.

I used that time to do some research.

A couple of weeks later, I was ready. I'd planned the night meticulously. It was early June. Jenn was at her boyfriend's and Tanis was at a friend's studying for an upcoming exam. It was just Tristan and me at home.

For the previous week, we'd had a semi-peaceful truce, both of us cautiously carrying on as if nothing had happened. On this evening, Tristan seemed sober and happy, and agreed to watch the new *Karate Kid* movie with me. He'd seen the original movie dozens of times and had watched all the movies in the series. Jackie Chan was his hero.

Most importantly, though, the movie was set in China and focused on a foreign kid learning kung fu.

That was my new plan for Tristan.

After my hope of getting Tristan into rehab was smashed, and my attempt at tough love failed, I spent days on the internet, trying to answer the question, *What now?* I had to get him away from his friends and the daily routine he'd built around drug use. I explored the idea of military-style boot camps for troubled teens but quickly dismissed that. Crushing his already tattered spirit certainly wouldn't benefit him. I knew that, whatever I wanted for him, he needed to agree or else he'd just go live with his dad. There'd be no forcing him. And the only thing he'd ever wanted passionately, aside from drugs, was to be a master martial artist. So that was where I started.

Tristan had been taking taekwondo classes since he was six, got his first black belt at twelve, and had spent five years as part of an elite demo team along with Jenn and Tanis. He and Tanis had just started a new black belt training cycle and were scheduled to test for their adult black belts in November—but only if Tristan could keep his shit together long enough.

My research hit a series of dead ends. Every program in North America was outrageously expensive, competitive, or did not offer residential options. And then one afternoon I stumbled across a blog post about someone's experience of kung fu training in China. That opened a whole new rabbit hole for me to dive into. There I found options, and eventually saw one teacher's name popping up again and again.

Shifu—the Chinese term for master or teacher—Wang was a Buddhist monk who had grown up in the Shaolin Temple and had quite a following among foreign students. He was currently teaching at a kung fu school in rural China, in the Kunyushen Mountains. His students described him as tough but fair, caring but never indulgent, intense but approachable. He didn't speak much English but communicated well with the stick he carried, using it to whack students or adjust their postures as needed. Nobody wanted to make Shifu Wang angry, yet they weren't scared of him. They respected him. And they all credited him with life-changing experiences.

I sent the school an email and learned that, yes, Shifu Wang was taking new students. They charged five thousand US dollars per year, which included training, room, and board. It felt right. It felt *perfect*. There were still mountains of problems to solve to get from here to there, like money, permission from Brad, and a thorough investigation of everything before sending Tristan, alone, to the opioid capital of the world. But the first step was getting my son on board.

I made popcorn. I closed the blinds to shut out the late evening sun. Tristan chatted about Jackie Chan's superhuman talents as we settled on either side of the couch, popcorn bowl between us. Balloo jumped up and demanded we feed him the puffy parts of the buttery popcorn—his favourite treat. The evening felt almost normal to me, like I was a normal mom hanging out with my normal teen, rather than acting out a highly orchestrated plan in the midst of our swirling sea of dysfunction. Still, I took it as a good sign that my plan came together and my son was here, miraculously pleasant.

Tristan didn't watch *Karate Kid* with the same intensity he had *Intervention*, but he was engaged, interested, inspired.

"Oh man, Mom, can you imagine how amazing it would be to study over there with someone like that?" Tristan said, when the movie ended. He was up and moving, stretching. Two hours of sitting was long for him. I watched his lean athletic body move with grace and power, and knew he was envisioning himself on the mat, winning tournaments.

"I wanted to talk to you about that. It may be possible," I said, calm and cautious, as if not to spook him.

He stopped and looked at me. "What are you talking about?"

"I've done some research. There are schools in China that take foreign students and train them—intensely—in kung fu. You're not really going to school here, so I looked into it. It could totally be an option for you, if you wanted."

His mood darkened, instantly. "What the fuck, Mom? That's why you wanted me to watch that movie? That's bullshit. I need to graduate high school. That's what you're always telling me, right?" He walked away, shaking his head, then turned around. "Besides, I do taekwondo. I don't want to do stupid kung fu and start at the beginning again." He headed to his room.

"Well, think about it," I said to the back of his head.

I was disappointed he hadn't taken the bait, but not surprised. Tristan hated change. He hated thoughts that derailed him. His first reaction was almost always to reject anything new. He needed to sit with an idea and imagine it, over and over again, until it didn't feel new anymore.

Now the seed was planted, his imagination would get to work.

And I would wait.

AS SUMMER progressed and Tristan's silence remained steadfast, I began to think that sending him to China was a pipe dream. But on a muggy August evening, about two months after we'd watched *Karate Kid*, Tristan found me in the kitchen cooking dinner.

"So, Mom, are you serious about China?" he asked.

I stopped chopping vegetables and looked at him. He sounded earnest and hesitant, unsure of my answer.

"Yes. Very serious. But there will be some rules around that," I said, trying to look stern as happiness welled up inside of me.

I wanted to yelp for joy at the possibilities ahead, but I held his gaze, unflinching.

"'Cause I want to go. So don't fuck with me if you're not serious."

Suddenly, I knew this was going to happen. I would get Tristan away from drugs and into the hard, physical training he seemed to respond so well to. "I've never been more serious," I said, and smiled with such relief and happiness it brought tears to my eyes.

He met my smile with a broader grin of his own. "So, then... does that mean I'm going to China?"

"Yup, I guess it does!" I was laughing now at the excitement and incredulity on his face.

"Holy shit!" He yelled, punching the air and spinning around. "I'm going to fucking China to learn kung fu! Nobody will believe this. *I* can't believe it!" His face glowed with something I hadn't seen in him for so long. It was more than excitement. It was passion, hope, adventure. And pride. "With a kung fu master, right? A Shaolin monk?" he asked.

"Yup," I grinned. "Absolutely."

"But after my black belt, okay? I want to get that first, and that will get me in shape for training over there."

"Deal," I said.

"Fuckin' eh. I'm doing it. I'm going to China!" He wrapped me in a bear hug, lifting me off my feet, crushing the breath out of me.

I breathed him in—weed, tobacco, and Tristan—kissed his fuzzy cheek, and said, "Yes you are. You're doing it."

We both grinned like maniacs as we chopped the salad vegetables, together.

I knew then that our connection, though tattered, wasn't broken—that Tristan, though struggling, wasn't lost.

4

WITH TRISTAN finally excited about studying kung fu in China, I hoped to re-establish control in my home. I decided to set new boundaries and stick to them. Tristan would surely grumble but I figured he'd follow my rules for a few short months rather than jeopardize his opportunity for adventure. And my rules were simple: he needed to go to school, follow his training plan for his black belt and, most importantly, not use ecstasy or cocaine or any hard drugs. Tristan negotiated to continue to smoke weed—to help him sleep and manage stress—and I begrudgingly allowed it. I'd rather he was completely drug-free, but I knew it would be hard enough for him to stop using cocaine right now. And, anyway, it would be a major improvement if all he used was weed.

I sat at my desk in the kitchen and typed up our agreement—so proud of my rules and full of hope—then printed it out, got Tristan to sign it, and taped it to the fridge. Tristan promptly took it down the first time he went to get a glass of milk.

"I signed it already, Mom," he said. "I don't need to look at it every time I get something to eat."

Fair enough, I thought. I allowed him this tiny resistance and tucked the paper in my desk drawer where I could look at it, even if Tristan wouldn't.

I wasn't so naïve that I'd simply trust Tristan's word that he wasn't taking drugs, so I bought drug-test strips to use if I ever got suspicious. With our agreement signed and test strips in hand, I felt ready—for what, I wasn't sure—but I'd stated my boundaries and felt good about them. I had a kung fu adventure that I could dangle like a carrot or take away if I didn't like his behaviour. I finally felt in control again.

One Saturday a few weeks after the start of the new school year, Tristan came home around noon and kicked off his running shoes in the front hall. I hadn't seen or heard from him since he'd left for school the day before. I'd spent the night sleepless and seething. This behaviour wasn't new for him, but it was new since we'd signed our agreement.

I glared at him without saying hi. "Tristan, you need to do a pee test," I said, and held out a test strip for him.

"Fine, whatever," he grumbled and took it with him into the bathroom.

I sat on my bed and waited, pillows pulled around me for comfort, until Tristan came out and handed me the wet test strip. He made no eye contact and kept walking to the kitchen, where I heard him pour a bowl of cereal.

My heart was pounding, and I didn't want to look. But he was so willing to take the test, perhaps that was a good sign?

I peeked at the strip and saw some of the squares already showing coloured lines. There were multiple positives. My mouth began to water, and I swallowed a wave of nausea as I watched the results appear: cocaine, ecstasy and marijuana were in his system.

I pulled a pillow closer to me. I wasn't angry. I was defeated and exhausted. I didn't want to deal with this.

I waited for my heart to stop pounding, then tossed the pillow aside and went to find him.

"Tristan, you did cocaine last night," I said from the kitchen doorway as he ate his cereal. "And ecstasy. That wasn't the deal."

"Jesus, Mom, you never trust me so what's the point of me saying anything."

"You don't need to say anything. I have the stupid test results. I know what you took." I kept glaring.

He shook his head. "I didn't do coke last night. I smoked weed and took a bit of E. Really nothing. I don't know why coke is showing up. Maybe it's still in my system from weeks ago." He looked at me and held my gaze. "Whatever. You're going to believe what you want anyway." He stood up to put his bowl in the sink and moved to walk past me, but I blocked the doorway.

"Tristan, you said you'd stop using drugs. That was the deal for China. You signed an agreement!" I sounded like a shrieking shrew, I thought.

"Mom, you always think I'm doing horrible shit, even if I'm not. I was just hanging with a girl last night. Like a normal teenager wants to hang with their friends and girls and stuff, right? You make a big deal out of everything." He brushed past me, through the doorway.

I didn't think there was anything normal about a fifteen-year-old boy not coming home all night because he was hanging with "friends and girls and stuff," but I let that slide. Instead, I reached for the only leverage I thought I had.

"What about China, then? You're going to throw away that chance just to keep doing drugs?"

Tristan turned to face me and paused, studying me.

"You just want me to go to China so I'll stop getting high, don't you?" he said, as if accusing me of some horrible deceit.

I was stunned. I thought I'd made that crystal clear from the start. "Yeah, I do," I said. "I absolutely do. That's the reason for this whole thing. But, Tristan, that's not the *only* thing about China, is it? You want it too. Maybe not the no-drugs part, but the training and adventure and the skills you'll come back with. It's a killer opportunity for you, and you know it. Nobody else your age gets to do cool shit like that. Seriously. So, yeah, I want you to go so you don't do drugs. But I also want all those other things for you. The question is, what do you want? 'Cause you can't have both."

He didn't answer, just looked at me with disgust and walked away.

I didn't know if it was possible for the test to show positive for cocaine if he hadn't used in weeks. Tristan had always been a terrible liar; he usually just told me what I didn't want to hear and rolled with my reaction. But now he'd looked straight at me and showed no sign of shame. He'd either been telling the truth or had upped his lying game significantly. And since I held the evidence of his drug use in my hand, I knew he was probably lying. I chided myself for being too lenient. I should have withdrawn the offer of China right then.

But deep within me was a thick rope of fear that there were no other options for Tristan. I was out of ideas. China had to work.

I threw the test strip in the garbage, put the kettle on and sank into a chair at the kitchen table. Maybe it didn't matter, I thought. Tristan now knew the test strips worked and I was ready to call him on things. Maybe that would be enough. I held onto the hope—blind, baseless hope—that Tristan had somehow learned his lesson.

The next week, we repeated the exact same scenario.

And the next.

Eventually, he said to me, "Fuck, Mom, I'm not going to use drugs when I'm in China. That's gotta be good enough for you. There's only a couple more months before I go, and I'm gonna have fun 'til then. You're just super square. You get so freaked out about drugs, but really... you're the weird one here, not me. Lots of people do drugs, Mom. They live perfectly good lives. Drugs aren't this big boogeyman you think they are."

"Tristan, we're not talking about lots of other people, we're talking about *you*. And you're not living a perfectly good life right now, are you? How's school going for you? How's taekwondo? You can't tell me drugs aren't interfering." I waved his positive drug test strip at him as if it proved my point.

Tristan just shrugged. "I'm a teenager, Mom. I'm not perfect, okay? If you don't want to send me to China, that's on you. But you're right, I got nothing left here but getting high. It's why I wake up in the morning. So, you think about that if you want to keep me here."

He strode out of the room and I sat back down at the table where I'd been eating my breakfast before he'd come home. I took a bite of my store-bought lemon poppyseed muffin; it was dry and tasted like dish soap. I pushed it aside. Tristan was being a manipulative little shit but he was being more honest than usual and it was time to get honest with myself. I had no intention of keeping him home, whether he kept using drugs or not. Something needed to dramatically change, and I saw China as his only way through this. He'd called my bluff.

After that, we both dropped the pretense. I stopped pretending I had any control over what Tristan did. I didn't bother with any more drug testing. It didn't matter. There were no more requirements for him to go to China. He just needed to stay alive and sane enough to get on that plane.

SCOTT AND I had carried on in our bumpy marriage. Almost two years after we moved into separate homes, and almost as long since I limited his interactions with my kids, I needed to finally end it. No one thing had happened, or hadn't happened, to force a decision. I just knew, all of a sudden, I'd had enough. I was tired of trying to make the unworkable work.

It wasn't the first time I'd tried to end our marriage. Shortly after the incident of taking Tristan to the ER, I told Scott we were over. He suggested marital counselling, and I agreed. After only four sessions, he refused to go back, saying he felt ganged up on. A year later I tried to break up with him again and, this time, he suggested taking the vacation we'd never gone on, that I'd been asking about for years.

I felt it was only right to give our marriage every possible chance, to give Scott the benefit of every doubt. It was how I did things—with my kids, with all my relationships. I'd state my needs, and then, when they weren't being met, I'd lower my expectations. And then lower them again. But with Scott, I was forever lowering my expectations and now, with a kid in crisis, I just couldn't deal with a troubled marriage too.

I was nervous on the drive to Scott's house in the way I got nervous whenever I was about to hurt another person's feelings. But I was determined and even felt a bit powerful. At the very least, I could take control of my marriage, even if that meant ending it.

I noticed the early autumn leaves, gold and red and yellow, drifting from their branches and swirling their way to the sidewalk. Every fluttering leaf cheered me on, whispering that it's good to let go, sometimes. To begin a new season.

I knocked on Scott's door and walked into his small apartment. His dog, a Mexican rescue mutt, greeted me and I scooped him into my arms. "I'm gonna miss you," I whispered into his muzzle. Scott smiled and opened his arms, but I shook my head and stepped away. Without any preamble, I told him I was done.

Scott shut his eyes, as if to hide his hurt, or perhaps his exasperation, and let out a deep sigh. "I don't get it, Kathy. Why do you keep doing this?"

"Neither of us are happy in this marriage, Scott. We don't share anything that husbands and wives do. I can't continue to work on our marriage at the same time as I'm working through everything else. And we've tried. I just don't have it in me anymore. I can't do it all."

"And Tristan is your priority, I know, I know." He knew, all right, but he didn't like it. He pulled out a chair and sat down at the table. "I just love you so much. I don't know why you can't let me be a happy getaway for you. A place where you can relax and enjoy things a bit."

"I can't relax and enjoy things right now. It's impossible. I need somebody to be *with me* through it, or not at all. It takes too much energy trying to be happy for you." We'd been going around this argument for ages, but we sat at his kitchen table and went around it again, for as long as I could manage. And then I just let him talk, his words of love drifting around me, unheard. I noticed he was wearing his favourite button-up shirt with tiny blue flowers on it. I noticed the pain in his eyes and the tiny creases at their corners; he looked tired. I noticed the placement of his furniture and the bananas on his counter and was aware I might never see his place again. I noticed everything except his words because they no longer mattered.

Finally, I left.

On the way home I felt lighter. The weight of my marriage had pressed on me for so long I felt like I was floating in freedom—freedom to manage my own bumpy life, in my own bumpy way, without having to be responsible for the feelings of another grown adult.

As I pulled into my driveway, I took out my cell phone, called my friend Leigha, and asked her to come over with a bottle of wine. I decided I would celebrate. I would enjoy the sunshine on my face for one brief moment before the storm of my life thundered overhead again. I could do that with a friend.

Because left alone, I knew, I'd crawl into my lonely bed and weep for my failure as a wife as well as a mother.

5

A FEW days later I walked into the kitchen to find Jenn at the table, eating kimchi and rice.

"Did Sonia's mom make that?" I asked. Jenn loved the home-made food that her best friend's mom made.

She nodded her head, still chewing. "Oh my god, if I die and get reborn, I want to be Korean. They have the most delicious food. Also," she continued without missing a beat, "I'm for sure going to die. Probably next week. I'm going to have a heart attack."

"Oh, well, I'm glad to have a few days' notice. What do you want for your last meal?" I put the kettle on for tea.

"You're off the hook, I'm eating it already. But seriously, Mom, I've been asked to do a fashion show downtown, with all the big designers, and real professional models. I'm totally going to pass out and make a fool of myself."

"What? That's fantastic! So exciting." I laughed at her horrified expression. "But nobody's making you do it, if you don't want to."

"Oh, I *want* to, and I'm going to do it, even though I will almost certainly trip and fall on my face or have an aneurism."

I laughed and gave her a big congratulatory hug. Jenn had been modelling on and off for the past two years, but she preferred photo shoots to catwalks. Her beautiful face, feline eyes and natural thin-ness were classic, and her ability to radiate emotional energy played well for both camera and crowds. Thankfully, at five-foot-six, she wasn't tall enough to make it big, which comforted me. The last thing Jenn needed was a career built around partying and trying to be someone else's idea of beautiful. I'd watched Leigha go through that twenty years earlier and knew how damaging it could be. But with her average height, I could encourage Jenn to follow her passions knowing her wings were safely clipped.

"You'll be awesome, hun. You always are. Can I come watch?" She filled me in on the details and got up from the table, leaving her dirty dishes behind.

"I'm outta here," she said, grabbing her sweater from the front hall and checking her make-up in the mirror. "Only a few more weeks and I'll be gone for good!" She was almost nineteen, in the process of moving in with her boyfriend and feeling very grown up about it.

"Well, you'll always have your room here."

"I know. Love you, Mom." She gave me a quick hug and went out.

I smiled to myself as I cleared her dishes into the dishwasher, poured my tea and then opened my laptop to get work done. I had an important deadline the next day and wanted to double-check that everything was ready. I reread the report I'd prepared, looking for ways to clarify concepts and add more rationale to my recommendations.

Then a shriek pierced the silence: "Mom!"

Tristan was yelling for me. Wailing.

I ran to his room and saw him sitting on his bed, head in his hands, rocking back and forth.

"What's wrong?" I asked, panicked.

"I need money. I need *you*. To give me *money*. And I need it *now*." His voice was harsh, anxious, broken. He stopped rocking and looked at me. His eyes were red-rimmed and sunken. He looked desperate.

Jesus Christ. I froze. Then took a deep breath. "Tristan—"

"Mom, I need some fucking money, okay?" he yelled, rocking again. "What part of that don't you understand?" He hit his head with his hands, again and again, with every word he spoke. "I (*hit*) need (*hit*) Some (*hit*) FUCKING (*hit harder*) MONEY! (*hit harder still*)." He screamed this last part, bashing at his head.

I took a step forward to stop him, to catch his hands, to hold them tightly to me, to wrap him in love and safety, but I stopped myself.

This wasn't like the time he fell, as a toddler, and knocked out his front tooth, or got stung by a bee as a preschooler. I couldn't make this better with a warm hug and basic first aid. My boy was going crazy in front of me.

The whole world dropped away until nothing existed except that room and Tristan and me. No past. No future. Just now.

"Tristan, stop it." I spoke firmly, but calmly. "You need to stop hitting yourself so we can talk."

He stopped, clenched and unclenched his fists, and looked up at me again, still rocking. His eyes were teary now.

"Okay," I said. "Good." I took a deep breath, trying to spread calmness, buying myself a moment to think. "You want money for cocaine, right? But that's what got you here. It's what you need to get away from. More coke won't help you."

"You don't understand, Mom. You don't get it." He took a few laboured breaths, and I could see he was trying to form his thoughts. "Look. It's *not* having any that makes me crazy. If I get coke, I won't need to use it, I swear, because I know it will be there. Then I won't need it. If I have it, I don't need it. If I don't have it, I need it, but I don't need to *use* it, I promise, Mom."

He looked frantic, almost hopeful, searching my face to see if he'd made a clear argument, to see if I finally understood. I didn't. I was scared. It terrified me to see how Tristan's mind worked.

He must have realized his logic was lacking because he tried a different tack. "Mom, if I don't get something now, I don't know what I'm gonna do. I don't wanna live like this." His voice broke, with a sob. "I *can't* live like this. I'm going to fucking kill myself."

Even as those words cut me, I didn't think Tristan was suicidal. I'd heard his dad, in depression and guilt, threaten to kill himself dozens of times, always as a tactic for sympathy or... something. Something I could never quite fathom.

I was sick of manipulative threats, but I was not immune to Tristan's pain.

Instead of fear, my heart swelled with love and hurt for my poor, sick boy. This was the babe I held in my arms and nursed at my breast, the toddler who I taught to count by finding snails in our backyard—one and then two and then three. The boy with a heart so big he would help anyone who was hurting, spending his last dollar to buy his sister a stuffed animal to cheer her up, or volunteering to vacuum the living room when he saw I was stressed.

I had no idea how to help him now. Paying for his drugs wouldn't help him in the long run, I knew. But would it help in the short term? Would it help to get him through the next few weeks, until I could get him on that plane to China? Until I could see if he could start over, somewhere else, without relying on substances?

I looked at Tristan. Behind him, my own reflection stared back at me from his window, waiting to see what I'd do. Judging. I knew I couldn't make her happy, no matter what I did. There was no right answer, only pain. Pain now, or pain later.

I turned away from myself.

"How much do you need?"

"Just twenty bucks is fine," he said, then paused. "Forty would be better." He looked at me, and then said, "But I owe the guy some money and he won't sell to me until I pay him back first."

"How much do you owe him?" I asked.

"Eighty. Sorry, Mom." He sounded like he meant it, his guilt palpable. I suspected he was playing me, but also thought it might be true on some level.

I nodded my head. "If I do this for you, and I drive you, will you stay home tonight?" I had an urgent need to keep him with me. Not for his sake, I admitted to myself. He'd be fine once he got high. But I'd be up all night worrying and crying. I needed him home for my peace of mind. If I was going to do this for him, I deserved something in return. "And will you try to keep your shit together for the next few weeks? Please?" I added, for whatever it was worth.

"I will, Mom, I promise. Thank you. Thank you so much."

I drove Tristan to a high school parking lot five minutes from our house. It was almost nine o'clock by that time, pitch black, threatening rain. Tristan was quiet on the ride, twitchy and anxious. As

I parked, he told me he'd be back in a few minutes, then strode off through a path in the woods with the hundred and twenty dollars I'd withdrawn from a drive-through ATM.

It worried me to lose sight of him. I didn't know who he was meeting, or where. And Tristan would just turn off his phone if he didn't want to hear from me. I didn't know how long I should wait.

Ten minutes passed.

I wondered if Tristan felt remorseful. If he knew what he was putting me through and felt sorry at all. He said it often enough, but did he mean it? I felt better when I imagined he did.

Another ten minutes passed.

I figured I should probably go home. Twenty minutes was definitely longer than the "few" he promised to be gone for. I felt like such a stooge and was suddenly furious with myself for being duped. I sat in my car with the windows steaming up, tears of shame and anger streaking down my face, weighed down by my failure as a parent. *I'm driving my kid to drug deals now? Paying for them? How can I even try to justify that?* I couldn't.

"I'm sorry," I whispered aloud to the mom I had wanted to be and so clearly wasn't.

I sat in the chilly car, warm tears on my cold cheeks, and waited a bit longer.

Twenty-five minutes after he walked through the path in the trees, Tristan returned to the parking lot. He got in the car, looking like his old self. He wasn't anxious. He wasn't twitchy. His colour was better. Not good, but better than it had been an hour earlier.

"Thanks again, Mom. I'm sorry to put you through this shit. I won't do it again, I promise." He looked at me and seemed normal. Not that I knew what normal was anymore. Tristan was more normal on drugs than off.

I nodded my head at him, completely exhausted. I just wanted to crawl into bed. "Okay. Let's go home," I said.

As I started the car, Tristan reached over and gave me a shoulder rub. His physical touch comforted me, as it always did. He was here right now. He was safe. I was okay.

TRISTAN DROPPED out of taekwondo in mid-October and, for the first time in her life, Tanis kept training without him.

On the morning of Tanis's black belt test, Tristan was nowhere to be found. He hadn't come home the night before, even though he promised he wouldn't miss her test. But his promises meant nothing at all.

By 10 a.m., Mom, Jenn and I sat on the hard wooden benches of the training hall, waiting for Tanis to get started. Brad stood off to the side, chatting with some of the other parents.

Tanis walked over from where she'd been talking with Master Kenny. "Do I look all right?" she asked.

Her black uniform was impeccable. Her blond hair, still sweaty from the timed ten-kilometre run she just finished, was pulled back into a ponytail. The red and black belt she'd worn for the past six months was wrapped around her waist twice and tied in a perfectly centred square knot, her insulin pump clipped to its side. Today, she hoped to replace that belt with her second black belt.

"You look perfect, sweetheart," I said.

She scanned the room, her brain already running through her test requirements. She was pure nerves waiting for release. Whenever she heard the door jingle, she glanced toward it, hoping, I knew, that Tristan would show up.

I was furious with Tristan, both for not being there and for taking my attention away from Tanis on her special day. My mind spun through possibilities of where Tristan could be: passed out somewhere? Injured or dead? Feeling sorry for himself? I didn't want to be worrying about him right then but couldn't help it.

Just as Master Kenny called Tanis to the mat to begin testing, Tristan flew through the door.

"Hey, Tanis!" he called, clapping his hands. "You got this!"

Tanis glanced at Master Kenny, who gave her a tiny nod, allowing her to back off the mat, bowing as required, so she could give Tristan a big hug. He was her training partner, her sparring partner, her brother, and a big reason why Tanis was testing for her black belt that day. Tristan's pride boosted her confidence and she relaxed more than she had all morning.

As Tanis resumed her place on the mat, Tristan yelled "Go get 'em!" and slid next to me on the bench. My fury vanished in a wave of gratitude. Everything was now as it should be.

"Glad you made it, hun," I said, and smiled.

"Of course," he said. "Where else would I be?" as if doubting him was the most unreasonable thing in the world.

6

OUR TRAVEL plans fell into place beautifully. I would wrap up my current contract by the end of November and had secured a new contract to start in early January. That gave me the money for Tristan's year in China, as well as the time and job security I needed to spend the first five weeks with him. I'd also train as a student at his school but only in tai chi and meditation—the intense physical aspects of martial arts held no interest for me. And then if all seemed well, I'd leave him there to complete his training. If either one of us was not comfortable with that, he would return home with me in January.

But Tristan was like a sandcastle in a storm, his features fading, his size diminishing. His eyes became sunken and dull. He acted more like an emotionless zombie or outraged lunatic than a teenage boy. I knew in my bones that the plan to get Tristan to China was a good one, but it was clear it wasn't helping either of us in the here-and-now. Tristan was spiralling, body and soul, his addiction a runaway train, and I couldn't think of one damn thing to change the situation.

I was a problem-solver by nature and profession. As teenagers, Leigha and I had lived by the mantra, "If there's a will, there's a way." We carried out sometimes elaborate schemes to get what we wanted: money to buy concert tickets, or a weekend at a local hostel while our parents thought we were at each other's homes. Now, as a content strategist, I spent my days helping companies solve their content problems. I'd been successfully finding solutions for decades.

But I'd never encountered a problem as difficult as saving Tristan.

Searching online, I found a six-week program for parents with kids at risk of drug abuse. It started the following week, was free, and took place fifteen minutes from my home. I could attend the first five sessions before we were scheduled to leave for China.

Driving to the first meeting, I was concentrating on the glaring headlights that pierced the rainy darkness when Simon and Garfunkel's "Bridge Over Troubled Water" came on the radio. I turned up the volume. One of my all-time favourite songs, at different times I had wondered who the "I" was—the "I" who would lay themselves down, creating a bridge above troubles and pain. As a teenager, I'd imagined it to be a boyfriend, protecting me and cheering me on, though nobody had ever lived up to the romantic altruism the song suggested to me. Later, I saw *myself* as a bridge for others who walked through turbulent waters—my children, or my friends. But now, on this wet night in October, it suddenly struck me that the bridge was God and he—she? they? it?—was there for me.

My body relaxed and the tension I didn't know I was holding faded away. The fact that this song came on at just this moment did not seem coincidental. This God, this *something*, was telling me directly that it would take my part through the darkness and pain that inevitably lay ahead. I somehow knew that this bridge was made of love and hope and peace. I knew that if I could tap into love, hope and peace—if I could walk on the bridge God would create for me—I would rise above my pain and the whole world would lay itself down to comfort me and lend me its strength. I would no longer be alone. I'd be held safely as this *something* shepherded me to solid land.

If I couldn't find that bridge, I'd be carried away by the surge and drown.

I pulled into the parking lot, lay my head on the steering wheel, and cried the deep-release sobs of a drowning woman who was unexpectedly rescued. It felt like I had the start of a solution. I didn't know the *how*, but I knew the *what*: love, hope and peace could give me strength, if only I could find them.

I wiped away my tears, got out of the car, and let the cold air hold me until I began to shiver. Then I walked into the government-funded centre, following signs to a bland, all-purpose room with a dozen plastic chairs arranged in a circle. I was anxious in this small crowd of strangers and out of place as the only single woman in a room filled with couples. I helped myself to chamomile tea and browsed mental health brochures to avoid small talk, seating myself when the two facilitators announced they were ready to start. One guy and one girl, they both looked barely out of high school: clean, shiny, preppy. I didn't trust they had much life experience with drug addiction, or anything else for that matter.

That evening I learned that Tristan did, in fact, meet the textbook definition of a person with substance use disorder, also known as addiction. I became familiar with the downward trajectory of addiction and what to expect if Tristan continued to spiral. I heard countless stories from other parents: stories of lying and cheating, stealing money, dealing drugs, breaking-and-entering; stories of arrests and jail time, lost jobs, homelessness, attempted suicides, overdoses, and psych wards; stories of exhaustion and despair and fear, of shattered dreams and heartbreaking love wrapped in a complete lack of hope. Everybody had a beautiful story of who their child was before, in stark contrast to the nightmare they'd become in addiction.

We were a worn out, depressed group of parents with lost kids. Over the course of the program, we never discussed recovery or the hope to be found on the other side of addiction. It just never came up.

When the other parents exchanged phone numbers and email addresses, I opted out. I didn't need to hang out with more drowning people. I would do better on my own.

MY MIND was not my friend. I began to obsessively imagine worst-case scenarios. I pictured Tristan homeless and dirty on the streets of Vancouver's Downtown Eastside, begging for money, committing crimes, selling his body and soul for drugs.

I planned his funeral in my mind: I imagined choosing photos from happy years, showing Tristan with his sisters, climbing trees, eating ice cream, competing in taekwondo tournaments. I'd choose music from his favourite artists like Bob Marley and the Beatles. I'd have to ask Jenn and Tanis about the current stuff he listened to. The guest list stumped me. I didn't know most of his friends and decided I didn't want to invite them anyway. It would be a very small gathering.

I imagined Tristan's death more times than I could count, always on the long nights when he didn't come home and often while driving alone, crying in rush hour traffic before stopping at the grocery store to pick up something to make for dinner. The world went on around me and I went through the motions of living while I was killing myself inside.

One morning when I hadn't seen Tristan for days, I stood at the kitchen sink washing the previous night's dinner dishes, absently noticing the last few leaves struggling to stay on the branches of the maple tree outside the window. Suddenly, I felt a physical pressure in my sternum that stopped my breath. I was flooded with thoughts of the brutality Tristan must have been exposed to through his addiction, and how it barely scratched the surface of where he was headed. I struggled to breathe. I didn't trust my legs to hold me. Leaving the dishes, I checked on Tanis, who was watching an episode of *Dog the Bounty Hunter*, ran to my room, threw open my closet doors, and collapsed into the darkest corner behind the overflowing laundry basket. I barely got a dirty T-shirt stuffed in my mouth before a long wailing sob escaped me and I gave in to my dark fantasies.

How would Tristan survive, homeless? What horrors would he live with and need to perpetrate? I could feel what it would do to his sweet, sensitive soul, and how he'd become hard, empty and isolated, turning only to drugs and a filthy sleeping bag for comfort. And who could blame him? Who wouldn't want comfort, any way they could get it, from the world he was creating for himself?

I curled into a ball, my head against my knees, my eyes clenched shut. The worst part of this nightmare was that it would never end. I knew addiction was a progressive spiral downward. Sure, some peo-ple lived as highly functioning alcoholics or addicts for decades at a time, even a full lifetime, but once a person slid lower, could they rise again? Tristan was sliding at supersonic speed. The idea of him living in the darkest depths of addiction for decades upon decades, building his whole world on the twisted, rotting foundation of drug abuse until the last of his life's energy sputtered out, seemed more than I could bear.

This nightmare sat heavy within me, like fact. I began to think I'd rather see him dead, and that realization slayed me. What kind of mother could give up on her fifteen-year-old son, even in her night-mares? How could I even imagine a situation where I would wish him dead? I told myself it was unnatural—that *I* was unnatural. I didn't deserve to be his mother. He deserved—he *needed*—a mom who could help him. Not me. I lashed myself with these thoughts until I could take no more and I lay my head on a pile of dirty laundry and cried myself into a foggy sleep.

A FEW days later, mid-afternoon sun reminding me the windows needed washing, I walked into the kitchen and saw Tristan sitting at the computer desk. He'd come home, finally, the day before.

"Hey, how's things? What are you up to?"

He turned to me with a wild look in his eyes, his face red.

"Fuck, Mom, just shut the fuck up, will you? You're such a fucking cunt, you're ruining my life, just leave me the fuck alone!" Spit flew from his mouth and he looked like he wanted to punch me.

I froze. His reaction was so bizarre and extreme that, in some odd way, it centred me. It clearly had nothing to do with me and everything to do with Tristan and his pain. I vaguely noticed the tag sticking out of the back of his T-shirt and resisted the urge to tuck it into place.

Tanis came into the kitchen to see what the yelling was about. "You're going to let him speak to you like that?" she asked me, incredulous.

"Just get the fuck out of my life, both of you!" Tristan yelled and stood up, holding his arms in the air as if he were trying to scare us away with his great size, with a threat of violence neither Tanis nor I believed.

Tristan's outrageous behaviour made Tanis pause, and he pushed past her, grabbed his backpack and left the house again.

"What was that about?" Tanis asked.

I just shrugged and shook my head. "I asked him about his day," I told her, tears welling in my eyes. I had to get away before Tanis's concern melted me into a blubbery mess.

I held up my hand, as if to say, "I'm okay." Or, perhaps, "I need some space." Or, maybe, "Not one snarky word from you. I can't take anymore." I don't know what I meant and didn't stick around to see Tanis's reaction. I just hurried to my bathroom and ran the bath water, full blast, so that Tanis wouldn't hear my sobs, my gasping breaths.

I sat in the bath, sobbing, my mind in hysterics at the unavoidable terrors ahead. I screamed silently to myself, *I can't do this!* over and over and over again, for I don't know how long. There were only two weeks left until we'd planned to leave for China, but I was sure we wouldn't make it. Tristan would continue to disintegrate before my eyes. Soon there'd be nothing left of either of us.

I can't do this! I can't do this! I can't do this!

My panic didn't abate, as it usually did when I let myself cry. Instead, it grew, and every gasping breath confirmed I could not continue on this impossible road. I wasn't skilled enough, or strong enough, or stable enough to save my boy. Nobody could help me. The demons had won; they would take Tristan to hell, and me along with him, because I was tied to my son and didn't have the strength to fight anymore. I simply could not go on.

I can't do this! I can't do this! I can't do this!

And then, without warning, my entire body felt the words: *Yes. You. Can.*

And everything stopped.

I stopped crying. I sat, stunned, in the reverberating silence.

A lone drop from the faucet plopped into the water, causing tiny concentric circles to radiate outward toward my raised knees.

The voice was so unexpected, so out of the realm of my reality, that I had to assure myself that I had, in fact, heard those words. But "heard" wasn't quite right. The words weren't attached to a voice. They didn't sound male or female. It was more like I *felt* the words echo through my body. And not just the words—those three simple words, *Yes. You. Can.*, clear and sharp and loud. I felt the *truth* of the message, that I could do whatever needed to be done. *I can do it, I will do it, and it will be worth it.*

Suddenly, I knew those things to be true. I had absolutely no doubt.

I wondered if I'd just heard the voice of God, or if it was a desperate message from my inner self. Was there any difference? It certainly felt like something bigger than me, beyond me, both of me and outside of me—a bridge back to sanity, perhaps.

The warm release of relief washed over me. I lay naked in the tub, humbled, grateful and suddenly very powerful. I knew I would keep going. I was ready.

I sat for a while longer, then stood and took a deep breath. I stepped out of the tub, dried off, got dressed, and went to prepare the evening meal.

THE SATURDAY before our Monday morning flight, Tristan told me he wouldn't go to China unless he could bring marijuana with him.

"I don't care what a sweet experience it is to train with freakin' monks," he said. "I won't be able to eat or sleep or relax or do anything if I don't have something. Seriously, Mom, I'm not going without it." Tristan paced the living room floor, looking more agitated with every lap.

"How is that even possible?" I asked. "Weed is illegal. You can't take it on an airplane."

"A doctor can prescribe medical marijuana, Mom. I know a friend who got that."

"It's Saturday morning. The doctor's office is closed. And she won't just give you a prescription for weed just because you ask for it. That's not a thing."

"Yes it is, Mom. And I'm not going anywhere without *something*, at least." He stopped pacing and went to his room. I heard him flop on his bed. "Whatever. I guess I'm not going," he called out. "I don't care, anyway, it was a stupid idea."

"Oh, for god's sake, Mr. Dramatic!" I yelled back, frustrated and a little scared. He *had* to go to China. There were no good alternatives for him. I put the kettle on for tea and tried to think things through. I could wait to see how he felt on Monday morning. I knew he didn't want to pass up this opportunity but he may not have fully bought into it either, and drugs may be the stronger pull.

I didn't want to lose half a day at a walk-in clinic when I still had so much to do before we left and so little time with the girls, but I saw no choice. "Okay, Tristan," I called. "Put your shoes on. Bring your Nintendo because it will be a long wait."

Hours later, he was finally called in to see the doctor. "Do you want me to wait here?" I asked, taking his Game Boy and putting it in my purse, "or come in with you?"

"I don't care." He shrugged. "Come if you want."

I followed Tristan to a small cubby of a room, off-white, sterile, bland. The doctor soon came in and asked how she could help. I sat back, deliberately silent, and let Tristan do the talking.

"Unfortunately, Tristan, I can't just prescribe you marijuana because you're travelling," she explained. "Why do you feel you need it?"

"Umm ... I've been smoking weed every day to help me to sleep and eat and whatever," he said. Then he told her about the kung fu training in China, and how he'd phase himself off marijuana when he got there.

"That sounds like a wonderful opportunity, and it's smart you've got a plan to wean yourself off of weed," she said, as if Tristan were her nephew embarking on an exciting excursion rather than a young teenager with substance use problems. Then, with curiosity rather than judgement, she asked, "What other substances do you use, and how often?"

My heart began to pound and I took a deep breath. I knew Tristan would be honest with her in a way he wasn't with me and I listened intently to his answers. He used cocaine daily when he could, but at least a few times per week. Ecstasy too. The doctor asked about other drugs, but suddenly there was such a roaring in my head that I couldn't hear Tristan's answers. I saw his mouth move, rattling off a list of other drugs and—*did he just say something about heroin?* I didn't know. I watched him and this young doctor talk about his drug use as if I were watching TV with the volume turned low and a jet plane roaring over my head. The next thing I knew, they were both standing, and the doctor was handing me a bottle of Ativan.

"Tristan can have these when he starts to feel agitated or anxious," she told me. "No more than two every four hours, and no more than six a day."

She spoke to Tristan as she walked us out. "Exercise is one of the best ways to help your body detox; it will minimize many of the uncomfortable symptoms. Be sure to drink plenty of water, take electrolytes if you can, and you'll be just fine. Sounds like quite an adventure you'll be having. Enjoy!" She smiled and said goodbye.

Outside, I was confused. *What just happened? What did I miss? Why can't I remember the doctor getting up to get the Ativan?*

If my mind wouldn't hear what Tristan said about his drug use—if it blacked out that discussion and the aftermath—it must have been truly horrifying. I wanted to ask him to tell me again but decided not to. If his drug use was worse than I suspected, I didn't want to know. I couldn't bear any more pain.

I tucked the Ativan into my purse beside Tristan's Game Boy, and we went home.

7

TRISTAN WAS excited and engaged throughout our thirty-six hours of travel, including an overnight stay in Beijing and a ninety-minute cab ride from Yantai to the training academy. Only twice did he become agitated enough for me to give him the Ativan. Mostly, we felt like children let loose to explore a magical land where every piece of artwork, every traffic sign, every pork bun was a mystery for us to unravel, a treasure to unwrap.

We stepped out of the taxi and glanced around. The late November cold stung our cheeks, brilliant blue skies dazzled us with their vast beauty, and the air tasted of frost and soil. The training academy was nestled between a rocky hill on one side and cherry orchards that slept peacefully under a light blanket of snow on the other. Kunyu Mountain towered over us, its shadow looming in the late afternoon.

The school itself consisted of four buildings. The main building was three stories of yellow brick and housed the administration offices, dorms, first aid room and a common lounge area. The mess hall jutted out of one side, containing twelve round tables that seated six people each and a buffet area where staff served meals to students. There was a sprawling concrete yard spotted with basketball hoops and punching bags that separated the main buildings from the big training hall—a large, glistening, white room holding four matted areas and a fighting ring on one side. Swords, staffs and other traditional Chinese weapons lined the walls. A dog kennel sat against the far edge of the yard where a fluffy white Japanese Spitz roamed in the run, always ready for pets and playtime, and a couple other working dogs watched warily from cages.

Behind the administrative building, past a row of brick sheds, and beside a small courtyard where students hung their washing to dry, frozen, in the cold winter sun, was a small brick building. This was the "old training hall" where I was scheduled to train in tai chi and meditation with Master Lee.

After a quick tour of the grounds, however, the translator told us the dorms were full until after Christmas and handed us a note. "Give this to the man at the front desk," she said. "It's just down the road. Only four weeks, then there will be room for Tristan here. Maybe a room for you too."

I glanced at the scrap of paper with Chinese writing I now held in my hand.

In the waning light, we dragged our suitcases half a kilometre down the lane to a dirty, dilapidated building. Tristan and I looked at each other and burst out laughing at the expressions on each other's faces. This was not the kind of place we'd ever stay at in Canada.

"We're not in Kansas anymore," Tristan said, quoting *The Wizard of Oz*.

Inside, we handed the note to a stooped, elderly man. He clucked and nodded and showed us up two narrow winding flights of creaking stairs. Tristan carried both our big suitcases while I struggled under the weight of our carry-ons. The old man unlocked our room, pointed to the broom and cleaning supplies leaning against a plain wooden wardrobe, and then pointed to me and Tristan. He repeated his pointing until I nodded my head, then handed me the key and left us to it.

The room had two single beds with yellow flannel blankets, a small side table, two chairs, a wardrobe and dresser, and a bathroom. Flies dotted the ceiling.

Tristan unpacked his clothes and put them away in drawers, which seemed like good hiding places for bugs, dead or alive. I decided to live out of my suitcase. Through the dusty window I could see the lane and a small military base across the way, a long row of trees with swaying branches, a few magpies, and one scraggly tabby cat sauntering toward town.

"The shower is beside the toilet!" Tristan called from the bathroom.

The entire bathroom was barely bigger than a shower stall and covered in off-white tile. The toilet and small sink were well within reach of the shower spray. A small towel rack was tucked in the far corner with wishful thinking it might remain dry. The floor sloped gently toward a drain set against the back wall. The toilet paper dispenser had an industrial plastic cover to keep it dry but was empty, of course. We had brought our own supply.

Too tired to make our way back to the school for dinner, we had a quick snack of beef jerky, apples, granola bars, and our last precious bottles of water. It was cold—so cold that Tristan tried to blow rings with his breath—but we couldn't figure out how to turn on the heater. Tomorrow I'd ask for help, but in the meantime we crawled into my single bed together, wearing our coats and toques and mitts, and talked with wonder about the flies and the cold and the hardness of the bed—was it made of solid wood?—and the life-changing adventure ahead of us.

WE AWOKE at 6 a.m. to begin a routine we'd follow for the next five weeks: a predawn walk to the school, mesmerized by the silhouettes of trees above the lane, the warm steam of our breath in the freezing morning air, and the eerie silence beyond our footsteps. Seven minutes later, we'd pass through the red metal gates of the academy to join the jostling queue of people filing into the mess hall. The buffet was filled with hard-boiled eggs, apple slices, orange segments, and a warm, milky soy broth. Slices of fresh white bread and pots of green tea were set at each table.

Like most students, we had brought our own instant oatmeal with nuts and seeds, cinnamon and brown sugar. We each grabbed an egg and some orange slices, added hot water to our oats, and watched as others ladled the soy broth into theirs.

We stuck to ourselves that first morning, both of us shy and uncertain but anxious to get started. We noticed the other students—

mostly men in their twenties—bundled in parkas and scarves and sweatpants. Some laughed loudly; many ate silently. We heard many different languages, but English predominated.

We smiled and were friendly, but the early hour and jet lag didn't lend itself to socializing and our priority was to memorize the schedule: 6:30 breakfast, then nap at the hotel before an 8 a.m. jog down the lane with the other students. At 8:30 we'd split into small-group training sessions. Lunch was at noon (which, we learned, consisted of various stir fries six days a week, with the addition of much-anticipated chicken wings and soggy french fries every Friday), with rest time until 2 p.m. and then afternoon training sessions until five. Dinner was at 5:30, always similar to lunch, and free time in the evenings. Lights out by 10 p.m. Weekends were unscheduled, except for mealtimes, but we were expected to practice our lessons.

Every morning, promptly at 8:30, I entered the tai chi training hall. It was an old brick building the size of a small barn with wooden rafters and stone floors worn smooth by centuries of people practicing martial arts. It felt rustic—romantic. I imagined I was the heroine from *Crouching Tiger, Hidden Dragon*.

There were a dozen guys in my training group, all men in their early- to mid-twenties. Many of them were long-time students who chose Master Lee because he specialized in wing chun, a form of self-defence relying on lightning-quick arm strikes and incredible leg strength. And then there was me, a middle-aged, unathletic woman who had never taken physical activity seriously. I was the girl who always walked in PE class when others were jogging.

After a gentle warm-up came drills. In three lines of four, we traversed the length of the training hall doing a complicated series of kicks, punches, and hops, each needing a high degree of concentration and intensity. Uncoordinated and awkward compared to the young men, I slowed my drill line. *There's a limit to what can be expected of me*, I thought as my arms and legs lurched, almost randomly, out of sync with each other.

After a warm-up session a few days into my training, I approached Master Lee.

"Master Lee," I said, "can I practice my tai chi instead? I can't do these hops and jumps and I'm slowing everyone down. I don't need to train like they do."

Master Lee looked closely at me with an expression I couldn't read. Seconds passed and he held my gaze. I looked away.

Finally, he asked, "You want to do tai chi?"

"Yes, please," I said, hopeful.

"You can't jump like these boys?"

"No, Master Lee." I shook my head.

He grunted, clearly disappointed. "Go practice drills. Very important for tai chi. You must be strong, flexible. Not easy. Practice, practice, practice!" He pointed to the boys lining up for drills, a sour look on his face. "Those boys practice," he said, and then walked away.

So, back to drills I went.

Most days, I had two hours of meditation and three hours of tai chi. Master Lee was right, tai chi wasn't easy, or even all that enjoyable. I was surprised by how much physical strength it required, but at least it wasn't a cardio workout, and I could go at my own pace without slowing down the group.

One morning a few weeks into my training, as I practiced tai chi under the frozen pants and shirts suspended on the clothes lines above, I had the seed of a realization that would take years to grow.

That day I counted eight T-shirts, four pairs of shorts, three pairs of Chinese-style pants, two pairs of jeans, and one jacket fluttering on the clothes line along with four small brown birds. I hoped the birds weren't pooping on anyone's clean clothes. I noticed that my wrists were cold, so I pulled the sleeves of my sweater to meet my knitted gloves. Before I knew it, I had forgotten all about the two new tai chi moves I was supposed to be practicing to perfection so I could eventually thread them, and others, into a sequence, like beads on a string. As difficult as tai chi was to get right, physically, the biggest challenge for me was my mind.

I refocused and concentrated intently on what I was doing—but what I was doing was jagged and stiff and wrong. I needed to clear my mind, let go of impatience and connect with the flow of energy through my body. *That* was what I needed to learn. I felt a flicker of excitement—of possibility. The goal, I sensed, was to relax my mind and be aware of my surroundings, but not focus on them. To stay in tune with my body, but not fixate on it. To allow my body the freedom to feel its way through the form, correcting itself as needed, and carrying on.

Unaware of their importance, I'd begun to practice critical skills I'd return to over and over in the coming years: surrender, acceptance and letting go.

I ACHED with the absence of Jenn and Tanis; I'd never been away from any of my children over Christmas before. Tanis was splitting her time between her dad's and my mom's, and Jenn was living with her boyfriend and planning a New Year's getaway to Cuba. A better friend than husband, Scott was helping to make sure things ran smoothly back home: he'd take the girls to spend time with our cat, drive Tanis to her dentist appointment, and make sure my bills were paid on time and cheques deposited. Everyone would be fine, I knew.

And yet . . . I wasn't sure.

When arranging details with the admin staff before our arrival, I'd been told I could train in the mornings and take afternoons off to stay in touch with people back home, get some work done, or watch Tristan train. But Master Lee seemed to think I was there to participate in *all* the exercises, all the time. A week into my training, I decided to clear up the misunderstanding once and for all.

"Master Lee," I said after one morning session, "I won't be in class this afternoon. I need to get other things done. The lady in the office told me this would be okay when I signed up."

Master Lee looked at me with his signature blank expression. He was an elegant man, slight, approaching middle age. He walked beside me gracefully, hands behind his back. I wasn't sure if he understood my English, so I was about to explain again when he held up a hand to silence me. It felt like a slap.

Then he shook his head ever so slightly and said, "Work in evening. Train in day." And with a quick scowl, he strode away.

I was stunned and a bit angry. I was paying for this experience and wanted it to be what I wanted. Why did Master Lee care if I didn't do drills or train for the full day? Who was he to disapprove of my priorities? I roiled with these questions, spinning them in my mind, not letting them land. Walking back to our room after lunch, I spun the questions out to Tristan so he could share my sense of injustice.

"What's the big deal, Mom?" he shrugged. "Just train. You'll probably never get another chance like this. What else do you need to do?"

At his words, my questions disappeared, like balloons bursting. Tristan was right. Nothing urgent required my time. Why was I resisting the experience in front of me?

I lay on my bed during our after-lunch rest period and thought about it. And the more I thought, the more complicated it felt. Part of my resistance to training, for sure, was my disinterest in physical activity—I would absolutely rather read a novel—but there was more to it than that.

Spending all that time on me felt selfish. Every minute I was training was a minute I wasn't thinking about Jenn or Tanis or Tristan, or what the future held for them. It was a minute not thinking about my next contract, my next paycheque. I felt panicked at the idea of not seeing life's inevitable curveballs until it was too late to respond. I had an urgent need to be ready for... whatever.

I had spent a lifetime being ready for whatever, managing situations and people's moods. It wasn't just Tristan, or Jenn with her party-hearty behaviours. Tanis's diabetes was a constant threat that demanded my vigilance, just as her celiac disease had when she was a toddler and I'd needed to keep a lookout for well-meaning neighbours with cookies in hand. Before that, their dad had relied on my predictability for his very sanity: if I wasn't where he thought I was, or with the people he expected me to be with, his old wounds would bleed red-hot jealousy and anger that I'd need to cool with soothing reassurances and self-sacrifice. Before that, I'd had to stay alert in case I said or did something that angered my first husband, my teenage love. I remembered the first time he hit me. We were camping. We'd been fighting about something or other and I'd tried to walk away and go into our tent. He grabbed my arm, swung me around and slapped my face, hard. "Don't you walk away from me!" he yelled. I looked at his face, contorted by alcohol and rage, and hated him with a fury that shocked me. But I stood in stillness and waited for his rage to run its course. By morning, I'd forgiven him—*he'd been drinking, he didn't mean to, he felt terrible afterward*. He must have taken forgiveness as permission because the blows kept coming, unpredictable but always anticipated.

And before that . . . well, that feeling of *needing to be ready* went back a long, long way.

I nestled deeper under my blankets, sweeping those thoughts aside, sensing that my resistance to training had little to do with that and everything to do with expectation and fear of failure. I carried a crushing hope to succeed, to train hard and impress everyone with my new skills. But what if I didn't? What if I was mediocre? What if I tried my hardest and was still mediocre? I could think of nothing more humiliating. And nothing more likely, given my lack of physical aptitude. I would be a laughing stock. Worse, I'd be dismissed, not worthy of time or attention. It would be safer not to try.

I didn't like the comforting familiarity of those thoughts.

I had grown up in a family that revered academic excellence: doctors, lawyers, educators, every one of them. I discovered early on that a poor attitude was more acceptable than a low aptitude. While my brothers were honour roll students, gathering full scholarships and multiple postgraduate degrees, I dropped out of high school twice before muddling my way through to graduation. I couldn't wrap my head around math or chemistry, and my memory wouldn't hold facts tightly enough to score well on exams no matter how hard I studied. Within the family and school system, I was labelled "unmotivated" and, eventually, nobody expected much from me.

As a teenager, I was the only one who knew my dirty secret: I wasn't unmotivated; I was stupid, or so I believed.

As an adult in the working world, though, I'd had a hard time reconciling this with my professional successes and accolades. Recently, my idea of "smarts" had broadened to include more than academic credentials. I now knew I was far from stupid, but here I was embarking on a new adventure and feeling the age-old pull to wear my unmotivated label rather than discover, once again, that I was incapable.

Suddenly, I was angry. Against all odds, I was in China. *How freakin' amazing is that?* I thought. Sure, I came for Tristan, but a new experience was being offered to *me*, and here I was approaching it as a salmon would a bear: writhing and resisting and not at all happy about it. *Fuck that!*

I lay on my hard wooden bed, gazing through the dirty window framing a slate-grey sky. Taking a breath, I committed to attending my training sessions after lunch that day, and every day. I would risk feeling left out or unneeded if I missed a moment in somebody's life back home and, instead, would spend time fully experiencing my own. I would court the humiliation of mediocrity and see what I could achieve. At least I would try. I would keep an open mind.

MASTER LEE made one exception for me: once a week, I was allowed one hour to watch Tristan in the large training hall. Rows of swords, spears and other weaponry hung on the back wall and polished tile shone beneath four large rubber-matted areas, each a home base for different training groups.

I learned that Tristan had three distinctly different moods when he was training.

If he was frustrated by not being as good as he wanted, or embarrassed by Shifu Wang criticizing his poor form, he'd smirk to look like he didn't care. But it was poor camouflage for his obvious pain and discomfort. Sometimes I'd see his eyes get teary, but by the time my heartbeat quickened in concern, he'd throw himself deeper into the task at hand, using more force, or restraint, or strength, or focus, or whatever it took to quash his emotions through physical exertion and his drive for perfection.

More often though, I saw him in community with his fellow students. They were all five or ten years older than Tristan, eight men and three women. These students came from five continents and eight countries, some for a few months and others for years, to learn kung fu and immerse themselves in foreign adventure.

I'd sit on a mat, back resting against the wall, and watch Tristan and the guys laugh and joke as they kicked pads and punched bags, or each other. They'd goof off in their brief rest periods. Tristan might grab somebody in a judo hold and bring him to the mat in surprise, only to get a good-natured beating in return. Or he'd be trying to find his breath after a particularly tough training session and another guy would walk by and push him in a way that caught my breath. I'd bite my tongue to stop myself from scolding them to settle down before someone got hurt, because nobody ever got hurt. These pushes simply set off a predictable chain of events that progressed from friendly cursing to more pushing and shoving, and ending, always, in laughter and sweaty arms around each other. Their joyful energy nourished me.

Occasionally, Tristan practiced a form and melted into it. His face lost its thoughtfulness and he found peace in the movement of his body. His arms and legs knew where they needed to be, and he moved gracefully to a rhythm others could feel but not hear. When Tristan found his flow, he was pure, beautiful energy. The other students would stop practicing their forms to watch him. Shifu Wang also watched, interested, without interrupting. He allowed Tristan to finish his form before telling him he needed to turn his toe more in one place or hold his leg higher or longer in another. Then he'd spend the next ten minutes making Tristan practice his toe points or leg holds or god knows what else until they were just right. Watching without interrupting, and then offering one-on-one attention, was the highest possible praise from Shifu Wang.

It didn't take me long to know that Tristan was exactly where he needed to be, and where he needed to stay. I smiled from a deep well of happiness I hadn't known was within me, my agonies of the past year slipping away, replaced by a lightness that mirrored Tristan's own.

FRIDAYS WERE the worst, and best, part of every week. In the mornings, we had power training followed by power stretching. I wasn't allowed to miss the power classes, though I could adapt the moves to my abilities. Nobody expected me to do one-handed push-ups like the other students, but Master Lee objected if I started with my knees down before even attempting push-ups from a proper plank position. Everyone knew I couldn't do the splits or anything like it but I still needed to rest one foot on the stone windowsill of the old training hall, about chest height to me, and keep my leg as straight as possible while another student pressed firmly on my back, lowering my nose ever closer to my leg until I begged for mercy. I often blinked back tears of pain and embarrassment on Friday mornings but, eventually, I learned to breathe *through* the pain, each breath bringing me closer to the second I could let go. And then I learned to breathe *into* it, feeling the pain as part of me, observing it, not rushing it, confident that the pain was not permanent.

Friday afternoons were the crowning jewel of the week, a balm after five days of torture. The run up Kunyu Mountain wasn't easy, but it was the last thing we had to do before two glorious days of rest. And along with our morning warm-up runs, it was one of the few times we didn't need to stay in our small training groups, so I could spend time with Tristan.

On our first Friday there, Tristan and I moved at our own pace. We jogged down the quiet lane, watching magpies watching us, to the base of a huge flight of wide concrete stairs that led to an ancient temple set into the side of the mountain. Some students were already running up the stairs, then down again, and then up. Senior students frog-hopped up: feet together, crouching low on each step, then bursting upward to land on the next. Some swung their arms for momentum, but a few held their hands in prayer position as they jumped. Then they descended, hands first—right hand on one step, left hand on the next—legs wide, in a bear crawl, repeating the hopping up and crawling down until their masters permitted them to continue their uphill run.

"I hope Shifu doesn't expect me to do that today," Tristan said, his eyes wide, fascinated by the challenge. I glanced at him and felt suddenly overwhelmed with gratitude that we were here, in China, together. What had started as a grasping act of desperation to get him away from drugs had become … this moment. After all we'd been through, it felt like a miracle to be standing beside him, each of us at peace with the other, with no greater worry than putting one foot in front of the other. Our past struggles held no significance, and my hopes were distant birds in the sky, requiring absolutely nothing from me. I was simply enjoying the beauty of a pause with my son before we climbed those stairs together.

Up we went, navigating around the frog-hoppers and bear-crawlers, up and up toward the entrance to the temple with its bright red doors topped with royal blue trim, sharply contrasted against the pale December sky. Up more stone stairs, through the original twelfth-century temple, past stone plaques and statues worn away by centuries of wind and snow, and shrines that blasted us with brightly painted blues and reds and yellows.

Continuing to a rest area lined with stone benches and a walkway to an open pagoda overlooking the valley, we took a few minutes to admire the sweeping view below us: vast orchards, stark in their winter barrenness; a silver river separating the valley bottom from the blue-grey mountain ranges above it; and the kung fu academy, tiny and barely recognizable in the distance.

Tristan's Shifu found us there. "Up! Up!" he said sternly to Tristan, pointing to a small pathway leading to narrow stone steps.

"I'll see you on your way down," I said, smiling, and continued to admire the view.

Master Lee had been sitting on a stone bench, chatting with another instructor. As Tristan bounded up the stairs, two at a time, Master Lee approached me, pointing to the stairs and nodding. My face must have shown my exhaustion and distaste at the idea of more stair climbing, but he nodded again and said gently, "Go slow. You be happy." He didn't smile, but his eyes held an uncharacteristic kindness.

The stairs were steep and narrow, with many loose stones. Nobody was hopping or crawling on these. I relished my aloneness and the silence as I walked to the rhythm of my heartbeat, comforted by the knowledge that Tristan was not alone, that he was part of a group that held him and energized him.

Happy in my thoughts, surrounded by evergreens, I listened to the thwap-thwap of my feet on the stairs for almost half an hour. Then the sound of people laughing jolted me from my reverie as I rounded a corner to a wide, rocky outcrop. A dozen or so students, Tristan among them, were messing around, striking kung fu poses both serious and silly.

"Mom, you gotta see this!" he said, running toward me and pulling my jacket in the direction of the mountain.

He led me through an arched entrance set into the mountain face, to a cave that had become a shrine to a hermit monk who meditated there in the early twelfth century. Inside, behind a grey brick altar, nine stone monks were carved into the wall, each one about three feet tall with a red silk cape tied in a simple knot at his chest. The soft scarlet fabric set against the hard, grey stone made for a startling contrast. An apple, incense and silk flowers were carefully arranged on a stone altar along with a value-sized plastic tub of tealight candles and a donation box. These stone monks had been tended to, daily, for almost nine hundred years. The idea of such continuity stretched my short-sighted Canadian thinking.

Back outside, we found more treasures: a waterfall of mysterious origin and magical properties, where people came to pray and be healed; an old well, ringed by a two-foot circle of stone, that any child or animal could stumble into and never get out of; and a breathtaking view of impossibly steep mountain faces set within a landscape of blues and greens, silvers and greys, every hue distinct and sparkling as if competing for attention.

Standing beside Tristan, both of us silenced by the majesty of the mountains and sky, and the miracle of the valleys and rivers, our troubles seemed trivial compared to the wonder, power and grace of the natural world. I imagined that the monk who had meditated on this view almost a millennium earlier had felt the same magic. For him, it would have been stronger, undiluted by the modern world, amplified by his devotion. And I felt sure it would have illuminated, for him as for me, the sharp edge we're all balanced upon, between ego and impermanence.

WE NEVER talked about drugs. When we'd been in China for two weeks, and Tristan hadn't asked for Ativan since the flight over, I flushed the remainder down the toilet. By then, he'd gained his appetite back and was sleeping well every night. Colour had returned to his cheeks, his acne had cleared up, and his eyes shone brighter—interested, curious, alive. His body was taut with energy, and he laughed easily and often.

Outside of training, our world revolved around food and relaxation. On Saturdays, we'd taxi into Muping and lose ourselves in the street market, vibrant and dirty, where scrawny cats and dogs followed us, hoping for scraps. After eating our fill of egg tarts, dumplings or crêpes from street vendors, we'd go to the supermarket to stock up on water and toilet paper, peanut butter and jam, potato chips and apples. In the bakery section we'd add custard buns, mooncakes and Shanghai bread to our buggy before heading back to our makeshift home, where we'd spend the afternoon reading or watching movies we'd downloaded to our laptops.

Sundays we slept in, skipping the school's breakfast in favour of a few extra hours of sleep and some pastries we bought the day before. Then we'd practice our forms together in the big hall. Without Master Lee's disapproving glare, I'd string my tai chi steps together and let Tristan be my teacher—laughing at me, encouraging me, correcting my posture.

"Oh my god, I'm a doofus! I can't even lift my leg up two feet without falling over!" I chastised myself one afternoon, frustrated by my inability. "You can hold your leg out perfectly straight for ages. I'm too uncoordinated for this."

"Don't say that, Mom. It's not easy and you're just learning. I've been practicing martial arts for ten years already. What do you expect after two weeks? You're doing really well," Tristan assured me. "Try again but tighten your core and then bring your leg up on your in-breath and extend on your out-breath. Don't worry about the height."

I tried again, tightening, breathing, lifting, extending—and then losing my balance and falling dramatically to the floor.

Tristan laughed. "Mom, you forgot to breathe at the end. You were holding your breath, I saw you." He reached his hand out to help me up, pulling me into a warm hug.

I was grateful for the many hours we spent together, but rooming with me in a hotel, rather than with other students in the dorms, made it difficult for Tristan to make friends. In the early days, he'd spend hours playing with the dog, throwing sticks, and giving it snuggles. But as the weeks went by, he relaxed more around others and chose to spend less time with me or the pooch. Rather than practicing forms with me on Sunday, he'd arrange to practice with other students in his class. Instead of sitting with me at dinner, he'd sit at the table where he and his friends ate and laughed at ridiculously juvenile jokes.

"Does it bother you, Mom?" he asked one evening as we walked back to our hotel. "You know you're welcome to come eat with us, if you want."

I'd taken to having my meals with a few older students, two French men in their thirties and an American ex-army man in his forties. They were comfortable enough company. While I felt Tristan's withdrawing keenly, I was happy for him. I wanted to see him settled before I left and enjoyed seeing him find his place among peers. It felt right for him to step away and reassuring that I could see what he was stepping into.

"What? And listen to all your bathroom humour and loud chewing?" I laughed. "I think not."

Tristan laughed, put his arm around me and kissed the top of my toque. "Thanks, Mom," he said.

We continued through the cold darkness in comfortable silence, my warm heart weaving dreams of happy times ahead.

8

—

THE FIRST two months back home were blissfully quiet. Tanis was in her final year of high school and working as a hostess at Boston Pizza, saving money to travel to Australia after she graduated. Jenn popped by now and again for a visit or a meal or to do her laundry, but her dramas were small and the joy I felt to see her was large. My work was as stable as a short-term contract could be and more interesting than difficult.

I chatted with Tristan on Skype every few days. I managed his money, which always disappeared more quickly than it should and left him asking for more. We talked about his training and his weekend trips into Muping, and I told him to buy more bananas and less candy. I reminded him to brush his teeth.

I began to relax into my world with Tristan gone, and I didn't find that very relaxing at all. I was relieved that all my kids seemed to be okay, but I had no idea what to do with myself when I wasn't busy trying to save someone. I didn't know how to just *be* in the world. I became bored and restless, tense and unhappy.

And then, in early March, I got an unscheduled Skype call from Tristan. He was in a panic.

"Mom, all hell's broken loose. It's crazy here. Shifu left suddenly to set up his own school near the Shaolin Temple, everyone is deserting, and the school is mad at us like it's our fault. I have to go too, because Shifu's the only one I want to train with. He's why I'm here in the first place, right? All my friends are going."

My heart sang with the comforting familiarity of crisis. Here was something that I could do. Here was something that mattered, that I could manage. I was in my element, fully awake, fully alive, as I took a deep breath to ease the adrenaline coursing through my body.

The next two weeks were a flurry of emails and Skype calls while I made arrangements to transfer Tristan to the new school Shifu Wang had set up on his own. I sent money to Tristan to buy a sleeper ticket for the sixteen-hour train ride, had a Skype call with Arash, the student who'd travel with Tristan to the new school, and made sure everyone was on the same page.

And then, two days before his scheduled departure, I got an urgent Facebook message from Tristan, telling me to go on Skype. I left the bag of groceries I'd just brought home on the kitchen counter and opened my laptop.

"Mom, something happened with Arash's student visa and now he can't go with me, so I have to come home." Tristan looked heartbroken.

"What about you travelling there by yourself? If we made sure someone was there to meet you?" I suggested.

"Mom, I don't even have a fucking phone. And I can't read Chinese to know when it's my stop. The train travels all the way across China. It's like . . . a whole day of travel or something. Who knows where I'd end up? It doesn't matter. Just book my ticket home. Whatever. It was good for a while." Tristan sounded like he was talking through a soggy blanket.

"Don't tap out this quickly, sweetheart. Let's see what we can do."

Calling it quits at this point seemed like defeat to me and I didn't want Tristan to feel defeated. More than that, I didn't want him home, tempted by his old lifestyle when he was doing so well over there. After another twenty-four hours of frantic communications, I called Tristan back.

"Okay. Here's the plan," I said. "You're going to—"

"I know already, Mom. Arash is going to give me his phone and Andrei will pick me up, but I'm not going. I'm not going to travel all that way by myself. It's ridiculous. I'm only sixteen. I can't travel across China. I don't speak the language. I don't have any money. I wouldn't know what to do if something happened. It's fucking stupid. I just want to come home." He was tired and almost in tears.

"Tristan." I spoke clearly, firmly. "You're not *only* sixteen, you're *already* sixteen. And you've accomplished so many amazing things that most people of any age haven't. You can do this. And you're not alone. Arash will still be there to get you onto the train before he heads to Hong Kong to renew his visa, and he'll preprogram any phone numbers you need into his phone for you. Andrei will be waiting for you in Dengfeng; he'll make sure you get off the train. I'll put extra money in your account for emergencies. Even if you're travelling by yourself, you're not alone, Tristan. You can totally do this."

Tristan paused for a while. "Do you really think so, Mom? Not like, you believe I can do anything because you're my mother, but like, for real, you think so?"

"Hun, you can absolutely do this. And think of the great story it will make! You can tell your friends you travelled across China by yourself. It's crazy! But totally doable crazy."

His breathing shifted and I knew he was envisioning the possibilities.

"Okay, Mom, but if something goes wrong it's on you," he said, not really joking.

"If something goes wrong, Tristan, you'll figure out how to fix it. That's what life is. But I don't think anything is going to go wrong. We have a good plan."

We chatted a bit more, going over the details again and again so Tristan could internalize them. Finally, I said goodbye and told him to message me as soon as he arrived.

On the day of his scheduled travel, I waited. And worried. I would never forgive myself if something happened to him.

I watched the clock as the minutes inched forward and absently sipped my tea. I tried to sleep, unsuccessfully. I tried to read, unsuccessfully. Every hour felt like ten.

Finally, a full twenty-two hours after Tristan boarded his train, a Skype call came in.

"Tristan!" I cried, relieved to the point of tears.

"Hey, Mom, what's up? How are you?" he asked, as if it were a regular day.

"How am I? How are *you*? You made it!"

"Yeah, I'm good. It was good. Well, not good really, the beds were tiny and mine was close to the ceiling so I couldn't sit up, but I didn't want to lie down either because I was scared I'd miss my stop if I fell asleep. So, it was pretty uncomfortable. But there weren't any problems, and Andrei was waiting for me. I would have called sooner but the internet was down at the school."

"What was the trip like?" I asked. "What's the new school like? Was everyone happy to see you?" I wanted all the details so I could live it along with him.

"It's all good, Mom. The school is tiny, but it's nice to be with just my training buddies. But I'm so tired I just wanna go to sleep. I haven't slept in like a million hours. Can I call you tomorrow?"

"Of course, sweetheart. I'm so proud of you. Congratulations on doing that. It was brave."

"Thanks, Mom. I love you."

"Love you too, Tristan," I said, and hung up, profoundly happy.

WITH TIME on my hands and Tristan settling in well at the new school, I threw myself into work. I focused on building my career, working day and night, weekdays and weekends. I worked so hard that I had no time to be bored, to notice how very little else I had in my life. I worked because I could manage my career, shape it, control it and feel successful. And because, like caring for my children, it gave me something other than myself to look after, an explanation for why I never had quite enough time to continue my tai chi or meditation practice, go to yoga, explore new hobbies, meet new people. *If only I had more time*, I'd say to myself, *I'd be so fit, so spiritual, so interesting!* And then I'd overfill my days with work and more work.

I told myself I could wait. My career needed me now.

But when I secured my next six-month contract, I finally did something for myself: I booked a two-week vacation to visit Tristan at his new school and spend a few days with him in Beijing, being tourists. And so, toward the end of May, I was back in China, in a tiny rural village beside the Shaolin Temple, in Henan Province in central China. I couldn't wait to watch Tristan train again, to be enthralled by his power and grace, this time without the distraction of my own training.

The first morning after arriving I watched Tristan's conditioning class, held in an outdoor field the students had cleared a month earlier. They were "conditioning" their bodies to withstand pain by systematically killing the nerves in their forearms and shins so they could more effectively block blows from opponents. I watched the students pair up and rhythmically whack their forearms against each other in elaborate movements that reminded me of a violent version of the hand games I played as a child. Then they moved on to whacking tree trunks until their forearms were red with broken blood vessels. When their arms could take no more, they tortured each other by rolling a wooden rod back and forth over their partner's bare shins until they could not stand the pain for another second.

I was horrified, watching this, but the students found their pain hilarious and laughter rang out as loudly as shrieks of pain. I watched them as if they were an alien species I couldn't fathom, equally appalled and amazed.

For the last exercise, one person stood in bow stance—similar to a high lunge position—while their partner repetitively kicked their forward thigh. Tristan was paired up with Shifu Wang. I could hear the thwack of Shifu's foot against my son's leg, again and again, until Tristan's wince turned into a grimace and then, finally, a howl for mercy.

"Close your mind, Baby," Shifu said quietly, still kicking.

Tristan gritted his teeth and shut his eyes. Time slowed down as I watched him take blow after blow until he suddenly jumped back, out of reach of Shifu's kicks, and bent over, hands on his knees, breathing hard.

I thought he might be crying. My body tensed and I held my breath but when Tristan raised his head, I saw he was laughing. "No more. No more, Shifu, please," he laughed. "My legs are on fire!"

Shifu smiled broadly and patted Tristan on the back. "Well done, Baby. Well done." And then he moved on to a new victim.

Walking back to school after class, I listened happily to the chatter and laughter of students, to chickens clucking as they fluttered off the tree-lined path ahead of us, and to goats bleating behind wooden fences. I breathed in the country air and felt complete.

Shifu caught up to me, matching his pace to mine. He was small and lean, in his early thirties. Like Master Lee, he moved with the grace of a dancer, but had a more youthful energy and kind eyes. We greeted each other.

"Kathy," he said, after we'd walked a few breaths in silence. "I want you to know, Tristan is very good boy. Smart boy. Hard trainer. Very dedicated. I'm happy to have him at my school."

"Thank you," I said, filling with pride from tip to toe. "I know he loves being here."

"And you must know that I call Tristan 'Baby' as endearment. Not an insult. He is so young. He is the baby here. Everyone's baby, but he is *my* baby, like my son. I mean no disrespect. I thank you for letting me look after your son. It is very big honour, and I will take care of him like a son." He looked directly at me.

His sincerity was startling. It struck me that it *was* an honour for him to care for Tristan. I'd given him full responsibility for one of the three most precious people in my world. I could see the love he held for Tristan and was deeply grateful. Because of this love, Tristan had found a home as well as a school; a father figure as well as a coach. And seeing how Tristan thrived under his care allowed me to rest, knowing he was well looked after.

I couldn't possibly communicate the significance of all of that to Shifu. "Thank you so much for saying that," I managed, my eyes tearing up. "It means so much to me." I brought my hands into a prayer position, hoping that might show the gratitude I felt.

I knew then that I'd never regret sending Tristan to China, encouraging him to follow Shifu, alone and scared, halfway across the country, or spending my meagre savings on a trip to visit him. Seeing him, here and now, as part of this group, with his friends and Shifu, was worth the price of airfare ten times over.

The week unfolded naturally and I basked in the warmth of seeing Tristan surrounded by friends. We practiced tai chi together before breakfast, in the early morning sun, listening to the soft melody of bamboo flutes drifting out from the boombox in the training hall. One morning, he was goofing around—showing me what tai chi might look like if practiced by a chicken—when some other students entered the courtyard and saw him. They couldn't stop laughing and called Tristan "Chicken Man" for the rest of the day. He took it as a badge of honour.

I had thought I could watch Tristan train forever, endlessly admiring as he stretched and sparred, but by the afternoon of the second day the repetition was killing me. My brain was about to burst from boredom. I started going for daily walks, which became a focus and an adventure. I'd see shepherds and goats, chickens and pheasants. Once, I saw a monk peeing against a tree. I accompanied the students on their Friday afternoon mountain run where Tristan now frog-hopped up and bear-crawled down flight after flight of stone stairs winding down the mountain behind the Shaolin Temple.

Here, Tristan was not simply surrounded by friends; he was part of a community, a community whose members supported each other in growing into their potential. Sometimes the support came with a grumble or a thwack of a wooden staff on his butt. More often, it came with laughter and patience. Close friendships formed, but it was equally clear that some people irritated each other. Regardless, they were a team and they looked after each other, inside training and out.

This kind of community had never been possible for Tristan at home. The intensity of training, the anxiety and excitement of being a foreigner in an unfamiliar country, and the immersive nature of a dozen young men living together created camaraderie and connection that just didn't happen in a Canadian suburb.

I remembered Tristan telling me he didn't feel like he fit in at school or on sports teams. At times, he broke my heart by telling me he didn't even feel like he fit in at home. He said he felt different, out of step with others. I knew using drugs had been an easy way for him to fit in, and a way to dull the pain when he didn't. But here, he fit. He'd found his people. I was overjoyed by where he was, and so relieved by the emotional respite it gave me that I was okay with my lack of involvement. I was satisfied to have done my part.

Maybe having been part of something like this, knowing these guys were here for him, would always be part of him ... maybe Tristan wouldn't need to return to drugs. Maybe he'd return home knowing what real friendship felt like and how good it felt to be healthy. I allowed myself to hope things would be different for him. *Maybe, just maybe*, I kept telling myself, and I knocked on wood to not jinx it.

9

TRISTAN COMPLETED his year in China and came home fit and healthy. I was happy to have him home. He picked away at his self-paced school classes, completed Grade 10 and started on Grade 11. He formed a close friendship with another kid from his school who shared his goofy humour and love of video games. He stayed in touch with his friends from China, some of whom were now scattered across the globe.

And he began his love affair with kitchens.

Before he'd unpacked his suitcases, Tristan got a job as a dishwasher at Mr. Mike's, a casual family steakhouse just down the hill from us. He liked the physicality, the rhythm and practical accomplishment of transforming dirty dishes into clean ones. He liked being part of a team and knowing the whole kitchen depended on him. There was an energy in the kitchen that charged him. He soon got promoted to plating desserts—defrosting frozen chocolate brownies and scooping ice cream on top, or slicing pieces of cake. Then he was trained to chop vegetables and finally, after months of hard work, he earned the title of "cook." He could make anything on the menu other than meat and seafood.

One evening in mid-April, while Tristan was at work, I waited for Jenn to return my car. She was planning to have dinner with me and Tanis, who'd recently returned from her travels in Australia golden-skinned and glowing. The menu was fettuccine primavera, with chicken for extra protein and gluten-free pasta for Tanis. The pasta was cooked and drained, but Jenn had not yet shown up. It was unusual for her to be late.

I called her and got no answer.

"Can I eat yet?" Tanis asked. She couldn't see why Jenn's lateness should affect her sustenance.

"Let's give it a few more minutes," I said.

Just before I was about to give in, Jenn walked through the door, her hair a new shade of blond, pulled back in a simple ponytail.

"You're late," I said, stating the obvious.

"I know, it's been a bad day and I just crashed your car," she said and plopped down on the couch.

My eyes opened wide, questioning. For Jenn, this could mean anything. Given the fact that she was here, in one piece, and hadn't called me from the scene, I figured she was probably being dramatic.

"Okay, not crash, exactly, but I rear-ended someone coming up the hill. He was really nice about it. There weren't any scratches on either of the cars. I checked, he checked, you can go check for yourself, but it was stressful and that's why I'm late," she said, looking like she was about to cry.

"Oh, hun." I gave her a big hug.

"Okay, I'm eating now!" Tanis called from the kitchen, like we'd been waiting for hours instead of minutes.

"Yeah, let's dish up," I said. "You want me to bring you yours, Jenn, or do you want to wait a bit?"

"I'm not hungry. My stomach's felt sick for three days."

"Maybe you're pregnant?" I said as I dished up my pasta, half joking. Birth control and Jenn had always been a difficult combination. She didn't remember to take it and it gave her intense mood swings. I was grateful she hadn't gotten pregnant before now and was always half-scared she would.

"I probably am, knowing me, because that's my luck," she said, her head falling on the seat of the old couch, like she was dying.

"It's not luck, Jenn," Tanis said. "It's called birth control. It's called being responsible."

"Blah, blah, blah, blah, blah," Jenn said, into the pillows.

"If you really think that, let's get a pregnancy test after dinner and find out," I suggested.

"I don't want to know," Jenn said. "I'm going to a party tonight."

I sat with the backwardness of that statement for a bit, waiting for my mind to form something both compassionate and constructive to say. Tanis beat me to it.

"Oh, great idea. Go drinking tonight and give your baby fetal alcohol syndrome. Nice one." Tanis lacked the compassion I might have used but she had a point. When Jenn partied, she wasn't moderate.

"Fuck my life, just shoot me now!" Jenn said and put a pillow over her head to shut us both out.

Watching her, face down on the couch, it occurred to me then that Jenn really thought she might be pregnant. This was a first. I'd asked her time and again over the past few years, in my half-joking, half-questioning way, but I'd never seen her respond like this. A pregnancy now would not be wonderful. Jenn and Alan were not a happy couple. They didn't have any financial sense, let alone stability. Their only hobby was drinking. And at twenty, Jenn was too young. My heart pounded but I tried to remain calm and take things one step at a time.

"Okay, let's get a pregnancy test and go from there," I said.

While Tanis and I finished eating, Jenn gathered herself together and drove the few blocks to Shoppers Drug Mart. She was back in ten minutes.

"I don't want to take the stupid test, Mom. I'm going out tonight." Jenn was no longer humorously dramatic. She was stubborn and serious and scared.

"Well, what if you're pregnant? Don't you want to know before you put things in your body that could be risky for the baby?"

"Can't I have just one more night to not think about it?" she pleaded. "And anyway, even if I am pregnant, I don't know if I'm going to keep it." She said this last part defiantly, but I knew Jenn. I suspected she would very much want to keep this baby.

"You don't know yet that you *aren't* pregnant. Until you know whether you're pregnant or not you need to be responsible. First things first—go pee on a stick."

Jenn went into the bathroom, and I began to clear up the dishes. Before I had the dishwasher loaded, she called, "Mom, come here!"

Tanis ran to the bathroom door. "I want to see. Are you preggos, Jenn?"

"Tanis." I gave her the evil eye. "Go wait in the living room."

I opened the bathroom door and Jenn was sitting, fully clothed, on the closed toilet seat. She passed me the test. It showed positive. Elation and excitement swirled together with desperation and despair. I decided to take my cues as to how to react from Jenn. I looked over at her. She was crying.

"Oh, love," I said, and wrapped my arms around her.

When Jenn was ready, we came out and the three of us sat on the couch in stunned silence. Even Tanis knew not to tease Jenn in that moment.

When Jenn finished crying, she wiped her nose on her sleeve and asked, "Now what?"

"Now," I said, "you take whatever time you need to figure out what you're going to do. You don't need to decide tonight. You *can't* reasonably decide tonight. I'll support you one hundred percent in whatever you want to do—except for partying tonight. You have to give up on that idea right now."

Jenn simply nodded her head.

Underneath my carefully neutral attitude, I fiercely wanted Jenn to keep this baby. My first grandbaby. I knew Jenn was young, and her relationship was not stable or loving, but lots of women had babies at twenty-one and did just fine. And maybe it was what both Jenn and Alan needed to grow up a bit, to pull back from the partying and be more responsible. It was possible a baby would bring them closer together, though a long shot. Still, I reminded myself there were worse things than being a single mother, if it came to that, and few things more wonderfully miraculous than a child. And Jenn would have support. She'd have me and her dad, who loved children. Alan's parents would be supportive and loving. That baby would be so, *so* loved by so many people.

A few days later, Jenn told me she and Alan were going to be parents. Already, her maternal instincts to protect and provide for her baby were fierce: she set up an adorable nursery with mint-green walls and white furniture, and she didn't smoke, drink, or use drugs for almost a year.

I OFTEN stayed up late to chat with Tristan when he got off shift so he could tell me about the intricacies of loading an industrial dishwasher, the joy he felt in cooking, or his humiliation when he screwed up. We cooked dinners together, me shifting easily into the role of sous chef, supporting him in bringing his culinary visions to life. I relished the peacefulness of it all.

By spring, Tristan had been home for five months. He was smoking weed daily again, but as long as he was in school, going to work and avoiding hard drugs, I was okay with that. I hoped the lifestyle he'd lived in China and his new passion for cooking would keep him on a good path.

And then one Friday night, he didn't come home after work. I went to bed but didn't sleep, listening for the door to open, waiting for the thud of his shoes on the floor as he kicked them off. Nothing. In the morning, I called him. No answer. On Sunday afternoon I got a call from Mr. Mike's, asking for Tristan. He'd missed his shift.

On Sunday evening Tristan waltzed through the door as if nothing had happened.

"What?" he asked when I pressed him for his whereabouts. "I was just over at Zane's. My phone died. Check with his mom if you want to."

He kicked off his shoes and they thudded as I knew they would, albeit two days late. Balloo greeted Tristan by rubbing against his legs, and Tristan scooped him up like a baby and kissed the cat's belly.

"And what about work, Tristan? You missed a shift."

"Oooh, shit." He looked upset about that. "I totally forgot. I'll have to talk to them. I know they're happy with me so it should be okay. First, I need a shower." He carried Balloo with him to the bathroom.

Mr. Mike's gave Tristan's shifts to someone else for the next week and told him if that happened again he'd be fired. I was ecstatic to have someone else impose consequences on him. He loved his work. He'd step up, I was sure.

He began skipping school and regularly didn't come home at night. Without missing a beat, I joined our familiar dance, stepping into my old behaviours as easily as Tristan had stepped into his: I searched his room when he wasn't at home and read his Facebook messages when he left his laptop open. Both confirmed what I already knew: he was using cocaine again. And he'd often offer to share his drugs with girls he wanted to hang out with.

In the year Tristan was away from home, I'd gotten out of the habit of worrying about him. I hated the weight of worry and didn't want to carry it anymore. I was angry, disappointed and scared but I tried not to fixate on him and his drug use. He wasn't as vulnerable as he'd been before he went to China, I told myself. He was seventeen. His addiction may be raising its serpentine head but it hadn't yet swallowed him. He was still pleasant and polite—most of the time, anyway. I could imagine Tristan losing his job, even dropping out of school, but he was not at the point where I could see him living on the street.

I threw myself into my career with a focus that left no room for worry.

"I NEED to go back to China, Mom," Tristan told me over dinner early in June. Mr. Mike's had finally fired him for not showing up to work the previous day. "I need to get my shit together and I can't do it here." He dished some grilled asparagus onto his plate.

Hearing those words filled me with hope but also caution. I'd been wanting him to acknowledge that he couldn't manage his life but I knew his next steps would be critical.

"You've tried that already, Tristan. You need to learn to get your shit together while you're here, living your life. What about rehab?" I asked, taking another mouthful of barbecued salmon.

"No way I'm going to one of those places. What do you think I am? A loser addict?!" That word—*addict*—held the weight of a million poor souls who were not smart enough or strong enough to avoid addiction. *Not like me*, was Tristan's underlying message. He slammed his fork down and then took a breath, calming himself. "I just need to get away for a bit, train hard with Shifu and the guys, and get reset. I'm living my life over there too, you know."

If Tristan refused rehab, I didn't see many options. I wouldn't pay for it myself this time, though, I told him. I couldn't even if I wanted to, so that decision was easy. But my aunts had set up an education savings fund for Tristan and my girls when they were small. If his school in China qualified as an acceptable educational institute, and we could legitimately withdraw funds from his education savings plan for that purpose, then I agreed he could go. I told myself he was getting an education there, if not an academic one. And I shivered as I felt my aunts, both teachers and strong academics, roll over in their graves.

By the end of June, only eight months after returning from China and less than a month after losing his job, Tristan boarded a plane to spend another year training in kung fu. At least, that was the plan.

SHORTLY AFTER Tristan left for China again, Scott phoned to tell me his new girlfriend, Carly, was moving in with him. Fifteen years younger than either of us, professionally employed, she happened to be between homes. "It just makes sense," he told me.

Scott and I had remained friends since our separation, getting together for bike rides and evenings of Netflix and popcorn. I knew he had met Carly only a week or two earlier.

A few days later, he asked to meet me in person. He sat on my couch, drinking jasmine tea, and told me that he and Carly were trying to have a baby and wanted to get married when our divorce was final. "So, I'd like to get the paperwork started on that," he said.

"You've known this woman for what?" I asked him, incredulous. "Two weeks? And you want to start a family? You're almost fifty!"

"I know, but it seems like I've known her my whole life, Kathy. And she's known another friend of mine for years, so I've met her before now."

"And you couldn't have told me this over the phone, why?" I knew I was being snarky but didn't care.

"It seemed right to tell you in person. I hope we can still be friends."

I wished I could have hung up the phone and been done with it but, because of Scott's relentless sense of right and wrong, I had to keep staring at his face and make small talk until he finished the tea and cookies I'd made especially for his visit.

At first, I thought I was upset because I didn't want to see him hurt. But over the next few weeks, it became clear I was mourning the death of our marriage for the first time. When we'd separated, all my emotional energy had gone toward Tristan—to getting him to China, to saving him. Afterward, my friendship with Scott had felt like a successful and natural transition rather than the end of something. But now, a strong resentment bubbled up from deep within and demanded my attention: Scott had never been a true partner to me.

This was the man who took a full year before "deciding" he was in love with me, who would buy chicken breasts and organic vegetables for himself, which he'd keep in "his" section of the fridge, when I could only afford hamburger and frozen vegetables for me and the kids. This was the man who, more than once, asked me to move away with him and leave my kids behind with their dad. Who, after we'd moved into separate homes, berated me and threatened divorce if I filed my taxes as if we were separated so I could claim the child tax benefits available while I was out of work. This was the man who refused to contribute to me financially, because I'd "just spend the money on the kids, and that's their dad's job."

I had accepted his lack of partnership as something to be endured. Who was I to expect deep partnership, anyway? An uneducated single mom with three difficult kids couldn't set her standards that high.

But it occurred to me now that I had deserved more. I deserved to not feel alone in a marriage. I deserved the kind of partnership that, I was sure, Scott was now offering this new woman.

He wanted me to meet her, to remain his friend and become hers. I would miss Scott's friendship greatly, but I'd be damned if I'd watch him give everything to her that he never could to me.

After the legalities were settled, we never spoke again.

SHIFU WANG'S school had moved up north where winter set in early and with blistering cold. As a senior student, Tristan was left to practice on his own for large parts of each day, and without constant camaraderie he found it hard to stay focused.

"Mom, I can't stand it here anymore," Tristan told me one Skype call in October, only four months after he'd arrived. "I'm freezing my balls off and I can't concentrate. But I have a plan—it's all worked out—I just need you to listen properly, with an open mind."

Another student was going to study muay thai—Thai kick boxing—in Thailand for six months. Tristan wanted to go with him. I tried to convince him to stay out the year in China, to persevere past the uncomfortable parts, but it wasn't going to happen. He was determined to come home or go to Thailand. The cold, dark days in northern China had lost their shine for him.

I researched the training academy he wanted to go to. They'd provide meals, accommodation and training, but nobody was going to whack Tristan with a stick in the morning if he didn't get out of bed for his first class. Nobody would even notice, or care. If he wanted to train, he'd train. If he didn't, he wouldn't. They weren't babysitters.

"Mom, I'll train hard, I promise," he reassured me. "Brent's getting ready for competition and he'll kick my butt if I don't get out of bed. And I don't want to spend all that time and money and not learn anything."

His words meant nothing to me. He might believe them, but I didn't. He'd go where his desires pulled him. I told him I needed a few more days to think about it. I walked through the house gathering up Tanis's clothes to wash—*how did her bra find its way under the couch cushions?*—and then collected the crusty dishes from her room as I thought about her brother.

I was concerned about leaving him unsupervised in Phuket, a tourist beach town where there were sure to be drugs. I didn't think he would search them out necessarily, but he wasn't likely to refuse if offered. Prostitution was prevalent there and I didn't think Tristan had the moral compass to pass on those offers, either. But he'd be eighteen, I told myself. Old enough to make his own decisions, even if they were bad ones.

Turning the dishwasher on and giving the counters a quick wipe with Fantastik, I was a little alarmed at how easily I accepted the idea of Tristan going to Thailand, where he could slide smoothly into a world of trouble but would have to work uncharacteristically hard to stay focused on his training. I saw where that would lead him. And yet, I'd let him go. Mostly, I admitted to myself, I didn't want him home. If he was not able to go to school or hold down a job, if he was not willing to stay in China or come home and go to rehab, then I couldn't see much good in having him rattling around home getting into trouble and then more trouble. I didn't want to deal with his lies or disappearances. I didn't want to worry about him daily or spy on him to know what he was up to. And I sure didn't want to be his emotional punching bag when things went badly for him, as they inevitably would.

Still, I paid attention to my deep-rooted feelings, the part of me beyond thought and reason where my bones vibrated with motherly instincts, and they were not in a panic at the thought of Tristan in Thailand. My head told me it was a bad idea but my gut told me it wouldn't be tragic.

Before going to Thailand, Tristan returned home for two months to earn a bit of extra money, spend Christmas with us and, most importantly, welcome the arrival of his niece. In the early morning hours of Christmas Eve, we greeted Emily Louise, a fresh spring bud, full of potential, unblemished by the storms of the world. I vowed to do everything in my power to fill her life with warmth and security and love and cupcakes and all good things that might protect her. Because while both her parents loved her to madness, it soon became clear they no longer loved each other. Emily was born smack in the middle of their emotional hurricane.

IN EARLY February, Tristan boarded a plane to Thailand, where he planned to spend five days a week for three months training in muay thai.

Tristan and I had prearranged Skype calls once a week but we usually spoke more often. On our first call, he walked around with his laptop so I could see the guava and lime trees just outside his window, and his tiny, sparse living quarters. Tristan said the people were friendly, the food was spicy but good, and the beaches and girls were gorgeous. I reminded him about the importance of training hard.

Tristan regularly ran out of pocket money and asked me to release more of his funds. He said it was for gas for the mopeds he drove to the beach, for eating out when he didn't want to eat at the school, and going out in the evening with Brent and the other guys. His poor money management had been a contentious issue when he was in China too, and I was sick of it. He needed to learn to live within his perfectly reasonable budget. Still, I sometimes sent him an extra twenty dollars. Occasionally, I knew his dad sent him money too.

Then in early March Tristan told me he was getting a tattoo.

"Tristan, that's a terrible idea," I said, making a sour face. "You don't know if it's sanitary or if they're decent artists. It would be better to save your money and find a good, reputable artist back here."

"Mom, it's fine. There's a guy at the beach who does really good work for, like, twenty bucks. I'm just letting you know."

And so, Tristan got his tattoo: a huge tiger face, the size of a salad plate, on the left side of his chest. Over Skype, I begrudgingly admired the beautiful line drawings in black with sapphire eyes for colour. I had to admit it looked good if you liked that kind of thing, which I didn't.

"How's your training going?" I asked for the hundredth time.

He usually avoided this question if he could, or lied, I suspected, when he couldn't. But now he had an excuse. "I'm not allowed to sweat for two weeks while my tattoo heals. But after that, I promise

I'll buckle down and put crazy energy into it. I don't want to waste my time here, don't worry."

I was livid. "Tristan! You didn't go to Thailand to get tattoos!"

"It's what everyone does, Mom. You can't go to Thailand and *not* get a tattoo."

But the final straw came a couple weeks later.

Tristan Skyped me on a Friday evening, sounding panicked.

"Mom," he said quietly, like he was deliberately keeping his voice down. "I need you to send me fifty dollars right now. I really, *really* need you to do this for me. It's the last time I'll ask for anything, I promise."

My stomach clenched and I wanted to throw my computer out the window so I didn't need to have this conversation with him. Again. I was sick of it.

"What happened, Tristan? What's going on?" I felt cold and steely.

"Mom, just send me the money, pleeease?!"

"I'm not sending you anything unless you tell me why you need it. You had your money for the week on Monday. It's not my problem if you can't figure out how to make it last."

"It's not for me, okay?" He paused, maybe hoping that would be enough. It wasn't. "It's for a girl, all right? She's here in my room, and she's scared, and she says she won't leave unless I give her fifty bucks or someone is going to beat her up. I'm trying to help her out, Mom."

I sat with that for a bit, my mind spinning, my stomach churning.

"You want me to send you money to . . . pay for your prostitute?"

"No, Mom, don't be disgusting! It's not like that. Really. She's just a girl I met, and I want to help her. It's not like that."

Clearly, it was exactly like that: a girl he just met who wouldn't leave his room unless she got money because she was afraid of getting beaten up if she left empty-handed.

I didn't want to hear any more lies, so I asked no more questions.

"If I send you money, Tristan, you need to come home. I'm not putting up with this shit anymore. This is way too far." I opened up another window on my laptop and began searching for flights to bring him home.

"Don't be like that, Mom! I'll do better, I promise. I can start training again now that my tattoo is healed. I won't get into any more trouble. I've learned my lesson. Mom, please!"

I wanted to tell Tristan to figure it out on his own, to clean up his own mess, for once. It would have felt good, so justified, if I had simply hung up on him and turned off my phone, shut down my computer. I imagined the sweet silence of that.

But it wasn't just about Tristan. There was a girl who was trying to survive any way she could, and I had no doubt she was fearful to leave without her money. To me, she seemed the innocent victim who'd pay the price for Tristan's irresponsibility. His immorality.

"Tristan, I'm sending you fifty dollars now. And I'm booking you on the next flight home. That looks like Monday. I'll email you the details." I hung up, disgusted—at Tristan, for being Tristan, and at myself, for somehow allowing this to happen. I'd paid Tristan's drug dealers in the past and now I was paying his prostitutes.

I felt like throwing up.

IO

I OPENED the door to my local Tim Hortons, a blast of cool air welcoming me as I scanned the crowd looking for Conrod. I'd only met him once before though he knew Tristan a little. As a youth counsellor of Tristan's best friend and many others, he'd worked with teens in various stages of drug abuse and dysfunction, and I hoped he'd help me figure out what was realistic for my son.

With Tristan home again, I was once again dedicating myself to answering the question, *What now?* He'd gotten his job back at Mr. Mike's and managed to hold on to it, so far. But once again, he'd stopped going to school. Occasionally, he'd go to drop-in jiu jitsu with a friend but wouldn't commit to regular martial arts classes. A few weeks earlier, he'd begun not coming home at night; more recently, he'd gone AWOL for days. I knew where this was heading.

I crossed the room to Conrod and shook his hand. He was the far side of middle age, with kind but tired eyes, a face etched with decades of love and loss, and a decidedly no-bullshit attitude—everything I thought a youth counsellor should be.

I sipped my Earl Grey while he had black coffee and listened patiently as I explained the situation. Tristan was now eighteen, that tricky age where he could be considered an adult, or not. Developmentally, he was not. Other than working as a cook in a family chain restaurant for near minimum wage, he had no ability to make his way in the world. I knew I'd need to step back and let him live his life at some point, but not yet. First, I needed to make sure he was prepared. And while I was beginning to suspect I might not be able to stop his addiction, I needed to know I'd done everything possible to set him up for success. I figured I had one more year in which to make a difference.

I told Conrod I'd begun to investigate culinary schools for Tristan. Though he was not yet trained to cook meat or seafood at Mr. Mike's, Tristan was the master of potato skins and side dishes and his passion for cooking kept growing.

"He literally dreams of the day he can professionally grill a steak." I smiled, shaking my head a bit. "Searing scallops or frying fish is like finding the Holy Grail—he says he can't even imagine what that would feel like. I haven't seen him this passionate about anything for such a long time."

Tristan had never completed Grade 11 so his options were limited. But the culinary program at Vancouver Community College had a good reputation and only required a Grade 10 education. Even after paying for his last stint in China, and the debacle of Thailand, there was plenty of money in his education savings fund to pay for culinary school.

"It's only a one-year program but I'm not sure Tristan can hold himself together that long. I don't like the direction his addiction is pulling him in."

"Well," Conrod said after I had run out of words, "if Tristan's using cocaine and other drugs the way you say he is, there's no way he'll complete school. You'd be wasting your money. In an ideal world he'd go to rehab. But if he's not ready for that, there's not much you can do."

I stared into my tea, thinking. Trying to find an angle around reality.

"There has to be something," I said. "I can't just leave him to end up on the streets. What would you do if it were your kid?" I was genuinely interested. I needed to know what someone who knew what they were doing would do.

He set down his coffee and sighed. "I've had dozens of kids in that situation," he said, gently. He then gave me the name and contact information for the director of a good rehab centre I could speak with.

"I know this is hard, but here's the thing," he continued, leaning toward me, holding eye contact. "Until Tristan's ready to get help, you need to let go. His addiction is not your problem. You can't change him, and you can't stop it. Your job is to make sure he doesn't pull you down with him. Set whatever boundaries you need to keep yourself safe and sane, and then stick to them. It's okay to say no to him. It's okay to say he can't stay with you if it comes to that. Your only job is to look after yourself. That's it." He leaned back and smiled. "It's not so easy looking after yourself, is it? It gets easier with practice."

Hearing his truth and compassion brought tears to my eyes, but I blinked them back while I entered the contact information for the rehab centre he recommended—Westgate—into my phone. As we were leaving, I asked Conrod if I could follow up with him again if I had any other concerns about Tristan.

"Well, now, I was very happy to meet with you this time but, no, I generally choose to spend my personal time with family and friends. It's easy in this field to get caught up in the urgency of everyone else's problems and end up creating problems for yourself. I've been there and I've learned to draw boundaries. It's part of that 'letting go' I was telling you about. I hope you understand."

I assured him I did, but I was taken aback. Only then did I realize that I'd put him out, that I'd expected his desire to help Tristan to be as overpowering as mine. But of course it wasn't. It couldn't be—shouldn't be. In my experience, most people cushioned a negative response in vagueness or falsity; I admired his directness even if it bruised. Perhaps he thought I could learn something from hearing what a direct refusal sounded like. If so, he was right.

When I got home, I investigated Westgate treatment centre online, read through their website, watched their videos and looked up reviews. I liked what I saw. But Tristan was still opposed to addiction treatment or counselling of any sort. In his mind, he didn't have a problem: life was good.

I didn't contact Westgate. I couldn't bear the thought of being told by one more person or place that they were not able to help. I was tired of hearing I needed to look after myself when I was not the one who needed saving.

Despite Tristan's lukewarm interest, I signed him up for culinary school.

THE FIRST two weeks of school did not go well. Tristan wasn't used to getting up at 5 o'clock in the morning to get himself ready and bus downtown for a 7 a.m. start. He was late a few times and missed two days of school. He got a warning: three absences in any six-week unit and he was out.

On the Friday evening after his second week of school, Tristan and I were home while Tanis was at a friend's. I was curled up on the couch, reading Stephen King's latest novel, *Mr. Mercedes*. Tristan was in his room playing a video game.

He came out, agitated. "Mom, I need twenty bucks."

I looked up at him and sighed. I was so tired of these requests, of not knowing what to do about them. If I gave him money, it never felt right. If I didn't, it still never felt right.

"I fucking need twenty bucks, okay? Just give it to me and I'll go. You don't need to see me again tonight, just give me the money!" Tristan was wild, frenzied.

"No. Tristan, you can't just be rude and demand money and expect me to give it to you."

And then all hell broke loose.

Tristan grabbed the lamp from the side table and smashed it, again and again, on the floor, its linen lampshade crumpling, its metal bending, until it resembled a dead bug. Then he took a counter stool and began smashing the broken lamp with that.

"You want me to break everything in the house?" he yelled, wild-eyed, sweeping dishes off the counter between the living room and the kitchen. "I'll break every fucking thing in this entire house. You don't even know. You have no fucking idea what it's like. I'm going to fucking kill myself. I swear to God I'm going to kill myself, you have no idea. No idea at all."

He kept yelling but his words lost their meaning and blended together. All I could hear was noise as I watched Tristan, shirtless, in pajama bottoms, smashing things. He seemed equally violent and vulnerable. I stood, terrified, heart pounding, at the far end of the room but my terror felt distant, like it belonged to another person. This other person yelled for him to stop, to no effect. She told him she'd phone the cops. No effect.

I went to my room and called the police.

When I came out, he was back in his bedroom, door closed. I could hear him sobbing. I was suddenly *so* angry. But still, my heart broke to hear him in pain. It hurt in every possible way. And I couldn't go to him. I couldn't make it better. All I could do was wait for the police to arrive.

I contemplated cleaning up, so the police didn't see a mess, and then realized what a ridiculous thought that was. Then I figured I should leave everything exactly as it was, as "evidence" of what Tristan had done, but that was equally ridiculous. In the end, I just dropped onto the couch and stayed there, listening to Tristan's cries slowly subside, and then stop, until two burly police officers arrived less than ten minutes later.

I explained the situation.

"Are drugs involved?" one of them asked.

"Almost certainly," I said.

"Do you want to press charges?"

"No. I just want him out of the house. And I want his key. I don't want him coming back in the middle of the night without me knowing."

The officer nodded his head and then knocked forcefully on Tristan's door, telling him who they were and that he needed to come out and talk to them.

Tristan opened the door right away. He was fully dressed. He had his suitcase open and half-packed. He knew where this was heading. He asked for a few more minutes to finish packing.

I agreed.

I absently picked up a broken dish and placed it on the counter, and then righted what was left of the stool and leaned it against the wall. Tristan had never been violent before; I'd never felt unsafe around him. This was a whole new world. I looked around, unsure of what to do with myself. I certainly never thought I'd find comfort in having the police present.

When Tristan came out of his bedroom, suitcase in tow, the police asked where he was heading. Tristan said he'd go to his dad's. I was relieved. Even like this, *especially* like this, I didn't want him wandering around. The police offered to drive him, but Tristan refused, saying he'd rather walk. There was no way Tristan would feel good about getting in a cop car, and a thirty-minute walk might clear his head. I told him I'd drive his suitcase over to his dad's later if his dad was cool with him staying there.

And then everyone was gone and I was left standing alone in the middle of everything that was broken.

I DIDN'T see Tristan for weeks after that, but I stayed in touch with his dad. Apparently, Tristan went to school every day, on time.

I was happy for the break; it was peaceful and pleasant with just Tanis at home. I could replace the dishes and make do with one fewer stool and table lamp but, inside, I was badly shaken. How could I have Tristan back if that was how he acted?

I poured my energy into work.

I'd recently expanded my business and was hiring and training employees. I spoke at conferences and ran a local content strategy meetup group. I started a new contract with Samsung. Like blinders on a horse, work kept me focused forward. In work, I could feel successful and in control. Hard work gave me a chance to rest. But as time went by, I began to miss Tristan and wanted to connect with him again. So I reached out.

"Hey, Tristan, you look good!" I said as he got into the car. And he did: clothes clean, eyes clear. I leaned over for a hug. Over burgers and shakes, he told me about school, the most amazing peach flan he made, and how he'd be learning to cook meat next. "And the manager at Mr. Mike's said they'd move me to the protein station once I finish the meat unit. And they'll give me a raise too!" he said, proudly, as he ate his last few fries. We chatted happily about school and food, and then headed back to the car.

"How's Balloo?" he asked as I dropped him back at his dad's. "Can I come by and see him sometime?"

"He's good. And of course, you can. Tanis is fine too, by the way." I raised my eyebrows.

"Oh, yeah. Tanis too. I haven't seen her for so long I forgot I had a sister. Oh wait . . . I have two!" Tristan laughed. "Just kidding, Mom. Thanks for lunch." He leaned over and gave me a long hug. "I love you. And my sisters too." He got out of the car and headed up his steps. "But I love Balloo most of all!" he called to me, laughing, before opening the front door and disappearing inside.

We'd had a good time together. I hadn't mentioned his violent episode and neither had he—not even to apologize. We both acted as if nothing had happened and that was okay with me. I wanted to strengthen our connection rather than relive the past that had torn us apart. There was nothing to be done about that, anyway.

Six weeks after he went to his dad's, and with a perfect school record during that time, Tristan came home again. The reason for his return wasn't our renewed positivity, though. It was the desperation in his voice when he phoned me.

"Mom, I can't stay at Dad's anymore. You gotta come get me. I'm in front of his place with my suitcase. If you can't come now, I'll walk."

I'd been enjoying a rare relaxing Saturday catching up on *Downton Abbey* episodes, and I would have preferred to stay embroiled in the Crawleys' dramas rather than deal with Tristan's. But theirs could wait. I turned off the TV and headed for my coat. "What happened?"

"It's stupid. I was playing around with Dad's machete, the one he keeps on his wall, and he thinks I was threatening him with it. I wasn't! I was waving it around, but not *at* him. And then Dad started yelling, and his girlfriend started freaking out, and then he called the cops on me. I don't even know why! I was just playing around. Dad's crazy, you know him. He totally overreacted. He just doesn't want me there anymore, Mom." He paused, his voice broken. "It's a small place, I get in the way of him and his girlfriend. I can't stay if he doesn't want me."

I was sure his dad had a very different version of things but it didn't matter. For years now, whenever emotions got too hot, Tristan had bounced between our homes like a hot potato. In his absence, I could recharge and get ready for the next round. I was sure Brad felt the same way. Clearly, tempers had become too hot at his dad's, and it was my turn again.

Back home, Tristan seemed steadier. He set his alarm for 4:45 every morning and was out of bed by 5 a.m. He liked to take his time in the morning, having a leisurely cup of coffee and bowl of cereal before showering, putting on his checkered cook's pants, and making sure he had a reasonably clean cook's jacket in his backpack. He was out the door by 5:45 a.m. and home again by 4:30 p.m. Two or three nights a week he'd grab a quick bite to eat before going to Mr. Mike's for an evening shift.

Tristan didn't miss another day of school all year. His enthusiasm in the kitchen became all-consuming. I wasn't sure where his preternatural focus on food came from. It might simply have been the newest outlet for his obsessive personality. Or maybe he was in the honeymoon phase of a new love, wanting to drown himself in every aroma and glory in the sensuousness of his hands kneading dough or the sensations of his tongue tasting champagne sorbet. Then again, cooking may have been his way of trying to keep himself from falling apart. Most likely, it was all three.

One time, Tristan spent all day in the kitchen, filling our world with the fried, yeasty scent of gluten-free doughnuts, which he topped with a sweet maple glaze and served to us for dinner, at 4 p.m., with a side of thick-sliced, apple-smoked bacon. Tristan didn't want Tanis to go through life never tasting a warm, homemade doughnut just because she couldn't eat wheat.

"Come and get it!" he called, setting the first batch in front of Tanis and placing more dough in the fryer. The doughnuts were puffy and golden brown, dripping with a rapidly hardening glaze. As Tanis took her first bite, Tristan stared at her, his grey-green eyes nervous and hopeful. He wore nothing but MMA shorts with a kitchen rag tucked into the elastic. He was lean and muscled, his hands and forearms scarred from cooking.

He's too skinny, I thought.

When Tanis finally gave him a thumbs up, her smiling mouth too full to speak, he whooped in a Rocky Balboa impression, his grin radiating such happiness I had to laugh. He danced around the kitchen island to wrap Tanis in a bear hug and kiss the top of her head.

For Tristan, if his cooking turned out well, he was on top of the world.

"I'm fucking awesome, Mom!" he yelled one afternoon, licking warm caramel sauce from his fingers, shimmying around the kitchen while singing along to Elton John's "I'm Still Standing." "This is fuckin' eh! All the girls are going to want this caramel sauce."

But if his cooking didn't turn out well, he was unpredictable. I learned to watch closely, barely breathing, to see if he'd just shrug it off and try again, or if things would fall apart. In the split second I saw his mood shift, I'd jump in to try to salvage whatever went wrong—a sagging soufflé or a broken bearnaise. Of course, I never could salvage a thing, because even if I did, it was too late.

Many times, after a cooking failure, he'd lock himself in his room and smoke weed, hurling obscenities if I tried to talk to him.

"Fuck off, Mom, it's all your fault," he'd say, whether I'd been in the kitchen with him or not. Sometimes I cleaned up his messes and encouraged him to try again. Sometimes that worked.

Other times, Tristan blamed himself for his culinary mishaps. He'd throw his cooking in the garbage and then lie comatose for half the day, speaking only to say how pathetic, useless and stupid he was. His words seemed true to him, and it broke my heart. I'd tiptoe around, to avoid being a target and upsetting him further by simply *being*.

On Tristan's worst days, after a cooking failure, real or imagined, he'd threaten to kill himself, demand money from me—which I sometimes gave him and sometimes didn't—and then take off. He never told me where he was going, and I rarely asked.

If that happened on a weeknight, it wasn't so bad. I knew he'd be home in time to change into his checkered pants and white jacket and head out to school before 6 a.m. But if it was a weekend, I wouldn't hear from him until Monday morning. Then my fear of what might happen to him was equal only to my relief that he was away.

When it was just the two of us, I could manage Tristan. But if Tanis walked into the room in the middle of one of her brother's dark moods, she had little patience and refused to coddle him. I'd try to catch her eye and shake my head, silently begging her, *Please, just let him be!*

But Tristan's moods were heavy, and hard to be around. If it got too much for Tanis, she'd tell him to get over it.

"It's only a coffee cake, Tristan. Make another one," she said one Saturday afternoon, as Tristan lay on the couch cursing himself.

In an instant, he leapt from dejection to rage.

"Fuck off and die, Tanis!"

"*You* fuck off, Tristan," she responded. "Nobody wants you here anyway, you're so fucking miserable!"

My world exploded.

My two beautiful children raged at each other, putting their martial arts training into practice. Feet and fists flew at each other. Forearms and shins blocked the blows.

I yelled for them to stop. I yelled that I'd call the cops. But they couldn't hear me over their furious cursing and exaggerated shrieks of pain.

My head throbbed and my chest felt like it would burst. My vision narrowed.

And then, suddenly, I was oh . . . so . . . tired.

I folded to the ground and sat with my head against the wall and waited, resigned, for my kids to wear themselves out. I had learned by now that they fought like cats: loud and terrifying but doing little damage.

Eventually, they retreated to their respective rooms. I remained on the floor, held only by the cold wall.

None of us talked to each other for the rest of the day.

For some reason, they both blamed me.

11

WINTER DRAGGED on and the world outside was grey and wet and monotonous. I began to worry that Tristan's mood swings were symptoms of something larger, more than just drugs, and combed the internet for diagnoses that seemed to fit: manic depression or perhaps bipolar disorder. I hoped for these diagnoses; they seemed more manageable than addiction.

I spoke with my doctor. She said Tristan's mood swings could certainly be caused by drug abuse alone, and it would be difficult to know if there were underlying mental health concerns as long as he was abusing drugs. He should come in and talk to her, she said, which, of course, he refused to do. "There's nothing wrong with me," he said. "You're the one who's stressed out all the time, Mom. *You* go see her!"

With Tristan refusing to get any sort of help, I once again wrestled with how I could make a difference. And then I had a radical idea. Perhaps, I thought, Tristan was behaving badly because he was angry that nobody trusted him. I had taken to sleeping with my purse in my room and hiding it away during the day. I didn't want to have doubts, and then accuse him, and then hear him lying to me whenever twenty dollars went missing, which had happened more than once. I didn't want him to steal my Visa card, which he had done more than once.

I had begun to bang on the bathroom door if he was in there longer than five minutes. *What is he doing in there?* I'd ask myself, and him, multiple times a day when he'd lock himself away for half an hour at a time, or more. I hated how my mind worried at that question, painfully and obsessively, assuming he was using drugs in the bathroom but not knowing what or why. He had a bedroom, for god's sake. Once, when I didn't trust him to stay home at night, I hid his running shoes. It didn't work because he had other shoes.

I hated that feeling of distrust; it corroded the better parts of me. It occurred to me that he must not like it either. Knowing I expected him to do the wrong thing must be eating away at the goodness inside of him. He often said, "Why should I even bother, Mom, if you don't trust me anyway? I might as well do what you think I'm doing!" An excuse, sure, but maybe there was some truth to it.

So, I decided to trust him and see what happened. Perhaps if I showed him more trust, he'd work hard to be worthy of it. Perhaps he would see himself as worthy, and then become worthy.

I began to look for opportunities to show him I had faith in him. I'd give him my bank card when he needed to pick up an ingredient for something he was cooking, or I'd ask him to get a few groceries and hand him twenty dollars like it was no big deal. Occasionally, he'd ask if he could buy some smokes with my card, as well as the groceries, and I usually said yes. Then I'd surreptitiously check the receipt and my bank balance. Over the next few months, other than the odd unapproved pack of cigarettes, I didn't notice any unexpected charges or withdrawals. I still slept with my purse in my bedroom—I wasn't stupid—but I was encouraged.

During this time, Tristan once again brought up the idea of getting his driver's licence. He was nineteen and had been longing to drive for years but, between his time overseas and his drug use, it had never happened. I'd always shut down the conversation. I wasn't sure if this was the perfect opportunity to show trust in him, or sheer madness to let him behind the wheel. All I knew was that I had committed to trusting Tristan and that, so far, it had not turned out badly.

And just like that, we had something to do together on weekends. We weren't fighting constantly anymore. We'd drive out and around a nearby lake or hit the highway and zoom downtown. Once he got the hang of it, he was a relaxed driver, and we used his driving practices to chat about school or his plans for the future. Sometimes he'd ask me about my work or other things going on in my life. We were rebuilding our relationship, one drive at a time. I was never nervous riding with him. He was a skilled driver.

In the spring of that year, Tristan earned his driver's licence and was able to drive without me in the car. I continued to choose to trust him.

Over the next couple of years, he took my car without asking on more than one occasion. Many times, when he did have permission, he failed to bring it back when he was supposed to. I paid countless parking tickets and, a few times, had to fetch it after it was towed. Once, I had to find my car after he ran out of gas and left it on the side of the road, not remembering exactly where. But he never got a speeding ticket or had an accident more serious than a small scuffle with the post in our parking stall. I thanked God for that because I knew, deep down, it could have gone either way. And if something terrible had happened, I would have been more guilty than he was.

TRISTAN WORKED hard through culinary school, finally learning how to grill a proper steak, fry fish and sear scallops. When he felt ready to move on from Mr. Mike's, I updated his resumé, hunted through job postings on Craigslist and used his email account to send out applications for him, checking in with him to make sure I was using the kitchen lingo correctly. I told him when and where to go for his first interview, and he was offered that job as a full-time cook at a fine-dining seafood restaurant overlooking the marina in Yaletown, a trendy neighbourhood in downtown Vancouver.

At last, I'd done all I could for him. He was no longer a minor. He had marketable skills and a career he was both passionate about and good at. His martial arts successes were rooted within him, ready to flourish again whenever he chose to return to them. And I was tired of living with him—tired of tiptoeing around his moods, tired of my continuing suspicions, despite my decision to trust him. I was exhausted. I wanted peace and quiet.

In September, I told both Tristan and Tanis they needed to move out by the end of the year.

Tanis was twenty-one. She'd spent the previous year in college but decided to take some time out and was now working in retail. Having her at home was no more trouble than cleaning up after her, but I felt done with that too. She fussed for a bit, not wanting to jump fully into adulthood, but then moved in with her boyfriend for a while before happily renting her own basement suite.

On November first, one week after Tristan's twentieth birthday and two months after he graduated from culinary school, I moved him out of my home and into an affordable room I'd found for him in a house with five other young adults. It was in Mount Pleasant, a vibrant Vancouver neighbourhood full of interesting and affordable eateries. It had a large, shared kitchen and was close to his work and transit. It was perfect.

I paid the damage deposit and half of the first month's rent and filled his cupboards and fridge with food. I bought him new sheets and blankets and towels. Tristan proudly paid the other half of his first month's rent.

The landlord asked if I'd guarantee Tristan's rent payments since it was his first time renting. I told her, "No, it's important he feels independent. He has everything he needs to make it work."

I looked away so she wouldn't see the lie. Sure, Tristan had a secure job that paid well enough. He knew how to get to work on time and work hard, and he did. But I knew that wouldn't be enough. Far from it. He was an addict. His brain didn't work like other twenty-year-olds' brains. His obsessions and compulsions were not something he could rein in, no matter how much he wanted to. Withholding this from his landlord seemed unethical—*was* unethical, and I felt terrible about it. But I needed him out of my house, and I could not be responsible for my grown son's inevitable financial blunders.

Tristan was angry at me for kicking him out and wasn't happy about sharing space with other people, but he was proud to be renting his own place in Vancouver. He had his life planned out: he'd work hard and get promoted from line cook to *chef de partie*, get a raise, and finish his apprenticeship and Red Seal certification. He'd start going to the gym again and get back into martial arts. In six months, he figured, he'd rent a small place on his own where he didn't have to share the kitchen. He'd buy a cheap car and save up so that in two years he could go back to China and spend another year training with Shifu Wang.

He truly believed this.

"This is your life now," I told him. I made it clear I'd no longer support him financially in any way. I'd no longer rescue him if he got into trouble. I wouldn't drive him around or do his work for him. As I said those words aloud, I prayed for the strength to make them true.

"Whatever, Mom," he said, unfazed. In his mind, he didn't need me.

While Tristan focused on his new life of independence, I braced myself for his downward slide. I'd done enough research to know what I had to do—nothing—but it wouldn't be easy. Tristan still didn't think he had a drug problem. Why would he? He had a good job, which I'd found for him, and he went to work every day. I'd always provided him with food and a clean bed, and I'd spoon-fed him opportunities since he was fifteen. I didn't regret that, but I was drained and he was an adult now. It was up to him.

I bought two votive holders and some beeswax candles, and placed them on my bookshelf next to a picture of Tristan. I lit them every night and said a prayer for him: *Please, let Tristan do as little damage as possible to himself and others while he learns what he needs to learn in order to get well and live a long, healthy life.*

As if addiction could be cured by candles and wishes.

A FEW weeks after he moved into his own place, I took Tristan to Hawksworth Restaurant to celebrate both his birthday and graduation from culinary school. It seemed fitting to take him to one of the best restaurants in Vancouver, the one that he considered the epitome of fine dining.

I put on a dress and some make-up and arrived outside the restaurant early, but only waited a few minutes before Tristan showed up. He wore his usual running shoes and jeans, but they seemed clean. He had on a wrinkly, dark blue shirt with a black nylon jacket over top. His button-up shirt told me he'd made an effort, but his face shocked me. It was gaunt and sallow, speckled with scabs. His hair was overgrown and sticking up; his eyes were sunken, but at least they seemed clear. It had only been two weeks since I'd last seen him, but the change in him was alarming.

"Hey, Mom!" he said, greeting me with a warm hug. He seemed sober, another indication he'd made an effort tonight. I hugged him and took a deep breath, reminding myself to focus on him, *my son*, and not his physical appearance.

We were seated at a table by the window, directly across from the open kitchen. I slid into the window seat, giving Tristan a better view of the city lights and people passing by on the sidewalk.

The waiter greeted us. "Are you celebrating any special occasion?"

"No," Tristan said.

"Yes," I said. "My son just graduated from culinary school. We thought this would be a good place to celebrate."

"Congratulations!" the waiter said to Tristan, who looked embarrassed by the attention. "You've definitely come to the right place. I hope you enjoy it."

We ordered a six-course tasting menu, complete with wine pairing. I'd always wanted to do this but had never been able to justify the cost. *This night*, I thought, *cost be damned*. We were together to enjoy ourselves.

"Mom?" Tristan said, looking uncomfortable. "Would you mind if we changed seats? I want to see the kitchen and the service."

"Of course! I was thinking the window was the best view but, yeah, obviously that's more interesting." We changed seats, and Tristan immediately relaxed, filled with new and exciting sights, sounds and smells.

I chided myself. Of course, Tristan would be more captivated by a bustling kitchen than a busy sidewalk. He was a young man who dreamed of becoming a chef, not a middle-aged woman who liked to imagine the lives of every passer-by. I had offered him *my* version of best, without thinking through what "best" meant for him.

Tristan watched the cooks in the kitchen and the wait staff flowing smoothly between the kitchen pass and tables. He was in his element, riveted by the action of the restaurant like it was a blockbuster movie. He gave me a running commentary.

"Those plates barely landed on the pass before the waiters picked them up. They got them from pass to table in less than two seconds! Oh my god, Mom, the food looks amazing."

The food resembled art more than any food I was used to eating. Each course required two staff to serve us: the waiter to describe the food and its ingredients, and the sommelier to describe the wine, why it was a perfect accompaniment to that course and how to drink it to get the most flavour. I didn't understand how they could communicate all of this without sounding pretentious, but they managed. It was like they were friends sharing what they found most fascinating in the world, sure that we would share their fascination. And we did. I had no idea that anything could taste so good, or that wine could taste so different depending on what you were eating with it.

Conversation between Tristan and me flowed easily, with so many new experiences to comment on and flavours to analyze. Every time a dish was served, he was like a kid with a Christmas present, admiring the beautiful presentation and enjoying the mystery of what he'd discover when he took that first bite. He'd ask the waiter questions like, "How was the scallop foam prepared?" and "How long did the duck marinate?" and "What's the seasoning in that sauce on the sable fish?"

He glowed with excitement, present in each moment, every one of his senses stimulated and thrilled by the food in front of him. I watched the city lights behind him, blurred through the rain on the window. I tried not to notice Tristan's hollow cheeks, sunken eyes and scabby chin. They didn't belong here, right now, in this room with us. They didn't fit with the clear light in his eyes, his enthusiasm, his knowledge of food and his eagerness to learn more. I tried not to feel my heart break, just a little, in the moments I couldn't help but see all that was before me.

After five courses and five small glasses of wine, I was comfortably full, dizzy with the richness of the food and my gratitude, and ready for the dessert course. Tristan, however, was still starving. I sipped mint tea while he ordered and ate a full chicken breast entrée.

"Chicken, Tristan? Out of all the amazing foods you can order from the menu, you choose chicken?" It didn't seem very adventurous to me.

"I need to see how they sear the skin, Mom. It's really hard to get right. The chicken usually ends up raw inside, or overcooked and dry. It's hard to get the skin golden and crunchy all over. I know it's just chicken, but it's not easy to do."

Of course, it was perfect—juicy and tender with a crispy golden skin packed with flavour. Tristan was impressed.

Finally, they brought us each a variety plate, with small servings of three desserts. Tristan's plate included a chocolate plaque with *Congratulations* written on it. "Well done on graduating from culinary school," the waiter said. "Chef says to drop off your resumé if you ever need a job."

I wondered briefly if the waiter saw Tristan differently than I did. Did Tristan look, to him, like a person anyone would want to hire? Did his interest in food overshadow the clear desperation of his physical appearance? Maybe Tristan didn't look as bad as I thought he did.

"That would be amazing, thanks!" Tristan said, eyes wide. "I'd love to."

We left the restaurant full of good food and good feelings. Tristan was proud of his past successes and inspired by future possibilities.

Six months later, he applied for his dream job at Hawksworth and was hired. The chef was enthusiastic about Tristan's talents and Tristan loved the job, despite the early morning start. But it took less than a month before his addiction stepped onto centre stage. After missing a few shifts, Tristan quit before he could be fired. It was what he had done at his previous three jobs as well. After that, he only applied for jobs he could walk away from without breaking his heart.

12

WITH TRISTAN out of the house, I had more time and energy to find new ways to help him. In my research, I stumbled across a book called *Beyond Addiction: How Science and Kindness Help People Change.* It outlined a methodology called Community Reinforcement and Family Training, or CRAFT, which balanced compassion with statistics, practical advice with personal choice, conceptual overviews with specific exercises and checklists. This, I thought, was a book that could change my world—and more importantly, could change Tristan's world. It promised answers and the power to make everything better. It claimed that most people who abused drugs ended up agreeing to go to treatment after their family members attended about five sessions of CRAFT, even if they were initially resistant to treatment. There weren't any in-person CRAFT sessions in my area, but I sure as hell could learn the methodology and practice the principles.

I bought four copies of the book, one each for Mom, Jenn, Tanis, and myself, determined we were all going to get on the same page. The book offered tips on how to keep myself calm through stressful situations and conversations. It reminded me of the difference between enabling dysfunctional behaviours (like driving Tristan to his drug deals) and rewarding healthy ones (like letting Tristan choose the menu or cook when he came to visit). Most of all, it encouraged me to interact with Tristan from a place of acceptance, understanding and love without judgement, and to treat myself with that same acceptance, understanding and love.

The principles were straightforward but living by them was not easy. Every interaction with Tristan was a minefield. If I made the slightest slip, my good intentions could explode into colossal failure.

Sometimes, I did okay. A month or so after reading the book, I sat at my computer reviewing my post-Christmas bank statements when I noticed some cheques had been cashed that I didn't remember writing. When I went online to view images of the cheques, I saw they were written to Tristan, in Tristan's handwriting, signed with a signature that looked nothing like mine. Four cheques for eighty dollars each.

My brain spun. This was bad. I needed to deal with this, but I didn't want to. I wanted to pretend I didn't see it. I didn't want to confront Tristan. What good would it do? It wouldn't bring the money back. Tristan would be angry and hurt. He'd feel terrible. He hadn't written a cheque to himself for five hundred dollars, which he could have. I imagined it was because he was, in his own way, looking after me, taking only what he felt he needed.

I opened the book to the section about having tough conversations and decided this was a conversation I needed to have. But only after I was calm and figured out what I wanted to say.

I called Tristan the next day.

"Hey," I said. "There's something I need to talk with you about."

"Okay," he said cautiously. "What's up?"

I came straight to the point. "I was looking at my bank statements and noticed that in January there were four cheques written on my account. To you. In your handwriting."

He was silent for a while. Then, "Yeah." I heard him sigh. We both sat in silence for another moment. I suddenly became teary.

"I could call the bank and tell them they're forgeries. Get my money back. They could prosecute you."

"Yeah, you could," he said. "Probably should." He also sounded sad and exhausted.

"Tristan, it's just not okay. You can't do this."

"I know, Mom. It's just . . . I was at your place and saw your cheque book. I wasn't even really thinking. I just took a few cheques, I honestly don't know why I even did it. Just thought they might come in handy. When the first one went through, I was shocked. So, I wrote another one. And then another. I only had four. I'm sorry. I really am. You can turn me in if you want. I'd totally understand."

More silence.

"I don't want to turn you in, Tristan. I just really need you to never do that again."

"I promise, Mom. And I'll get that money back to you."

I thought maybe he meant it but knew he couldn't do it. "That would be great if you did but what I'm asking here is that you never steal from me again. If you do this again, I will report you."

"I won't, Mom. I'm sorry."

And we left it at that. To me, it was a success. I confronted him. He heard me. That, for me, was a big win.

But not everything was as straightforward as that. As the winter progressed, I wanted more support than the book was giving me. I wanted people to talk to. The book mentioned SMART, an acronym for Self-Management and Recovery Training. It was a recovery support group that followed many of the same principles as CRAFT, but there were no meetings in my neighbourhood and only one in downtown Vancouver. I briefly considered going to an Al-Anon or Nar-Anon meeting instead. These were counterparts to Alcoholic Anonymous and Narcotics Anonymous for family members and others who had loved ones struggling with addiction. There were lots of those in my area, one almost every day of the week. But the SMART program literature emphasized that these twelve-step programs didn't work, weren't evidence-based, and required a spiritual faith I didn't think I had. My only experience with twelve-step groups was what I'd seen in movies: sad old people sitting on fold-out chairs in grey church basements and exchanging their woes. I wanted none of that.

Instead, I found an online community of people that followed the SMART principles. It wasn't in-person, but at least there were real people to communicate and bounce ideas around with. Scrolling through the posts, I saw a mother asking for help looking after her teenage son as he detoxed, a wife sharing her story of finding her husband unresponsive on the bathroom floor, and a daughter telling how broken-hearted she was when she took her six-year-old son to her mother's for his birthday party and found her too drunk to stand. Many people shared encouragement, advice and similar experiences. Every story was full of horror and strength, hope and despair. I could relate.

By spring, I had a doozy of my own to work through.

Tristan called me one evening, sounding scared.

"Mom, I need your help. I know you're not going to want to do this, but I need you to lend me some cash so I can pay back people I owe money to. They're going to beat the shit out of me if I don't pay them, and I can't go home until I do. Seriously, they're waiting for me with baseball bats. So, I'm on the streets unless I can stay at your place until I come up with a thousand bucks." He paused and I listened to him breathing. "And I can't come up with a thousand bucks on my own."

I shut my eyes, as if that would shut Tristan out. *Oh, for the love of God why is this still happening to me?* I thought. *To him. To me. To us. What the fuck am I supposed to do?*

I reminded myself to breathe. I reminded myself to communicate. I reminded myself to be kind, non-judgemental and, most of all, to *not promise him money*.

"I don't know how to come up with a thousand dollars, Tristan," I said. "Even if I wanted to. And I'm not sure I do. I don't know what to say. You can come to stay here, though, for now. Until we figure this out."

I hung up and sat with my heart pounding.

I went online to the SMART community group and posted a message explaining my dilemma. Do I find the money, somehow, to give Tristan? Or do I let him face the "natural consequences," as the SMART principles suggest I should?

I soon had a full gamut of responses. Most people suggested I not bail him out; Tristan needed to face the consequences of his actions. A couple of people said, yes, give him the money, but give it directly to his dealers; the risks associated with him getting beaten were far worse than the risk of giving him money. He might never recover from the violence.

One woman told me a story about her husband paying somebody to punch him in the face, to give him a swollen eye and a split lip so he could be more convincing when asking for money to avoid further fictitious beatings. He then used the money to buy drugs. She warned me not to trust anything Tristan told me.

A thousand dollars was a lot of money for me. I was working, had a good contract and could probably take most of that off my next client cheque, which was about three weeks away. But I didn't have it at the time, and I had no savings.

Before Tristan woke up the next morning, I went to speak with Mom. She'd supported me through all my ups and downs as a single parent and knew my struggles. She'd spent years feeding my kids after-school snacks and driving them to taekwondo classes while I worked—the easy, natural help of a grandma who wanted her grand-children to feel loved and to have opportunities. But that was not what was needed now.

She was stunned, but not surprised. I sipped my tea and she drank her coffee as we talked through whether to come up with the money or let him ride out the consequences, but it wasn't much of a dis-cussion. Neither of us were willing to take the risk of Tristan being beaten by thugs with baseball bats.

Mom would take the thousand dollars from her line of credit and, if Tristan couldn't pay her back himself, I would pay her back when I was able.

"But this is it," she said. "It's the last time I ever do anything like this, and you can tell him so. I'll tell him myself. This has gone too far!"

I'd heard this from Mom countless times before, and from myself even more. It was so easy to set boundaries after the fact, and so easy to set those boundaries aside when the stakes were high. And there were no higher stakes than my child's life.

I berated myself for breaking my commitment to say no to Tristan, and wondered when it would end. This time, I caved after two simple words: baseball bats. Who knew what the next time would bring?

But for now, we had a plan. After letting him sweat for three days, uncertain of what we'd do, I told Tristan that Grandma had gotten the money but that I'd only pay it to his dealer.

"It doesn't work that way, Mom," Tristan said. "He doesn't want to see you. He doesn't want to be seen. I'm the only one who can go to him."

That sounded like bullshit to me, like something out of a movie, but I was so tired, and the truth was I didn't want to approach a stranger, a drug dealer, and give him money. Even if I knew it was the smart thing, the right thing, to do. I didn't want to. I only needed the slightest nudge to give in on that one, and Tristan gave it to me.

"Fine. But, Tristan, you can't ever ask us for money like this again. I don't want to see you beaten up, but I won't do this for you again. And neither will Grandma."

The next morning, Mom and I both drove Tristan downtown, where he was interviewing for a job in one of the best Italian restaurants in Vancouver. He'd been out of work for a couple of weeks now. These days, he rarely lasted past one payday, maybe two. *Maybe his love of pasta will somehow save him*, I thought, as I remembered the mushroom ravioli and tender gnocchi he'd made for me—and then let the thought evaporate as I navigated the traffic.

Throughout the thirty-minute drive, Mom told Tristan how unhappy she was and that she'd never give him money again. She reminded him that she lived on an old-age pension and couldn't afford it. I glared at Tristan through the rear-view mirror and shook my head in disappointment when I saw him watching me. He apologized to his grandma, thanked her and sat quietly.

When we arrived, Mom handed Tristan an envelope containing ten hundred-dollar bills. Nothing felt good about it, and by the time I got home I was feeling worse. I had done everything wrong. I hadn't followed the SMART advice or their principles. I knew I shouldn't have given Tristan the money. The odds of him not using it to buy more drugs were slim to nil. And since I *did* give him the money, I shouldn't have made him feel terrible about it.

I did the two things that SMART said never to do: I paid him, and I shamed him. As I cleaned up dishes he had left in his room, I realized I was far more disappointed in myself than I was in Tristan. He'd behaved exactly as expected but I thought I would have done better. Clearly, the online support forum wasn't working for me. I didn't know what would, but a few messages from random strangers was not enough.

That evening, I lit the votive candles I'd bought and said my usual prayer for Tristan, but it occurred to me that I should really be praying for myself.

13

I PULLED up to Tristan's house and parked in the shade of a maple tree, its fresh May leaves bursting with new beginnings. As I took a minute to stop and breathe, I rolled my head from side to side, releasing stress from the day and setting an intention to have a good time—to be pleasant and positive, to share a good meal, and to simply *be* with Tristan without judgement.

The past few months had been difficult. No matter how many times I reminded myself to let go, walk away, let Tristan figure things out for himself, I hadn't been able to. He was still able to *get* work, but he was unable to keep it. Every few weeks he'd ask for money. Sometimes I gave it to him, sometimes I didn't. Sometimes I paid his rent. Mostly, I resented it.

I glanced up and down the quiet sidewalk and said a quick, heartfelt prayer to whoever was listening for the afternoon to flow smoothly and without drama.

Then, I texted:

I'm here 😊

Tristan quickly replied:

I cant come out but I need some money for food. Can u send me $40. Its not for drugs I promise.

Here we go again, I thought. This time I called him.

"Why can't you come out? I thought we had a plan." I chose to ignore his request for money.

"Yeah," he mumbled, "I know, but I can't."

"How come? What's going on?"

"It doesn't matter, it's nothing to do with you. And it's not about drugs, I just can't go out right now. I need money to order a pizza. You were going to feed me anyway." He sounded sober but oddly muffled, and he spoke more slowly than usual.

"I wanted to spend time with you and eat together, not just give you money. And I won't give you money unless you tell me what's going on."

He paused for a bit. "If I tell you, will you give me money?"

I made myself take a breath. Two teens on skateboards crossed the street in front of me—probably fifteen or sixteen years old. I imagined their parents might worry about them not wearing helmets or using crosswalks, but I was sure these kids came home sober most nights and did their homework. I watched as the kids jumped the curb on the other side and carried on down the sidewalk.

"I'm not promising that," I answered. "But I promise I won't give you money without some sort of explanation."

I could hear him breathing. Then he said, "It's not a big deal but I have some sort of infection on my lip, or my cheek, that whole area anyway, and I look like a fucking freak. I don't know what happened, maybe it was from a pimple or scab I picked or something, but it's taken over my whole face and I can't go out."

I shut my eyes. "Well," I said, "two things: either it's bad enough to need medical attention which, from what you described, it does. You may need antibiotics. Or it's not as bad as you're making out and you can come out for dinner."

"Hold on," Tristan said, "I'll show you."

A few seconds later, I heard the ping of a text coming in. My stomach lurched when I opened the photo. I wanted to throw up. Tristan's face—his beautiful, gorgeous face—was grotesque. The left side of his lip was so bloated and swollen it filled that entire side of his face, turning him into a caricature with a superhuman snarl. It looked like he'd been punched in the face, not that I knew what that would look like. I imagined him being beaten and brutalized by punks he'd pissed off.

"Holy shit, Tristan. That looks terrible. It looks like somebody punched you."

"No. My lip started hurting last night and then it was all swollen this morning and just keeps getting worse."

I had no idea what to believe or think, but I knew it needed to get looked after properly. "Okay, hun, you need to see a doctor."

"I don't want to go out looking like a freak, Mom!" he said, sounding desperate.

"Doctors are used to seeing all sorts of things. And you're not a freak, love, even if your lip is a bit freaky right now. Hold on, I'm going to see what I can find and call you back."

I hung up the phone, not giving him a chance to respond, and took another deep breath. Whatever the hell was wrong with his lip, it did not look good. Something about it scared me.

I searched for clinics in the area and learned the one just down the road took walk-in patients until four o'clock. The same clinic provided outpatient addiction services, which I'd tried to convince Tristan to check out the previous month.

It was already 3:40. I called Tristan back and told him he had to come now. Right now, no arguments. He agreed, but it was eight precious minutes before he got in the car. I could barely look at him, his face made my stomach turn, not so much from the physical disfigurement as from the thoughts of what could have caused it.

We pulled in with four minutes to spare, but Tristan refused to get out of the car.

"I don't want to sit in the fucking waiting room with people staring at me."

I went in and registered him at reception. I had his Care Card number on my phone, as I did for all the kids, and explained the situation to the receptionist. She told me we could expect a wait of at least an hour and a half, but that Tristan would need to be in the waiting room by five-thirty in case his name was called.

I walked down the block to get us some sandwiches and drinks from the deli on the corner, glad to have a few minutes to myself. Tristan and I ate and waited in the car, in silence, checking Facebook on our phones now and again, until five-thirty when we went inside.

Tristan was called in just before six o'clock and came out twenty minutes later. He headed straight to the car.

"Can I come back to your place?" he asked, after I'd started driving. "I don't feel like sitting alone in my room right now."

"Sure," I said. "Are you going to tell me what they said?"

"Yeah, he took some samples from my lip and some blood work, so he won't know for sure until he gets the results, but he thinks it's herpes on my lip."

He explained how the doctor told him it can sometimes present this way, though I'd never heard of it. I wasn't sure if he was making up a story but couldn't figure out why or how he'd come up with that one, if he was.

"He said I'm also at high risk for having HIV," Tristan said, looking out the window, his voice breaking a bit. "So, I probably do. I'm probably going to die of AIDS."

Tristan lived a high-risk life, and these thoughts weren't new to me, but they still held power to frighten me. It seemed this thought was new to Tristan, though—or suddenly seemed much more real.

"Love," I said, trying to sound reassuring, despite my own alarm, "being *at risk* of something and *having* it are two very different things. Let's just go one step at a time."

"You don't get it, Mom," Tristan said. "I know people with HIV. Lots of people. This one friend I have, she's only nineteen and she has HIV. She's a really nice girl, too."

I felt like telling him that viruses don't differentiate between nice people or not-nice people; it was simply a matter of behaviour and luck. But I didn't think it would be helpful.

"Okay, look." I glanced at him, trying to catch his eye. "Let's wait for the results. Until then, you stay with me and try not to let your mind go to worst-case scenarios. Odds are, you'll be fine. And if it turns out you have HIV, it can be managed pretty well these days. It's not a death sentence anymore."

"It doesn't matter, Mom. I'm not going to live long anyway. I'll be dead before I'm thirty."

This again. It walloped me, every time. He'd been saying this on and off for years now, and I hated it.

"Stop it," I said, perhaps more sternly than I should have. "That's not true. You need to be careful how you think about things, and that kind of thinking isn't good for you. You deserve a good, long life, Tristan."

"No, I don't, Mom. You don't even know all the shit I've done." Tristan was still looking out the window, face turned away, distress and heartache in his voice.

"It doesn't matter what you've done, hun. I promise you, you deserve a good life."

He didn't seem to register my words, lost in his own world of pain. "So much stupid shit I've done, I don't know why I'm even alive right now. And I've seen people die. Mom, I've never told anybody about this before, ever, but I watched someone die and didn't do anything to stop it. I don't fucking deserve to live."

I couldn't reply. My body kept driving the car, on autopilot, but I couldn't form thoughts let alone words. Blood pounded through my head, and I felt like I was on a plane that was about to crash, my whole world about to smash into a million pieces. Finally, I was able to think, *this is not Tristan.* Tristan was the sweetest, most sensitive soul I'd ever known. He rescued bugs from busy sidewalks. He hurt when others hurt. He always gave money, if he had any, to home-less people. Or if he didn't, he'd say hello and give them words of encouragement. Tristan would not let anyone die. He *could* not let anyone die.

And then, I thought, if he *had* let someone die for some reason, it would fucking devastate him. I understood then that I wasn't seeing my world about to smash into a million pieces; I was realizing that Tristan's world had already been smashed apart. He had done things he could not reconcile with himself. He operated from a value system that was not his own, one his soul fundamentally opposed—the value system of a junkie.

My heart ached for my boy and what he must have gone through.

But my compassion was quickly eclipsed by a searing anger that he had watched someone die and done nothing.

Tristan's sense of self may have been smashed by his inaction, but he was still alive. And someone, somewhere, was not. Because of Tristan.

Some mother somewhere mourned her child, who might have been saved if Tristan had stepped up.

And Tristan *knew* better. Tristan was a good person, well raised. He had morals. How the hell could he have done something like that?

I wanted to slap him. Or rage at him. But mostly, I wanted to understand this thing that was so completely unfathomable. In some odd way I felt like if I could get Tristan to explain it to me, I could correct his thinking and make him do it differently.

"What...?" I said, not knowing if I meant, *What did you say?* or *What happened?* or *What the hell?* Probably all three.

"It wasn't on purpose. I wanted to save him." He was in tears now. "I wanted to call 911 but my dealer wouldn't let me. He had all these drugs around and wouldn't let me call anyone. So, we got my friend on his feet and we were walking him around. He seemed to be coming to. He seemed to be doing okay."

I was still hung up on his not calling for help. "Tristan, it didn't matter what your *dealer* said." I pronounced dealer as if I were talking about a sewer rat. "You needed to call 911. You needed to make that call. I don't understand how you could not see that." I was not questioning him; I was accusing him.

"Mom, the guy would have fucking killed me. You don't get it. You don't fuck around with people like that. And I thought my friend was doing better and it was all really stressful and so I just left." He paused for a shaky breath. "When I went back in the morning, they told me he died."

I wanted to know who these people were, to report the dealer. I needed to know what they did with the young man's body, and that his mother knew.

"Who—" I didn't get more than one word out before Tristan shut me down.

"Fuck, Mom, just forget I said anything. It doesn't matter now. It's done. It was ages ago. It wasn't anybody, and he wasn't right in the head anyway. I don't want to talk about it." He leaned back in the seat and shut his eyes. The swollen side of his face toward me, Tristan looked every bit the monster I saw him as.

THROUGH SPRING and early summer, I tried to let go of my fear for my son. I travelled for work once or twice a month; things were easier when I was away, but that didn't fix life at home.

I needed a different approach but had no idea how to go about it. And so, like a moth fleeing darkness, I flittered toward whatever resembled light. For me, the brightest lights in my world had always been my children, so that was where I looked. I might have asked myself, *How could I create light in my own life? What joy can I bring to myself? Why do I always turn to my children to fulfill me?* But I didn't. Those questions never occurred to me. Instead, I poured my energy into staying connected with each of my kids.

In many ways, staying close to Tristan was the simplest, because I'd already made that a priority. We continued our routine of going out to eat, and I tried to practice objectivity—to accept him as he was without judgement.

One evening, as we ate fresh pasta at a family-owned restaurant on Commercial Drive, Tristan said, "Mom, I gotta move outta that house. My roomies all hate me." We'd found out a week before that Tristan did not have HIV but did have herpes. His lip had mostly healed but his face was scabby and gaunt, his pupils dilated. "They sit outside my door at night listening to me. It's really fucking weird. I can't leave my room without them staring at me like they wanna kill me."

My mind struggled under the weight of his words and what lay beneath them. Part of me wanted to shake him and yell, *Of course, they want you gone! You're a fucking junkie and now maybe a crazy paranoid one! You're not exactly prime roommate material.* But a larger part of me needed to accept him as he was in that moment. I loved him fiercely and I wanted him to feel that. It was hard to tap into love when worry and fear and judgement overwhelmed me. I asked myself how an objective-but-supportive person might respond, and then tried to be that person.

I didn't believe his roommates listened at his door, but it wouldn't have surprised me if they gave him the evil eye and wanted him gone. "Maybe they're just not comfortable with your lifestyle," I said, spearing a small scallop with my fork, swirling it until it was wrapped in a cozy blanket of fettuccine.

"What the fuck's that supposed to mean?"

"Just that. I suspect you live differently than they do. People may not be comfortable with the hours you keep or how you spend your time. But that's not your problem. Your job is to be a good roommate, be polite and not leave messes in the common areas. If you're doing that, it doesn't matter what they think."

I was impressed with myself for sounding non-judgemental and gave myself an internal high five.

"I think they're planning something to get me kicked out. The other night I heard them talking, at least three or four of them. When I went to confront them, they all ran back to their rooms and shut their doors. Good thing too, or I would have fucking kicked their asses." He scooped lasagna into his mouth and washed it down with a long swig of cola.

"Did you actually see them in the hallway?" I was trying to discern the line between reality and Tristan's imagination.

He shook his head. "But I know they were there."

This is it, I thought. *Tristan's hearing voices; he's losing his mind.* I'd been bracing for something like this ever since I attended those depressing classes for parents of at-risk youth when Tristan was fifteen, when I learned about the downward trajectory of addiction and heard too many stories of good kids gone bad. I just hadn't known how or when Tristan's next spiral down would present itself. Now I did.

I felt remarkably calm, a little relieved even, to not have to fear what was next for Tristan. And perhaps even a little hopeful, knowing that when people experienced these downward slides, they'd either settle into a new normal or finally reach out for help. Maybe this would be Tristan's rock bottom.

Again I considered my words and the effect they might have. "Well, either you're right, your roomies are against you and it's not the greatest place for you. Or there's a possibility your brain is playing tricks on you. It's not uncommon. Do you think you could go see a doctor, even if it's just to rule that out?" Such a reasonable question, but it seemed emotionally loaded. To both of us.

"I'm not fucking crazy, Mom." Tristan didn't sound adamant; he seemed almost thoughtful. "I'm not seeing a doctor."

"You don't think drugs might be causing you to think this way?"

"I know what I heard."

I figured I wouldn't push it any further. "Okay. If you change your mind and want a check-up, let me know. Otherwise, just try to be friendly and stay out of their way."

We finished our meals and ordered crème brûlée. We continued to chat about food and family, and I dropped him off feeling good about the evening. I had walked the tightrope and managed to keep my balance, even while Tristan was losing his.

STAYING CONNECTED to Jenn was easy because of Emily, who was now two years old and bursting with joyful energy and bouncing golden curls. I remembered being a young mom with a toddler—or three—and there were many ways I could help. I was happy to babysit or take Emily to the playground or buy her new summer clothes.

But as much as Emily kept us connected, she was also a barrier. I rarely saw Jenn alone. At twenty-three, she was a busy mom with a full-time job as an office manager at a taekwondo school and had just started a side business as a photographer for newborns. When I was with Jenn, Emily was always with us and the centre of attention.

We read books together, pounded playdough, baked cupcakes and fought imaginary ghosts with our special magical powers. Despite her busy-ness, Jenn was a great mom, attentive and loving. When they were with me, my world opened up and the sun shone brightly, no matter the weather outside. When they smiled, a chorus of angels sang in my heart.

Over the past years, though, the relationship between Jenn and her daughter's dad had moved from bumpy to bad, from disrespectful to emotionally abusive. I saw it with my own eyes whenever I saw them together. Jenn ignored it, refusing to talk about it except when she called me late at night, drunk, cursing Alan for whichever way he'd belittled her in front of Emily this time, or frightened her, or punched another hole in the wall. Then she'd tell me she was done with him; she was taking Emily and leaving. But in the morning, when she was sober, she'd brush it off as nothing, a minor misunderstanding not worth talking about.

I wondered how Jenn was *really* doing, on the other side of all her busy-ness and mothering. On the inside.

One afternoon while Emily was quietly colouring and Jenn and I fixed Kraft Dinner, ham, and cucumber salad, I asked her. Jenn shrugged her shoulders and continued cutting cucumbers. "I'm good. I mean... Alan is who he is and he's not going to change but he loves Emily."

I'd heard that many times before. "At night you call me, telling me your world is ending. But in the daytime, everything's fine. What's up with that?"

Jenn laughed. "Yeah, that's true. Everything looks like shit when I've been drinking. And I do hate him—he's a fucking asshole a lot of the time—but I guess I also love him. And I can't afford to move out anyway, so whatever. I'll make it work."

"Sweet pea, you know if you need to get away, we can find a way to make that work too." Our conversation was sabotaged by a bubbling ball of joy. "Mommy, Mommy!" Emily sang as she ran into the kitchen, waving her colouring book. "I made you a kitten. It's pink."

Jenn squatted down to admire Emily's colouring. "It's so beauti-ful, Peanut! Just like you." She gave Emily a big hug and then patted her bum and told her to go wash her hands before lunch. Before I could say another word, Jenn was taking the food to the table.

I knew where Jenn was at. I saw myself in Jenn's active mothering, in her working two jobs to balance financial security with creative fulfillment, in her privacy about her personal and painful relation-ships. I could see the fragile shell she was developing around the soft part of her soul —the shell that allowed her to get so much done, despite her pain—and it made me sad. I wanted to crack it open and let her troubles spill into the light where I could share in the agony and confusion and failure that lay beneath the surface of her poise and perfection, so we could begin to make things better. But I didn't. I recognized the practical value of that shell, of a mother needing to keep her shit together until she was ready. And anyway, I didn't think I could keep my shell intact if I saw Jenn's break. It was enough for me to deal with Tristan's messy life.

TANIS AND I sat outside a trendy café eating mediocre gluten-free sandwiches, our jackets pulled tightly around us, poor protection from the chilly spring breeze. With Tanis, I had an opportunity to build a relationship with a grown child without a toddler distract-ing us or drug addiction interfering; it felt good. We'd been meeting every week or two for dinner or a movie, but this was our first ven-ture out for a patio lunch.

"Oh, man!" I said, after a particularly cold wind blew our napkins off the table. "When's it going to warm up?"

"It's warm in Mexico," Tanis said. "Maybe we should move to Mexico."

"Or at least go for a vacation. I'd be down with that."

"Are you serious, Mom? Because I would totally go to Mexico."

I paused to consider. "Paying for it's the tough part. I could pay for mine," I said, thinking of my credit card. "But I don't have extra money to pay for yours." I expected that to be the end of the discussion.

"I have savings," she said. Then, before I could respond, she stood up, brushed the crumbs off her coat and headed to the car.

"Come on!" she called. "We're going to a travel agent!"

It took me a beat to realize she was serious. "Who goes to a travel agent anymore?" I muttered to myself, clearing the dishes away before joining her. An hour later, we left the travel agency, tickets booked for an eight-day all-inclusive stay in Mexico, just outside Cancún—just the two of us.

For a full week in late June, we moved from sun to shade to pool as the mood struck. We ate when we were hungry and napped when we were tired. We took a day trip to go ziplining and snorkelling in the *cenotes*, and—after a long and lively debate about the ethics of keeping animals in captivity—spent an afternoon swimming with the dolphins anyway.

There was no internet at the hotel, so I enjoyed the peace of being unplugged. Thoughts and worries about Tristan crossed my mind during the day but I blew them away like dandelion fluff. In the evenings though, after I was in bed with nothing to distract me, I'd let myself think about him and wonder how he was doing. Sometimes I'd cry, knowing the painful journey he was on. I relished this private time to think about him—I *needed* it—but I was happy to keep my days focused on Tanis, allowing sunshine and easy human connection to strengthen me.

One afternoon toward the end of our stay, Tanis and I decided to go into Cancún. It was a last-minute decision based on a sluggish restlessness from too much sun and inactivity. There was a bus heading into town, and we decided to get on. We poked through the shops and grabbed a bite to eat, then decided to spend half an hour at a Starbucks where we could go online and check our messages. I was sipping my iced tea when I opened Facebook Messenger and saw five messages from Tristan sent less than an hour before. I clicked on them.

Hey
i wanna go to rehab. i need help

> i slept in today and lost my job
> im an idiot
> i suck

I was stunned.

"Tanis! Tristan wants to go to rehab."

"What?" She stopped what she was doing to read the message. "Holy shit. Good for him! About time."

I messaged back, hoping he was still online:

> Just got your message - I only have Internet for the next 20 minutes. I think that's smart. The only way we can pay for it is to close out your school funds account and use that. You should have enough for one full round of rehab. So think very carefully to make sure you're serious about this right now. I'll send you a number to call if you are.

I waited a while. No answer back. I messaged him again:

> Do you want me to let Gma know so she can help you get there if you want? Also, I'm really sorry that you're having to go through this Hun.

Tanis was leaning over my shoulder, reading the messages when Tristan replied.

> nvm
> i don't wanna use all my school money on this
> didn't know it would rinse me out clean

Tanis laughed and shook her head. "Tristan, you dummy. He doesn't get it, does he? Does he think Princess Charming will swoop down and make it all happen for him?"

I messaged:

> You won't be able to do school or anything if you can't beat this. If you're sober, you can literally be successful at whatever you decide, with or without your school money. Think about it. You really need to fight this thing.

He didn't answer back. We both stared at my phone for another few minutes, but still nothing.

"Well," I said to Tanis. "That was interesting."

"Yeah. Do you think he's actually going to go to rehab?"

"I do. Maybe not right away, but his wheels are turning. I think he will."

I'd been wanting to get Tristan into rehab for six years. I couldn't have been happier or prouder of my son if he'd been applying for an Ivy League university. It seemed unfair that most people express sympathy for a son going to rehab rather than the enthusiastic celebration it deserves. Not that Tristan had fully committed yet, but he'd expressed an interest and that was enough for me, for now.

Tanis and I both felt lighter as we finished up and left to catch the bus back.

"Isn't it a bit odd that the one and only time we were connected to the internet is the time Tristan decided to message me?"

"I know! It's crazy," Tanis said. "You gotta wonder about things like that. I'm telling ya, the Universe has a plan."

14

I LAY awake listening to the chickadees. I usually wanted to wring their sweet little necks. Anybody who chirps so loudly at three-thirty in the morning deserved a good swat, I figured. Pulling a pillow over my head to block their predawn jubilation was more my style, but on this particular morning they kept me company as I stared at the ceiling of my dark bedroom. They felt like friends bolstering my strength for whatever daylight would bring.

Their innocent songs held me while I listened for Tristan to come home. *Home.* He hadn't lived with me for almost a year, but it still seemed like his home was with me.

I prayed he'd remember today and have the strength to face it. I didn't know who I was praying to, but I prayed Tristan was alive and not damaged beyond repair. I imagined my prayers calling to him, finding him, guiding him home. I spent all night praying and trying not to cry. And almost succeeding.

Dawn had lost its glow by the time I heard the front door close and his sneakers thud in the hallway. Sweet relief lasted a brief second before anxiety caught up with me again; one hurdle down but many more ahead.

Today was the day Tristan had said he'd go to rehab. Finally, he'd agreed to use his education funds to do it. But time was not friendly to addicts, and every minute of every hour offered a thousand ways and reasons for him to change his mind.

I breathed in; I breathed out. I noticed my jaw clenching and tried to relax but my neck still twinged, and my stomach roiled. I decided to get my tea. *Just don't look at him*, I told myself. *It doesn't matter. He's here; that's what's important.*

I found my housecoat in the pile of clothing on my floor and went downstairs, glancing at the lump on the couch. I didn't let myself think as I made my cup of Earl Grey, focusing my mind on the mundane task in front of me, a task I could control: boil the water, get the tea bag, add a splash of milk, sit down in my chair by the window, look outside. Success.

I mindlessly watched birds flit from branch to branch. It struck me as odd that they could carry on as if this were any other day, as if there were anything more important in the world than what was happening inside, here, today.

Nine months earlier, I'd moved Tristan out of my home and into his rented room. The amount of time I'd needed to conceive and give birth to him was all he'd needed to burn his life to the ground, twenty years later. Amid the wreckage, though, there was hope. Today, there was hope.

It had been less than two weeks since Tristan had texted me in Mexico, finally admitting he needed help. He knew he couldn't keep a job and had given up trying. He was behind on his rent and his landlord was kicking him out. If he didn't do something he'd be homeless. That something needed to happen today.

I finished my tea, now cold, and looked outside. Soft morning light had given way to the stark brightness of day. Time to put my thoughts aside and focus on what needed to get done. Tristan had to call the rehab centre before noon, or he'd have no place to go. They'd held a bed for him all week and this, they said, was the last day they'd keep it for him.

I hauled my carcass out of the chair, put my cup in the sink and then went to look at my son. My breath caught when I saw his beautiful face, now scabby and gaunt with a newly swollen lip. I didn't let myself feel the pain rushing through me when I saw him. I held my breath when I dialled the phone and passed it to him, listening to him muttering incomprehensibly. I didn't know how they could understand him. Maybe it was enough that he grunted his assent when they asked if he was coming in. It felt like I was still holding my breath an hour later as he sat at the kitchen table, coffee untouched, lashing out at me. He was vaguely abusive, largely incoherent, and threatening to walk away from it all. I was focused only on my goal of getting him to rehab, so his words fell unfelt around me.

I looked at Tristan from across the table and gently asked him to pack his things. I was determined not to do this for him. This needed to be his decision; he was the one who needed to take action.

"Fuck off, already!" he moaned, wrapping his arms around his head as if to keep it from exploding, and then bringing it to his knees, burying his face. "You're such a bitch." His voice trailed off, broken. He muttered a few more muffled curses and my heart threatened to break. *This is not my son*, I reminded myself. This was addiction and desperation.

I tamped my emotions down and put one foot in front of the other, unthinking, unfeeling. I was just moving forward and trying my best to keep Tristan moving forward with me: cajoling him, feeding him, and ultimately telling him firmly there was no more time to delay. The treatment centre was only half an hour away, but if we weren't on the road in twenty minutes, he'd miss his two o'clock intake time—and he had no other options.

He went upstairs, had a shower and came down with his bag in hand.

As we walked to the car, warm sunshine washed over us and Tristan stopped to take a deep breath. In that moment, he seemed almost like himself again, his face full of love, fear and fragile determination. He looked me in the eye and said, "I'm doing it, Mom," then flashed a sad smile and put his arm around me.

My heart ached from the potency of hope and hopelessness, pride and shame, in him and in me. The final surrender. It wasn't a soft surrender, but a desperate tap out after a long hard fight. We were betting his life on something better arising from the ashes.

"Yes, you are, love." I smiled and hugged him back tightly, then kissed his fuzzy cheek. "You're doing it."

As we drove, I held my breath. I placed my finger on the auto-lock button in case he changed his mind and tried to jump out at a red light. I don't know what I thought I'd do if that happened. Kidnap and deliver him, against his wishes, to the rehab fairies to work their recovery magic on him? God help me. But Tristan was quiet, dozing, until he suddenly sat up.

"Wait!" he said, his voice coarse and crackly. He cleared his throat and tried again. "Which one are you taking me to? I'm not going to the shitty one with all the fucking doctors. I'll live on East Hastings before that. I want the fun one." Earlier that week, in return for a place to stay and food to eat, I'd made him phone three rehab centres. I'd read it helps when a person chooses their treatment facility. Tristan had made the calls but had no opinion, made no choice. Thankfully, the one I wanted for him, the one I'd added to my contact list two years earlier, was the "fun" one: Westgate. On the phone, the other centres talked about their routines, therapeutic approaches, and certifications, but this one told him how much fun they have in recovery. This one talked about good food, going to the gym, dirt biking, movies, laughter, being "a part of." Of course, Tristan wanted that one. What twenty-year-old wouldn't choose the promise of fun over therapy? Even if it meant he had to give up smoking, as well as everything else.

"It's the fun one," I said, relieved I'd chosen correctly.

TRISTAN FINISHED his last smoke and tossed the butt. We crossed the road to an unobtrusive low-rise apartment building, older but well kept. He carried his duffle bag with the few clothes and toiletries he'd haphazardly thrown in. Four or five guys sat out front. They each greeted us with a polite "Hi" or "How's it going" and plenty of eye contact. One tall, good-looking guy in his late twenties stood up, smiled at Tristan and said, "Hey, are you a new guy?"

"Yeah, I guess," Tristan mumbled, eyes down.

"Welcome. I'm Von." He shook Tristan's hand. "You're gonna love it here. They're going to fatten you up—you're skinny, bro! Come on, I'll find someone to do your intake."

Von held the door and got us seated in the foyer. While we waited, half a dozen men of all ages walked past. Every one of them welcomed Tristan. Many gave me words of encouragement, too. They told me he was in a good place, that I could stop worrying and sleep again. They called me "Mom." I smiled at them, blinking back tears at the simple feeling of being understood, of being in a place where young men smiled.

One guy asked if I wanted coffee and, when I told him I drank tea, seemed near giddy that he could get that too. He returned a minute or two later, apologizing for taking so long. "I didn't know what you liked so I brought one of each option." He grinned, pulling an assortment of crumpled tea bags from his jean pockets, front and back. I wasn't thrilled about the teabags in his pockets but he seemed so earnest that I couldn't say no. I chose Mint Medley.

An intake worker called Tristan into the office. Before I could follow, a stocky young guy in jeans and a Harley-Davidson T-shirt appeared and greeted me with a handshake.

"Hi, I'm Ben. You must be…" he looked down at a notepad. "Tristan's mom. I'll be his caseworker. Come on," he said, putting his notepad in his back pocket and running a hand over his buzz cut. "I'll show you around if you like."

The centre was spread across two small apartment buildings and one large heritage home on a typical suburban street. Nothing fancy, but clean, comfortable, homey. There was a huge bowl of apples, oranges and bananas in the living room, which felt good. Nobody was starving here. Some guys were playing chess, another strummed a guitar, a few wrote in notebooks, and a bunch sat in the sunshine talking. There was an abundance of tattoos, but everybody looked healthy and happy.

Just normal guys.

I soaked it in, knowing this would be Tristan's home for the next three months, at least. These were going to be his people. I began to hope. I wanted this so badly for Tristan. Seeing the guys, hearing their laughter, made it seem possible.

Back on the front steps I hugged Tristan goodbye, breathed him in, and told him I loved him. His arms hung at his side as I wrapped mine around him. He was uncomfortable in my hug, uncomfortable in his body. One of the guys walked by just then, chuckled and said, "Go on, give your mom a hug. She deserves it, man."

Tristan gave me a quick hug, all edges and nerves. "Love you, Mom," he mumbled, and went inside.

Driving home alone, I was overwhelmed by relief. I was still anxious: *What if he doesn't stay?* And scared: *He's not going to stay!* But above all that, I felt relief: *I've done my part. He's safe.* I felt like I'd been holding my breath for years, almost to the point of suffocation. Now, I let it out. I could breathe.

I had so much space around me and in me. Where did all that space come from? What was I going to do with it?

I WAS not even home yet when my phone rang, and I saw "Westgate" on the call display. *Oh god, what's wrong?* Even though I was driving, I answered the call, certain I'd need to turn around again, that Tristan had failed treatment in the first fifteen minutes and now I'd need to find him a homeless shelter. Or something.

"Hi, Kathy. It's Ben. Tristan's doing fine and getting settled in no problem."

I relaxed, immediately. I noticed I was holding my breath again and let it out.

"That's probably the first thing that crossed your mind with me calling: 'What did Tristan do now?' But he's great. It'll take some time to stop panicking whenever I call, so I just like to put that out there up front."

"Thanks, I appreciate that," I laughed, and then teared up at the novelty of being understood *again*—at knowing my fears were not unique. "You've done this before."

"Yeah. You've spent a lot of time worrying about him. It'll take a while not to. What I'm calling about, though, is to see if you can drop off some of his things at the house whenever you have time. He didn't bring much with him, so any clothes or toiletries he'll need over the next few months would be great. No rush. Whenever it's convenient."

I told him I'd stop by the next day. I hung up, happy to have a task, to still be helpful to my son.

The next morning, I woke from a restless sleep, sunlight streaming through the blinds. The surprising spaciousness I'd felt yesterday, which had seemed so full of promise then, now felt like emptiness. I had no crisis to manage, no problem to fix or avoid. It was Saturday, so no work. I had expected to feel more alive in my new-found freedom, giddy with the success of getting Tristan to rehab. Instead, all I felt was an absence of something with a rushing undercurrent of anxiety. An absence of *what*, though? I wasn't quite sure. Maybe Tristan? Or stress? Or purpose?

I tried to focus my thoughts on what was important: Tristan was in treatment. Then, a crashing wave of gratitude filled me to the brim, and I became fully awake. When I remembered I could take Tristan's things to him later that day, my residual anxiety washed away in a flood of happiness.

I spent the morning gathering Tristan's clothes and doing laundry. That afternoon, I drove back to Westgate. The sky was a brilliant blue and my mood was bright. I had a suitcase packed with Tristan's freshly laundered clothes, a new toiletry bag stuffed with masculine bathroom products, and a bag of candy—sour worms, skittles and mini peanut butter cups. It felt good to be doing good.

As I walked up the sidewalk, into the house and then into the office, I glanced around, looking for a glimpse of Tristan. He was on restrictions for the first few weeks, which meant he wasn't allowed to phone me, or anyone, and I wasn't allowed to phone him. Apparently, this helped the guys settle into new routines and learn to turn to each other for support. It prevented them from continuing dysfunctional dynamics they had with other people when times got tough. Tristan couldn't call me if he wanted to be rescued. I couldn't rescue him. The restrictions were in place to support us both in finding a new way of being. I appreciated that.

But if I happened to bump into him, that seemed like fair game. Short of wandering through the buildings calling his name, though, I didn't think that was going to happen. I decided to come right out and ask. Ben wasn't in the office that Saturday so I dropped Tristan's stuff off with another caseworker and asked if I could say hi.

"Oh, yeah, sorry, he's out with a bunch of the guys. Went to the aquarium. Beautiful day for it," he said, looking up from the old desktop computer he was working at. I was suddenly, inexplicably angry. On Day One, Tristan was out having fun at the Vancouver Aquarium?

I set Tristan's bag beside his suitcase and adjusted my purse to stop it from slipping off my shoulder—finding any excuse to avoid eye contact. Did they have no idea of the stress Tristan had put me through over the past week? Not knowing whether he was going to make it here or not? Disappearing for days, and me not knowing if he was dead or alive? And what about all the shit he put me through over the past six years? And the first thing rehab did was reward him with a field trip? I'd been at home worrying—no, *knowing*—that Tristan was feeling alone and miserable, angry, hating the place and wanting to escape. I hadn't even realized I'd been worrying about him until that moment. And here he was in rehab for less than twenty-four hours and was out watching belugas and dolphins—doing normal-people things I hadn't been able to do with him for years—while I worried about him, did his laundry and bought him candy.

Maybe my reaction showed, or maybe it was just predictable.

"He's with good people, Kathy," the caseworker assured me. "Some of the guys in transition were going to the aquarium and bought an extra ticket for Tristan, figuring he could use a distraction. The boys here look out for the new guys." He smiled in a way that reminded me of a proud father. "They know what it's like. It's early days for Tristan and he's feeling pretty low. That's normal. It's important for him to see the guys having fun in recovery, to know he can be 'a part of.' He's likely to feel like shit today, no matter where he is, no question. But it doesn't do anyone any good for him to sit here and mope. He can be with the guys and see them having a good time, sober. If he doesn't know he can have fun in recovery, he won't stick around for long. That's the truth."

"Oh, that's great," I said, nodding my head as if it helped me look more believable. "That's wonderful." I thanked him and went back to my car. I was happy for Tristan. I truly was. All I ever wanted was for him to be happy, to fit in, to have good friends and do fun normal-people things. So why was I so upset?

As I tucked myself into the privacy of my car, it dawned on me that Tristan had other people to look out for him now. He didn't need me anymore. He didn't need my sleepless nights and endless worrying. He didn't need me rushing out to him with fresh clothes and Axe body wash to make him feel better. He didn't need *me* taking him to the aquarium. He was doing just fine. And if he wasn't, there were other people for him to turn to, people who understood him and could support him better than I ever could—*or ever had*. I simply wasn't needed anymore.

It was a tremendous loss, like every bone in my body disappeared and I didn't know how to stand. It felt like I suddenly, truly lost my son. Our entire relationship was built around me looking after him, managing his moods, making his life work. I didn't know how to be his mom anymore.

While Tristan was wrapped in the comfort of new friends, a new program and a new life, I was left alone with the emptiness of having him gone from mine. I didn't have a group of people in my camp, distracting me with field trips and outings. I didn't know how to be "a part of" or how to have fun, and there was nobody to show me.

I started the car but just sat there, hands on the steering wheel. I didn't have anyone to go home to, nobody to wrap me in their arms and lend me their strength and tell me I'd be okay. I wasn't upset about Tristan going to the aquarium at all. I was upset at being left behind, alone.

After all I'd done for Tristan, it didn't seem fair.

II

THE NEXT
RIGHT THING

15

EIGHT DAYS after taking Tristan to treatment, Mom and I pulled into the driveway in the back alley behind the house where he'd been living. Morning sunshine swept aside some of my anxiety as I braced myself for whatever lay ahead. In the days before Tristan went into treatment, he'd started cleaning his room but hadn't finished. He'd been worried about his kitchen and cooking gear, so I told him I'd finish cleaning and bring his things home for safe keeping. If he was in rehab, it was the least I could do.

I was glad Mom had come with me so I didn't have to face Tristan's place alone. When I'd been a newly single mom, working and going to school, I'd struggled with the chaos of three children under the age of eight. Floors went unvacuumed, toilets were uncleaned, toys and clothes lay where we left them. Whenever it got too overwhelming, Mom would arrive, unasked, to put things in order. She'd spend the day cleaning and tidying, creating systems and storage spaces in the hope I'd maintain order. It never quite worked, because systems and storage were not the problem: it was time, energy, and inclination that I lacked. But I was as grateful to Mom then as I was now, looking at the house in front of us.

"Come on," she said, opening the car door. "No sense sitting here. It won't clean itself." Mom was a bundle of forced positivity, determined to look on the bright side. I dug Tristan's keys out of my wallet, took a deep breath and prayed we wouldn't run into the landlady. I felt embarrassed to be Tristan's mom.

We entered the large kitchen. Thankfully, nobody seemed to be home. Three large fridges and two stoves lined two walls, with a large double sink on another and a countertop island in the middle. I showed Mom Tristan's fridge area and she started cleaning out the few scraps of unrecognizable food and wiping down surfaces while I went up to his bedroom. His room had its own lock, and I slipped the other key Tristan had given me into the knob.

I could see where he'd cleaned up, somewhat. There was a path of bare parquet floor from the door to the bed to the walk-in closet. But the rest was piled high with dirty dishes, garbage, filthy clothes and pots and pans crusted with old food. The curtains were drawn, the room was dim and humid, and flies buzzed lazily.

Tristan had always been such a clean kid. Organized. He liked things being just so.

This is his addiction, I told myself. *This is not Tristan.*

I stepped over and onto piles of garbage to reach the window and pulled open the curtain. Summer light flooded in, making his room look even worse than before.

I noticed the square IKEA mirror I'd bought for Tristan when I'd redecorated his bedroom seven years earlier. He was thirteen years old at the time, on the verge of becoming a man, his whole life ahead of him like a blank canvas filled with potential. He'd needed a room suitable for a teenager, not a boy. Now, the mirror lay flat on the dresser beside his bed, covered with the residue of fine white powder. His rumpled blankets, the ones I'd bought him when he moved in, had smears of blood on them. From nosebleeds, I knew, and from obsessively picking at his skin and scabs. I'd read that people who use too much cocaine feel like they have bugs crawling under their skin. "Coke bugs" they call them.

I wrapped my arms around myself and stood, unseeing.

I thought about Tristan when he was thirteen years old. By then, I no longer needed Mom's help to keep things in order—Tristan was my cleaning buddy. We'd put on Bob Marley's *Legend* album and dust and vacuum and tidy the house together until the last song finished. When "Redemption Song" came on, we'd take a break and sit side-by-side on the couch, shoulders touching, and listen silently as Marley told us, "None but ourselves can free our minds."

"I'm coming up!" Mom called cheerfully, making me jump. I heard her footsteps on the stairs below.

"No, don't!" I went to the top of the stairs and looked down. "There's a ton of dishes to wash. I'll bring them down. Can you do that while I clean up here? You really don't want to see this."

Something in my face must have shown how upset I was. "You shouldn't have to do that alone," she said.

"Mom." I smiled. "I'm not alone. You're here, and you have no idea how grateful I am. But it's not going to help to have you up here, and somebody has to do the dishes. It's a nasty job. If it were just me, I'd throw them all away."

"No, you can't throw out dishes!" Born during the Great Depression, she was appalled at the thought of wastefulness. Plus she knew Tristan had spent years collecting his kitchenware.

"Well, then I vote we divide and conquer."

With a place to start, I carried dirty dishes downstairs until they filled the countertop and told Mom to let me know when she was ready for more. Then I armed myself with the box of extra-large garbage bags I'd brought with me and went to work.

Everything disgusting or remotely questionable went in the garbage. I didn't live by Mom's motto of "waste not, want not." If it grossed me out, it was garbage. But I picked carefully through everything, as best I could, and filled a suitcase with clothes I felt were salvageable. Slowly, I worked my way across to the closet.

There was no room to walk into the walk-in closet. Old garbage bags and loose moldy garbage spilled onto the floor. Tristan's best dress clothes still hung on hangers, squished by the garbage around them. As I pulled the rotting bags out, I realized they weren't all trash—some contained clothes or dishes, too.

My mind spun. Had Tristan deliberately thrown away his stuff? He loved his stuff! I decided he must have cleaned up by throwing everything into bags, garbage or not, and tossing the bags in the closet. In the summer heat, the stench was overpowering.

Pulling the bags from the closet, I found three Rubbermaid containers filled with . . . I wasn't sure. Urine? My stomach lurched and I retreated to the bed to sit down.

Was Tristan peeing in containers? Why in god's name?

I remembered what Tristan had told me about his roommates watching him, being out to get him. I imagined Tristan spending days in psychosis, so paranoid he couldn't make himself leave his bedroom. He'd be mortified if he knew I found this.

After a few deep breaths, I went back to the closet, scooped everything into garbage bags, barely looking, and carried them down to the dumpster. I didn't care at that point if I threw out valuable items. If Tristan had wanted to save anything, he should have done it himself.

Four hours after we arrived, I had Tristan's room emptied, mopped and scrubbed clean. Mom had Tristan's dishes and kitchenware washed and packed. We were exhausted. We hadn't cleaned his place to get his damage deposit back—Tristan owed rent beyond what his damage deposit covered—but it wasn't right to make anyone else deal with his mess. And we did manage to save a lot of his clothes and kitchenware. I needed a shower, but I was happy.

As Mom and I took the last load to the car, the landlady pulled into the driveway.

"Thank you for cleaning up," she said as she walked toward us. Then she shook her head and lowered her voice, like she was telling me a secret. "I think it was not very good."

"No," I said. "It was not very good. But it's good now. Ready to rent out again." I handed her Tristan's two keys.

"Tristan has not paid rent these last two months. He owes me twelve hundred dollars. Can you give me a cheque for this rent? I do not have a lot of money, and—"

"No, I don't have that kind of money, sorry." I shook my head and began to move away.

"I will take a payment plan. For you, you came back and cleaned, and I thank you. So maybe two hundred dollars each month until it's paid?"

I felt badly for this woman but I had hit my limit of cleaning up Tristan's messes for the day. I looked her in the eyes and said, "I'm sorry Tristan didn't pay his rent. I can't help you with that. That's his responsibility. You could take him to small claims court. But he's gone into an addiction treatment centre so ..." I shrugged. "I can't do any more."

I piled the last bags of Tristan's bedding into the car, and Mom and I drove away.

THE FOLLOWING Wednesday I worked from a Starbucks just a few blocks from Westgate. Not that I got much work done, but I didn't want to worry about traffic or be late to see Tristan. As afternoon rolled toward evening, I gave up even pretending to be productive.

I watched people pass by on the sidewalk: businesspeople, homeless people, students.

I checked the time—5:41—and sighed.

It was still too early to put my mind to answering the question that had been rattling in my head all day: Would Tristan prefer a strawberry Frappuccino or a vanilla one? I knew he'd be happy with either. I could put anything edible in front of him and he was like a puppy with a bowl of ice cream. But I also knew he'd *prefer* one over the other, depending on his mood, and I had no way of knowing if his mood that day was strawberry or vanilla. I was trying to remember how many times I'd seen Tristan order one of those flavours compared to the other when my phone rang.

It was Westgate. I had no idea why they'd call me now, less than an hour before I was due to arrive for my first visit with Tristan and then my first Parents' Group meeting.

"Hi Kathy, I'm just phoning to give you an update. Everything's fine and there's no reason to worry." It was Ben. He'd called a few times over the past week and still began every conversation this way. "But Tristan had a bad day so he won't be able to see you this evening."

That landed like a fist to my gut. I didn't know what a bad day might look like for Tristan now. Was it a bad case of the blues? Did he want to run away and give up? Did he punch someone? Did he go all crazy and psychotic?

"What happened?" I asked.

"Oh, he was butting heads with our director at dinner tonight. Dale called him out on his table manners and Tristan started mouthing off. That's not unusual for new guys. They rebel against authority and don't like to follow rules. I know," he chuckled. "I was the same way. And then they just get stuck in the anger. Haven't got a good range of emotions yet. I don't know if you've met Dale, but the guys don't get away with too much around him. He calls them on their bullshit."

I had met Dale, briefly. A beefy, middle-aged, biker-looking dude with sharp eyes, a foul mouth and plaid flannel covering a heart bursting with decades of service to others. But something didn't seem right. Tristan looked up to men in authority, showed them respect, even awe. He was a follower, not a leader. I'd have thought he would have tried hard to stay on Dale's good side.

"Well... what happened?" I still didn't get it, clearly.

"It's all good now. Tristan took it hard and wanted to walk out, but the guys talked to him and he had a bit of a cry in his room and then found Dale and apologized. They hugged it out, no hard feelings. Tristan just needs to learn when it's best to stay quiet. He says he's still committed to being here, but I think he could use a calm evening with the guys and we'll try again next week for a visit with you. But you're still coming to Parents' Group?"

"Yes, of course. Thanks for letting me know about..." my thoughts wandered off. I didn't know what I was thanking him for.

"No problem. I'll see you soon."

I stared out the window to the parking lot. I was deeply disappointed about being unable to see Tristan after twelve days of no communication. I'd never gone that long without speaking to him, even through all his travels and misadventures, and I'd been so looking forward to our precious half hour, much more than the weekly Parents' Group. Now I was stuck with the chaff of the evening, without the wheat. I sipped cold tea and swallowed my anger as Ben's words echoed inside of me.

It made no sense that Westgate hadn't asked for my opinion about how to manage Tristan. Who knew my son better than I did? They didn't know what he would respond well to, and what he wouldn't. They didn't know what made him tick like I did. They talked about including family in addiction recovery, but maybe that was just lip service to reassure me. They certainly weren't using me as a resource to help them understand Tristan.

It didn't seem like a good start to me.

STILL FRAZZLED and anxious, I drove to Westgate for Parents' Group. I tried to calm myself and focus on the experience in front of me. There was still so much I could learn about Tristan's environment, even if I couldn't see him tonight. And if Ben said Tristan was fine, even with the drama of the evening—that his behaviour was *normal*, even—I needed to try to believe that.

At 6:57, with three minutes to spare, I walked up the front stairs of Westgate's heritage house.

This is where Tristan lives, I thought.

I'd timed my entrance carefully. Not so late as to draw attention to myself, but not so early that I'd have to make conversation.

One of the guys saw me, opened the door and said hi. I said hi back as I scanned the living room for Tristan, knowing I wouldn't see him, and walked through the industrial-sized kitchen into the back multipurpose room where they held group meetings. I promptly sat in the first spare chair I saw and smiled and nodded at whoever looked my way, to be friendly. Then I pretended to answer imaginary but oh-so-urgent messages on my phone.

As a teenager, I'd been shy and anxious to fit in, fearful of rejection, so I'd made up an invisibility cloak for myself; a coping mechanism I'd wear when I walked the hallway of my high school.

With my cloak securely in place, I could proudly hold my head high, never looking anyone in the eye. I'd pretend not to hear the occasional "Hi, Kathy," until I no longer needed to pretend. In that way, I became invisible. Nobody could see the shy, anxious girl I was. If I was noticed at all, people thought of me as aloof, proud, snooty. That was far from the truth, but I could work with that. I gave the impression of not needing anybody, not wanting anything. Talking with strangers still wasn't easy for me and being in large groups of people made me anxious. But I would have endured any nightmare to get a glimpse into Tristan's new world.

There were about twenty or so parents, mostly women, mostly middle-aged, sitting on stacking chairs set in a circle around the perimeter of the room. These people didn't look like parents of drug addicts, to me. I felt out of place. Sure, some had a haunted look about them—I could relate to that—but most of the parents looked downright happy. I hadn't seen so many smiles in one room for I don't know how long. And the laughter! People greeted each other as if that alone were cause for joy.

Some people, like me, wore jeans or shorts and T-shirts. There were men with stubble and dark circles under their eyes, and women who didn't try to hide their worry lines with make-up. I felt a connection with those people. But most of the parents were well put together. They wore beautiful shawls with striking Indigenous designs, or delicate scarves in a rainbow of colours chosen, it seemed, to set off bright eyes or rosy lips. There were bangles and rings, leather boots and fashionable shoes, impeccable make-up and carefully styled hair. Casual. Not pretentious or over the top, but as if they cared about themselves.

They looked like normal people you'd meet anywhere, not parents of drug addicts.

That thought surprised me. Of all people, I knew that addiction could happen to anybody, in any family. Yet I still carried the idea that parents of addicts were poor, dismal and unkempt. I certainly felt poor, dismal and unkempt in comparison to these women with breezy scarves.

More stacks of chairs stood against the back wall, along with folding tables that would be set out at breakfast, lunch and dinner.

This is where Tristan eats his meals.

Two huge chalkboards hung on the walls, one at each end of the room. Scrawled on one were ten characteristics of low self-esteem. The other listed characteristics of high self-esteem. The low-esteem board described Tristan pretty accurately, I thought: self-critical, needing affirmation from other people. For myself, I had more high self-esteem characteristics than low and felt oddly proud—like I got a good grade on a test. Not an A, but a C+ at least, maybe a B.

This is where Tristan attends group meetings.

Ben came in and sat in front of the low self-esteem board. It was the first time I'd seen him since he'd shown me around during Tristan's intake. He waved hello to me as he continued talking to the woman next to him.

This is Tristan's caseworker.

Another man sat at the opposite end of the room, in front of the high self-esteem board. He seemed ageless but he was dressed like a teenager: jeans, a rumpled button-up shirt and sneakers. His face was neither young nor old, but he clearly had experience.

"I see some new faces tonight, so welcome," he said, looking around the room, eyes resting briefly on me and a few other women. "I'm Paul and, in addition to helping out with these groups, I'm the head counsellor for the youth program." That fit perfectly. Teenagers would feel right at home with him. He looked like one of them, but older.

I had expected to hear an overview of how these sessions worked, but Paul jumped right in with a story about his background and path to recovery.

"I told myself I had every reason to use," he began. "My birth parents died when I was young and I'd been in the foster system before my parents adopted me. Poor me. I was angry at the world. I fought, I stole, I lied to get drugs. I was the neighbourhood punk everyone stayed away from. One day, I went home and my key didn't work. My parents had changed the locks. I pounded on the door until my dad came down and told me he was tired of me upsetting my mom, and if he saw me around their house again, he'd call the cops. *Their* house, not mine. The nerve, right? I was like, 'Whatever, I don't need you or your stupid home!' and I stomped halfway down the block before realizing it was cold and I had nowhere to go."

Paul paused and laughed. "I felt like such a big tough guy, but I turned around and went back to the house and started yelling, 'Mom! Mommy, Mommy I want my blanket!' Seriously, I was nineteen years old and yelling for 'Mommy' to get my blanky. No joke. So finally, I leave, satisfied, with my favourite Snoopy blanket in hand." Everyone in the room was laughing now, me included. We could picture that scene.

"I couch-surfed with friends for a few nights, checked out a homeless shelter and decided I really liked being warm and comfortable. I wouldn't make a good street person. So, I decided to get help and I came to Westgate. That was twenty-six years ago."

Twenty-six years. It was hard to imagine. Proof that recovery was possible.

This is Tristan's role model.

Paul's story had soothed a part of me I hadn't known was aching. His story was tragic, in many ways, but he told it with such humour and happiness. I realized that while parts of his story were tragic, *he* was a triumph.

I felt a whisper of hope.

There was no real structure or logic to the meeting. After Paul spoke for a while, one of the women mentioned her son celebrated his one-year cake the week before, and another shared how she helped her son and another "Gate Boy" to set up their new apartment. A discussion ensued about when to help and when to step back. Everyone in that room knew it was a tricky tightrope to walk.

"What works for me," said one woman, "is asking myself whether what I'm doing is a *handout* or a *hand up*. For example, when Stu was six months out of Westgate, he asked if we'd lend him money to buy a car and we said no way. He could save up. He did, and he was really proud of that beater. Now, two years later, he asked if we'd cosign on financing so he could get a new truck. He loves off-roading and helps a lot of people in recovery to move and pick up furniture. He's been responsible with managing his money and making payments, so we said sure. Buying a car for him when he first got sober felt like a handout. Helping him to finance a truck now feels like a hand up."

Stories followed stories, and I started to relax. *Perhaps our kids can get better*, I thought. Maybe Tristan could get well, move out with a roommate, have a one-year cake, manage his money and buy a beater car one day. As impossible as that seemed.

Then a woman across the room mentioned she'd just got back from what she called "a few days of radical self-care" at her cabin. She was coping and focusing on her own health and well-being, even though her son had recently relapsed.

Relapsed.

Relapsed.

I couldn't hear what came next. My heart raced and I closed my eyes, willing myself away.

I wasn't stupid; I knew relapse was always a possibility. Some say a *probability*, until a person hits that seemingly magical moment when recovery sticks. *If* they hit that moment, which they don't always.

Jesus Fucking Christ, Tristan can't relapse, I thought. *I do not have another round of this in me. I'd rather die.*

My fear was visceral. My thoughts didn't feel dramatic. They were not an overreaction or exaggeration. They came from a place of deep exhaustion and certainty that I wouldn't have the strength to live through Tristan's addiction again.

My faith in recovery wavered as I watched this woman across from me, so strong and calm, talking about the joy and gratitude she found in hiking and spending time with her husband this past weekend, despite everything—despite *relapse*.

I studied her, like she was a bizarre creature I'd never seen before. A kid in relapse was a failure, worth screaming about, and grieving and shrieking and tearing yourself apart. Did this woman not understand the risks? Did she not see how quickly people lose themselves in addiction, sometimes forever? How could she possibly go off and enjoy herself when she should have been chasing her son down and tying him up if necessary to get him back into treatment? And if that wasn't possible, at least she could be in deep despair.

I decided this woman wasn't like me. She had a cabin. And a husband. She felt joy. She had a son who relapsed, and she still felt joy. Clearly, she was nothing like me. This was a good thing because if she was different, our sons must be different, and Tristan wouldn't relapse like her son did. I knew my logic was faulty, but it was comforting and I began to calm down and breathe again.

Paul closed the meeting after a fast ninety minutes, telling us we "didn't cause it, can't control it and can't cure it. If you could have, God knows you would have by now." Everyone stood up, formed a big circle with arms around each other's shoulders and said the serenity prayer together. I let the words wash over me: *Grant me the serenity to accept the things I cannot change, the courage to change the things I can, and the wisdom to know the difference.* It seemed a bit awkward and churchy to me, so I was surprised by the surge of emotion I felt as I listened. Even if I had known the words, I wouldn't have been able to speak them right then.

16

THE NEXT week I finally got to see Tristan. He was waiting for me as I turned up the sidewalk to the house.

"Hey, Mom," he said with a big grin and open arms.

"Tristan!" I walked into his hug and hugged him back tightly. He looked good. He'd lost his sickly pallor. He smelled good. No more tobacco or weed.

I gave him the extra-large strawberry Frappuccino I'd brought for him and he looked like he'd just received an unexpected birthday present.

"You look great," I said. "You've gained weight."

"Yup. Almost twenty pounds already. The food's pretty good here. I'm going to have to slow down, or I'll end up four hundred pounds. This isn't going to help," he said, holding up the Frappuccino, "but at least I'll be fat and happy!" He laughed and took a long slurp.

"Nah, it looks good on you." His cheeks had colour and filled the space between his jaw and cheekbone. His eyes were a clear, deep grey-green. His gaze was focused and aware. His body had filled out too. He was no longer all elbows and wrists, ribs and shoulder blades. He was almost stocky.

"Come on. I'll show you around," he said, holding the door open for me. The building had previously been residential apartments and Tristan's room was a one-bedroom suite he shared with two other men. The bedroom was given to the guy who'd been there longer and was already in transition. Tristan, as a new guy, got one of the two beds set up in the main room, which used to be the living room. The room also held two side tables, two dressers, and one floor-length mirror. There was a wall of windows overlooking the main house and back patio next door, a table with four chairs and a small galley kitchen. Clean. Comfy. Basic.

"Hey, that's great!" I said. "You can still cook or make snacks up here."

"No, we can't," Tristan said. "We can have water and stuff, but they don't like us eating up here. No food or cooking. We have to go down and eat with everyone else. They don't want us isolating. We have to be 'part of.'"

"I guess that makes sense," I said, though I felt oddly sad. I motioned to the table and sat. "So, how's it going? What do your days look like?" Tristan got a binder from his bedside table, sat down and pulled out his weekly schedule.

"Breakfast is early, at seven o'clock. If you miss it, it sucks because then you miss it. I did that once." He looked at me and smiled.

"So, you didn't get to eat breakfast?" I was appalled.

"Nope, but I can always grab cereal and a banana or something. I just miss out on the good stuff. Eggs and bacon and shit. And I get in trouble. We're not supposed to sleep in. We need time to make our beds and then be at our first meeting by eight o'clock."

"Meeting? Like with your counsellor?"

"No, our NA meeting—Narcotics Anonymous. We go twice a day, morning and night. They're out in the community. Then after we come back we have our sessions here. Usually as a group. Sometimes I meet with Ben or one of the counsellors, but mostly it's group stuff. Then lunch and chores."

My mind was swimming, trying to absorb every detail. "What chores do you do?"

"Right now, I'm sweeping the main house. I like it 'cause nobody bothers me. I can just get it done. Except when people start walking through where I'm sweeping, that kinda pisses me off." He shook his head as if remembering somebody walking through his dust pile.

"What about cooking?" I asked. "Is there a chance you could do that as a chore?"

"Yeah, but I don't want to. I don't want to cook yet."

I nodded my head like I understood, which I didn't, but I let it be. Tristan told me that after chores there was free time for anything that moved life forward: scheduling doctor appointments, doing your taxes, going to the gym, doing step work, meeting with your sponsor, doing volunteer work, going out for coffee and a conversation. Dinner was at five o'clock. Phone calls to family occurred between 5:30 and 7 p.m. although, he warned me, one landline for almost sixty guys made it difficult at times to get through. Tristan was officially off restrictions as of that day so I'd find out for myself soon enough. Then an evening NA meeting, a check-in with a caseworker, and journalling before bed. That was his life now.

"So, Tristan," I ventured. "How is it? How're you doing?"

He hesitated before answering.

"It's good. It is." He gazed out the window, then turned back to me. "But it's hard. It's really hard having emotions again. I haven't really felt anything for years. I don't know how to deal with emotions very well. I get really angry and then I cry and then I feel like shit for crying. Having feelings is hard and showing them is even harder. Like smiling, that's a big one. I'm literally learning how to smile again. Like, I practice in front of the mirror because I don't know how." He gave a half laugh and then a full, well-rehearsed smile.

We both burst out laughing, but my heart broke for him. Such basic things as emotions and smiling. I couldn't imagine how hard that would be. How did this happen to him? I didn't know what to say, so I said nothing.

"And thinking, that's another big one. Trying to pay attention to the stories I tell myself. It's all connected, I guess. 'Our thoughts create our feelings, our feelings create our behaviour and our behaviour creates our life,'" he said in a sing-song voice, as if he was mimicking someone. "Or something like that. It's pretty interesting, but ... my thoughts still kinda suck. They put me on antidepressants, though, and that seems to be helping a bit," Tristan said.

I was suddenly, acutely pissed off. Why was he on antidepressants so soon? I didn't like the idea of an instant diagnosis. He didn't seem stable enough yet for anyone to understand the root of the problem. It felt like they were throwing more drugs at a drug problem.

"Who put you on antidepressants?" I asked, willing myself to not leap to judgements. "You've only been here a few weeks, how do they know your moods aren't just because of using drugs, and then not?"

"It was the doctor, obviously. And, sure that's part of it, but I've been depressed since I was at least ten years old. Long before I did drugs. Anyway, it seems to be helping, so that's good."

"Yeah, that's good," I parroted. *Since he was ten years old*. I tidied up the papers on the table, for something to do while I gathered my thoughts.

It made sense, looking back. And I *had* been concerned. But it had been so easy to attribute Tristan's dark moods to his sensitive nature and the stress of our divorce and do nothing—just see how things progressed. That was on me. I should have dealt with that ten years earlier.

The guilt of leaving Tristan's depression unrecognized, untreated, stayed with me long after I left him that evening. I would have done anything to crawl back in time and do it differently. It didn't seem fair that I couldn't get a do-over when I finally learned something so pivotal, something that could make a difference. Why should *he* suffer because of *my* oversight? But there were no do-overs, and I had to learn to live with myself. It wasn't easy.

A few weeks later, as I was still trying to accept the past as past and focus on creating a better future, Tristan told me he'd also been diagnosed with ADHD and put on medication. "I can actually follow a conversation, Mom!" he told me during one of my visits. We were sitting on the front patio and he seemed relaxed as we warmed ourselves in the sunshine. "Remember all those times I'd just nod and say 'uh-huh' when people were talking? It's because everyone sounded kinda like the adults in a Charlie Brown cartoon: 'waa waa waa waa,' even when I tried to pay attention. Now..." he paused, looking for the right words, and then shrugged. "Now, I can actually take part in a conversation."

The guilt I'd been trying to push away came crashing down again, tenfold. Through the rest of our visit, through Parents' Group that evening, through that night and for many nights afterward, I wondered if I could have prevented Tristan's problems, his self-esteem issues, his addiction, if I had just paid more attention when he was young. If I had not been so quick to lovingly label Tristan as a space cadet at five years old when his mind wandered, or at seven years old when Tanis still needed to meet him on the playground at recess to escort him to the correct classroom on time.

By the time I found out about Tristan's ADHD, I'd been to Parents' Group a few times already. I reminded myself of the slogan Paul was so fond of, the "three C's": *We didn't cause it, we can't control it and we can't cure it.* And yet it seemed to me that Tristan's addiction *was* my fault. I may not have caused it, exactly, but I might have prevented it by getting him help and medication when he first needed it.

While Tristan was learning to smile and have conversations with people again, I was learning to live with guilt. I knew that feelings of guilt were normal, but not useful. I'd been practicing letting go of my guilt for weeks already but I was nowhere near skilled enough to be successful. I whipped myself with guilt, chose to wear it like a horsehair shirt because I didn't deserve anything else. I had thought, in Tristan's addiction, that I knew what pain was, but I was only just discovering the many different ways my heart could break.

THE SATURDAY after I first visited Tristan at Westgate, he phoned to invite the whole family to visit him at Redstone, their rural retreat in Mission, BC. He was spending the weekend there.

Mom, Jenn, Tanis, and I piled into my car and drove forty minutes to Redstone. Tristan gave us a tour of the house, which included a basketball court, media room, indoor swimming pool and beautiful kitchen with a sunny deck. Mom sat in a deckchair where she could admire the view while the rest of us explored the grounds. We walked past flower gardens, peeked into a greenhouse bursting with tomatoes and cucumbers and beans, and then down through fields of organic gardens with everything from kale and carrots to blueberries and strawberries and a small fruit tree orchard.

As we began the walk back to the house, three llamas left their grazing and followed us up the hill. They shifted from a lazy lope to a steady trot, closing the distance between us.

"Oh my god, run! The llamas are going to get us!" Jenn cried, more serious than not. She ran ahead on the long dirt driveway, positioning us between her and the llamas.

With Jenn's back turned to us, Tanis yelled, "Jenn, they've almost caught up to you, they're going to eat you, run faster!"

Jenn shrieked and ran in a burst of energy.

Tristan chimed in, "Watch out, one's coming out of the woods right at you. He's gonna get you!"

Jenn turned and saw the three llamas now walking slowly along behind us. "Fuck off, you guys. You're crazy for *not* running. Did you notice that brown guy's teeth? And the look in his eye? He's out for blood!"

We walked up the remainder of the road, laughing at and with Jenn. She stayed a good fifty feet in front of us, the llamas following twenty feet behind. I was wonderfully, blissfully content.

When we got to the house, Tristan ducked into the garage to get some llama treats, which they were clearly expecting. Tristan and Tanis and I fed them each one and then watched as they ambled back down the hill to the fields. Jenn continued to watch from a distance.

Back on the sundeck, we sipped fresh lemonade and visited with Tristan and some of the other guys. A fat old French bulldog wandered out for some pats and lay in the shade. The guys talked about their new "recovery bodies," wondering when the weight gain would stop, yet proud of the pounds they'd packed on. I sat back and let my mind wander, basking in the beautiful sober chatter around me.

After a while, Tristan asked if I wanted to walk down to the garden again, just the two of us, to see some amazing zucchini or something. It seemed like an odd request but I was happy to have some time alone with him. We walked at ease in each other's company, close together, chatting about easy, comfortable things.

Then Tristan asked, "So, Mom, are you happy I'm here? Are you sleeping better now?" He gazed ahead, still walking, but he seemed tense waiting for my answer.

"Of course, I'm *so* happy you're here!" I said and smiled. But then a nightmare I'd had the night before flooded back to me: Tristan was leaving treatment and I knew he was going to relapse, become homeless and die. I had lain awake for hours trying to shake that feeling.

"I did have a nightmare again last night, though," I said, thinking nothing of it until I saw his reaction. His face fell; he looked devastated. Only then did I remember another saying they had at Westgate: *You can judge a guy's recovery by how well his mom sleeps at night.* I realized my blunder and tried to pull my foot out of my mouth. "But it's all so new. I'm sure I'll be sleeping like a baby soon."

It was too late. Tristan, still needing external validation, was looking at my sleeping habits as a reflection of his success in recovery and I had as good as told him he was a failure. We went through the motions of looking at vegetables and walking back, but our lightness was gone. We were weighed down in our thoughts.

I obsessively replayed that moment in my mind, my sense of guilt and responsibility as strong as ever. When I got home, I desperately wanted to phone Tristan and explain, but I couldn't phone him while he was at Redstone. And anyway, what would I say? I felt like my nightmare told him, point blank, that he wasn't doing enough, wasn't good enough.

For the next two nights, I tossed and turned in my blankets, worrying about how that affected him. Instead of sleeping, I lay awake, imagining him wanting to give up, go back to drugs, because what was the point if his own mother didn't believe in him? The next day I still couldn't reach him, so I exhausted myself with self-recrimination. I was sick to my stomach.

Once or twice during this time, I heard a tiny voice inside me trying to cut through the noise in my head: *Thoughts create feelings,* it whispered. But it was like a signpost in a blizzard, and my mind skidded right on by.

Finally, on Monday evening, when Tristan was back at Westgate, I was able to call him. At 5:30 sharp, I was on the phone, grateful that Tristan answered.

"Hey Tristan! Thank you so much for inviting us to Redstone, it was so good to see you," I began.

"Hey Mom. Yeah, it was great to see you and everybody. It's a pretty cool place, huh?"

"It is. But look, I've been worried about something I said to you, and I need to explain." I took a deep breath and then carried on. "When I told you about my nightmare—of course, there's still a part of me that worries about you but your recovery is all so new to me and Saturday was one of the first times we've spent much time together and the first time I've seen you looking so happy and healthy and, truly, you know I've never slept well and that has nothing at all to do with you. I think you're doing a wonderful job and am so proud of you and I love you so much and I'm so sorry I had that nightmare because I know you're safe and solid in recovery now and I'm sure I'll sleep well from now on, honey." I stopped, out of breath, and closed my eyes. I was a bit shocked at my outpouring of emotional truths wrapped in illogical nonsense.

"Don't worry about it, Mom," Tristan said without a pause. And then he told me about the rest of his weekend at Redstone: swimming in the lake with the guys, visiting with his dad and uncle and eating fresh-baked pies made from berries in the garden.

17

ONE NIGHT, as I lay in bed, reading and sipping licorice tea, my phone rang. The call display showed "Westgate."

I looked at the time: 9:12 p.m. Westgate wouldn't be calling me at that time of night about anything good, and Tristan never called this late.

My stomach clenched as I answered the phone. "Hello?"

"Hi, Mom." It was Tristan after all, sounding chipper. "How are you?"

"I'm good," I said, cautious. "What's up?"

"Not much, not much. Just got back from a meeting, heard some good shares. I was thinking about you, so thought I'd give you a call." He paused, briefly. Then, "So, how was your day? What did you get up to?"

I didn't know what to make of that. Usually, if Tristan asked me about my day, it was to butter me up to get something.

"It was fine, nothing special," I said and paused, waiting for Tristan to come out with the real reason for his call. He remained quiet and then I heard voices mumbling in the background. It sounded like he was talking with another guy. "What about you?" I added.

"It's all good. I just called to say hi and find out about your day. Um...how's Balloo?"

Now that was downright weird. "What's going on, Tristan? Why are you so interested in my day and asking all these questions?"

He burst out laughing and I heard more laughter and talking in the background. "Oh, Mom, why do you have to be so difficult? I'm just tryin' not to be self-centred and pay attention to your needs. One of my friends is beside me making sure I ask about your day, and you're making it so hard!" They were laughing now like this was the funniest joke ever.

I relaxed and joined their laughter. Tristan was simply practicing what he was learning. He was practicing how to be a thoughtful person, how to be in healthy relationship with others. And, no, I sure wasn't making it easy, turning the conversation back toward him. It would take more than a few weeks for me to drop a decade of worry.

"In that case, I had a great day," I told him. "I took Balloo to the vet for his old-age check-up, got some work done, and now I'm just relaxing with my book."

We talked for a while about Balloo, and Tristan asked about Jenn and Tanis and my mom, and I shared the latest family news. I reminded him that I was heading out to Toronto the next day, for work.

"I gotta get going, Mom, there's another guy waiting for the phone. And I have a bunch of step work to get done tonight. Have a good night's sleep. Love you!" he said.

I told him I loved him too and hung up.

I couldn't remember when I'd had such a simple phone conversation with Tristan about *my* day. It was unfamiliar and energizing. Full of possibility. It occurred to me that I may actually get my son back and enjoy how he showed up in my life. That thought floored me. I hadn't realized I'd doubted it.

A week or so later, Tristan again phoned me after 9 p.m. I'd been speaking with him every few days and, this time, felt only the lightest breeze of anxiety because of the late hour.

"Hi Mom, sorry to call so late. I couldn't call earlier because I was busy saving some guy's life and then I had to rush to a meeting. But I wanted to check in and say hi." He paused. "So . . . hi!"

I laughed. "Hi to you too. Saving some guy's life? What's that all about?" I was happy to give Tristan the opening he clearly wanted.

"Yeah, it was pretty cool! Chris and I were walking back from the library, and we saw this old man—he was maybe sixty or so—stumble into the road and fall and crack his head on the curb. Then he was just lying there bleeding, so we got him to the grass and sat him up against a tree and called 911. Thankfully, Chris had a phone! He was a little bit out of it, mostly from being drunk I think, so we stayed with him and talked to him until the ambulance came. He said he was really grateful, and the ambulance guys said we did a good job."

"Aw, sweetheart, that was such a kind thing to do!" I said, full of mama-pride.

"Yeah, well, we were there and somebody needed to look after the dude. But it did feel really good. *Too* good, maybe, if I'm practicing humility—it's not supposed to be about me!" He laughed. "But, Mom," he continued, his voice quiet and full of emotion, "I never would have done that when I was using. It felt really good to be able to help someone."

"I'm so glad you were there for him, Tristan. It does feel good to help people, doesn't it?"

"Yeah, it really does." We sat in the warmth of our silence. Then, "So, how was *your* day, Mom?"

We chatted a bit longer before I hung up and got ready for bed. I felt a bit foolish at the smile stuck on my face as if it belonged there. As if making up for lost time.

"EMILY, WATCH out for the poo!" Tristan yelled, trying to avert a petting-zoo catastrophe.

Emily froze, arms spread wide, her chubby legs bent in a crouch, ready to spring or fly in any direction.

Tristan grabbed his niece around her waist and flew her over the pig poo, setting her down safely on the other side.

"Whew!" he said. "That was a close one. You'd have sunk right into the poo, and we'd never see you again."

"Ew," she said, looking at the pile of poo Tristan had saved her from. "But I wouldn't have sunk into it. I'm bigger than it is."

"I don't know," said Tristan, looking very serious. "It could be one of those terrible pig-poo holes I've heard about. They're really, really deep. You just put one foot into them and, *whoosh*! You're pulled right down into pig-poo world."

She listened, slightly concerned, until her two-year-old logic kicked in. "No, see Uncle Tristan? The ground is hard." She kicked the ground to prove her point and jumped up and down a couple times. "It doesn't sink. There's no such thing as a pig-poo world anyway," she finished, defiantly.

Tristan looked like he was going to argue the point, but I stepped in and told Emily she was exactly right and Uncle Tristan was being silly. "Come on, let's go see the baby goats. That one's still nursing from its mommy!" I pointed, and Emily scurried over to the goats.

Back at our picnic table, I felt elated to have all my people around me. We were at Queen's Park celebrating Tristan's first thirty days of sobriety and Jenn's twenty-fourth birthday. My mom sat on a chair in the shade with a book on her lap. Tristan needed to bring a recovery buddy with him for off-site family visits, so we were introduced to Luca, a guy slightly younger than Tristan who was nine months in recovery. They were goofing around blowing bubbles, while Tanis poked fun at them in their goofiness. Jenn, Alan and Emily rounded out the family gathering.

We took turns taking Emily to the playground, petting zoo and water park. We ate our sandwiches and Mom's signature Greek salad, and the oatmeal chocolate-chip cookies I'd baked that morning. I could have stayed well into the evening, but after a couple of hours Jenn and her family had to get going, and Mom soon followed. As Tanis helped Mom carry lawn chairs to her car, I began to tidy up the picnic supplies.

Tristan and Luca were playing Frisbee, and Luca caught the disc and walked over to me. "Hey, Kathy, you've done lots for today. Tristan and I will clear up." Tristan looked startled, but moved toward us, ready to help.

"No, please, don't worry about it," I said. "I love watching you guys play Frisbee, and I'm happy doing this." I tried shooing him away.

Tristan went to pick up the Frisbee from where Luca had dropped it.

"No, you deserve a rest, it's our turn. You did all the work making the food. We need to do our part. We'll clean up," Luca insisted. Tristan took a split second to see which way the tide was turning, then started packing up the food with Luca.

"Okay, thanks for your help." I smiled. I realized I'd been in my habitual mothering mode, assuming all the responsibility while Tristan's only job was to have fun. I thought about what I'd heard in Parents' Group: these guys need opportunities to contribute to the family, to take on responsibilities, give back and do their part. It was part of being an adult in the family and important to their sense of self and their recovery. One of the reasons a new guy always took a buddy with him was to catch opportunities like this one.

I silently thanked Luca and Westgate as I found a sunny spot to watch the boys clean up and pack the car.

But there wasn't always a recovery buddy around to notice and interrupt our old patterns. One evening after Parents' Group, Tristan told me he needed new running shoes. The sole was coming off one of his shoes, there was a hole in the toe of the other, and Westgate's sports day was coming up. I thought my days of buying things for him were over so I wasn't happy about it, and running shoes were expensive. I told him I'd think about it.

"I *need* them, Mom!" he pleaded. "I can't do sports days in these piece-of-shit shoes I'm wearing. I won't go. I *can't* go if I don't get new shoes."

That sounded like the old Tristan, but he had a point. It's hard to run around in shoes that were falling apart. "Fine," I said. "I'll bring you some before sports day. Size ten, right?"

"Yeah, but they need to be basketball shoes, Mom. Not running shoes or trainers or whatever. *Basketball* shoes. And not crappy looking ones. Something nice."

"Holy Mr. Demanding," I said. I didn't want to buy him shoes in the first place, and his attitude wasn't helping. "I'll see what I can do."

I resented buying his damn shoes, but I paid a hundred and forty bucks for black and yellow Nike basketball shoes. I didn't want to go out of my way to bring them to Tristan days before sports day, so he could break them in, but I did. It seemed easier to just get it done and out of my mind so I could stop being angry about it. It was so easy to do what I had always done that I didn't even notice.

As I walked up the sidewalk to Westgate, Tristan ran out to greet me.

"Hi, Mom. What's up?" he asked. He was wearing new all-white running shoes.

"I brought you your shoes," I said. I looked down at his feet, confused. "But you have new shoes already. Where'd they come from?"

"Yeah, they're pretty sweet, hey?" Tristan lifted one foot and then the other so I could admire them. "They were in grabs. There's a whole bunch of clothes that people donate or whatever—we call it 'grabs'—and these were just sitting there. A perfect fit!"

"But you knew I was buying you new shoes. *Basketball* shoes," I added, noticing that the shoes he had on were a different style entirely.

"Oh, yeah, thanks so much, Mom," he said, reaching for the bag I was carrying. "You can't have too many shoes!" He smiled but didn't even bother to look inside the bag.

I didn't stay long to visit with him. I was angry that I let myself be duped again. Ben had told me I wasn't supposed to buy expensive stuff for Tristan, *ever*—that he didn't need the latest, coolest brands—but especially when he was demanding. I knew Westgate would look after him, yet here I was. Again. Doing things I resented for Tristan—things I wouldn't do for myself. I couldn't remember the last time I'd spent that much money on a pair of shoes for myself.

I'd had lots of opportunities to do the right thing. I could have simply said "no" in the first place. I could have bought Tristan a cheap pair from Walmart. I could have taken them back and returned them when I saw he had other new shoes. But I didn't do any of those things. *Why?* Because I didn't want Tristan to be unhappy. I didn't want him to be angry with me. But deeper than that, down in that immensely powerful part of me beyond all thought and reason, I bought him the shoes because I didn't want him to miss sports day and feel bad and relapse and end up on the street and die. That seemed like a rational, predictable chain of events.

I realized I was still riding the same merry-go-round of bullshit I'd been on with Tristan for years, and the merry-go-round was in my head. If Tristan had a buddy with him, we were fine because someone else was looking out for our old, unhealthy patterns of behaviour. Tristan was working a program that would teach him new ways of being, over time, but what about me? I couldn't live my life feeling that if I didn't meet every one of Tristan's needs—no, let's be real here: his *wants*—he would relapse and die.

Your thoughts create your feelings, your feelings create your behaviours, your behaviours create your life. That tiny voice piped up again, sounding just a touch righteous. Damn her, but she was right. I had told myself a far-fetched story that terrified me and, to prevent an imaginary catastrophe from happening, I resentfully bought Tristan expensive shoes he didn't need.

I was suddenly so tired of being disgusted and angry with myself. I was tired of the shame and resentment I felt when I made bad choices, and a bit heartbroken that I was still in that space.

I decided that if I expected Tristan to go through the hard work of his recovery—of changing not only his behaviours, but his thoughts, his feelings, his *very brain chemistry*—the least I could do was pay more attention to my own thoughts and actions.

I'll bring it up at my next Parents' Group, I thought, not realizing how easily that idea came to me.

18

BY THE end of September, I'd been going to Parents' Group every Wednesday for over two months. After that first week, I'd committed to attending regularly, my motivation purely to better understand and support Tristan. Yet somehow, slowly, my focus on Tristan began to twist around and land back on me. It felt like every time I tried to learn something new about Tristan, I got a deeper, more important understanding of myself. Like when I began to worry that Tristan was struggling in his recovery.

"I'm not allowed to go the gym anymore, until I finish step four," he told me while we ate burgers at a local gourmet burger joint. He'd recently been allowed to visit with me off site and without a buddy, so it was just the two of us. "I've been on step four for a fucking month already. I don't know what's wrong with me. I get started, I mean well, and then I just zone out. I mean, fuck, I've been here over sixty days and I'm not even through a third of the steps. I'm never gonna get done."

"What's the gym got to do with it?" I asked, biting into a mountainous mushroom burger.

"They say I'm a bit obsessive with it. That's probably true. I certainly choose to go to the gym more than I choose to do my step work."

Step four was one of the more difficult ones. Tristan described it as "writing down all the horrible shit you've ever done," but I knew that was only partially true. I'd read the *Narcotics Anonymous Basic Text* a few weeks back and found the principles and stories inspiring. I knew this inventory needed to include both the good and the bad, and there were good reasons for that.

"Have you talked to Ben or your sponsor about it? Maybe they have some ideas to help."

"Yeah, I have. Their big idea is 'just do it.'" Tristan took a bite of his burger and washed it down with vanilla milkshake. "And now, to take away my gym privileges, which will probably work because I'll have nothing else to do. And I gotta get out soon. I know my money is almost out."

"Sweetheart, we've been through this before. You don't need to worry about money. You stay as long as you need. The only thing you need to think about now is your recovery. I'll deal with the money." My mom had offered her line of credit, and I had access to more credit myself.

"Mom, you don't have money, and it's not your problem, it's mine. I just gotta burn through the rest of these steps."

"Tristan, I'm serious. Money is not your concern. You can stay a year for all I care. I'll figure it out. Just take the time you need. There's no rush." I tried to catch his eye, but he just stared out the window.

Finally, he turned to me. "Yeah, okay."

But it didn't feel okay. It felt like Tristan was not fully engaged. I worried that he was either not doing the work or was rushing the work simply to get out.

That week, I went to Parents' Group concerned. I sat on my usual chair and let the friendly chatter wash over me until Paul started the meeting. He began by telling a story about how, after six years of sobriety, he'd become compulsively focused on buying an expensive couch that he neither needed nor could afford. But it was cool for whatever reason, and he had to have it. He had the entire room laughing as he told us about the emotional, financial, and relationship consequences of having an addict's obsessive mindset. The point was that recovery is more than not using drugs. It's a process that takes time and continual effort.

Tristan's caseworker, Ben, was cofacilitating that day. After a few moms shared stories of their sons' continuing compulsive behaviour, he told a story that shifted my thinking entirely.

"When I first came here, as a client, I didn't think I was an addict," Ben said. "Sure, I was a twenty-seven-year-old unemployed dude living in my parents' basement, playing video games and getting high all day. I didn't have a girlfriend, obviously, but if I couldn't blame that on the fact that I was brown—and back then I blamed every problem in my life on my brown skin—then I'd blame the girls for just not getting me. So, my life was working just fine for me until it stopped working for my parents." He paused and looked around the room.

"I ended up in rehab because my parents made me. But the thing about Westgate is that you're surrounded by all these guys living their lives and having fun, and you get pulled along. You go through the steps because you have to, and at some point, you begin to believe that maybe you *do* have a problem, and maybe recovery *is* possible. And then you go through some more steps, because you have to, and maybe you realize you want this and are willing to do the work for yourself, not because somebody is making you. But for some of us, like me, it can take a while. You don't need to believe in your own recovery to begin the process of recovering. The process is designed to get you there, even if you resist. Belief in yourself can happen later. You just gotta trust the process, not use drugs, and do the work."

I sat back in my chair. That was the message I'd needed to hear. I'd worried Tristan was not fully committed to his recovery, but he *was* working the program and that was what mattered. He was only sixty days in, still very new. I decided to trust the process. I would try not to worry every time I imagined he was internally conflicted, but to understand that conflict was part of the process. And to keep reminding myself that it was Tristan's process, anyway, not mine.

I hadn't taken any deliberate steps toward my own recovery, yet. But I had been coming to these Wednesday night Parents' Group meetings and surrounding myself with parents in recovery—parents who seemed healthy and joyful, even though their kids were in rehab, or were out in the world again in all their flawed beauty, or had relapsed and were back in active addiction. I wanted to be more like these parents who could have their own lives regardless of how their children were doing.

I knew then that I could hold my worry for Tristan less tightly than before. I could be more thoughtful about letting go of responsibilities that weren't mine. I could pay more attention to what I wanted and less attention to managing other people's lives. Nothing had changed in my life, but my thoughts and feelings had begun to shift in a way that felt significant. If I was already seeing changes in myself from passive participation, I thought, what might be possible if I poured my energy into it?

IN OCTOBER, I attended a special weekend session for family members up at Redstone. Summer was gone. Gold and yellow leaves danced their way from tree branches to the earth, ready for the next raking. The vegetable gardens were tucked in for the winter, but the llamas still wandered the fields.

Ten of us attended the weekend: four couples whose sons were at Westgate, a sister of one of the clients, and me. I recognized two of the couples from Parents' Group, but the others had come from out of town: Texas, Saskatchewan, Alberta.

We gathered on the forest-green faux-leather couches in the living room, nibbled on fruit and freshly baked pastries, and chatted until Carla, the lead counsellor at Westgate, came in. She had high cheekbones and a beautiful face that reminded me of Cher, and she brought a calming energy to the room as she passed around binders and opened a PowerPoint presentation.

We learned about the physiological changes in addiction and recovery. I already knew that Tristan, as a stimulant user, was spared the horrific physical withdrawal symptoms that opioid users experienced, but I hadn't realized that the psychological impact of stimulant withdrawal was among the worst and longest lasting: mood disorders, lack of emotion, depression, sleeplessness, anxiety and even paranoia could be expected for weeks or months. Intense cravings—feeling the *absolute need* to get high—could occur for well over a year. These symptoms were not a matter of morality or weakness; they were brain chemistry.

But the focus of the weekend was to learn about healthy and unhealthy responses to our loved ones in addiction, and what the recovery process looked like for *us*—how we could recognize our own codependent behaviours and move toward greater self-fulfillment regardless of what our children were doing. We journalled and worked through exercises and had opportunities to share.

Supreet was one of the moms I knew from Parents' Group. Her son had been in treatment for five months and, by all accounts, was doing exceptionally well both at Westgate and on his regular home visits. But Supreet was still struggling.

"I just can't imagine he'll go back to being a normal teenager, doing normal things," she said, one hand stroking her long braid. "I see him doing well now—he's even practicing his guitar again—but I can't get over the fear. It's like I have to expect he'll start using again to protect myself from heartbreak. I know that's not helpful." She brushed away a tear and then smiled, self-conscious. "I'm sorry; I just find it so hard to trust he'll be okay."

My heart went out to her. I knew her pain, intimately. But before I could open my mouth to offer understanding and support, one of the fathers from Parents' Group spoke up.

"You know," he said, his voice smooth and reassuring, "last weekend we took Michael and five of his recovery friends up to our cabin for the weekend. They had such fun! We built a stone path down to the water and they drove the boat and roasted marshmallows. They're such helpful and polite guys I would honestly trust them with anything. That's what recovery does. You don't need to worry about Benji; he'll be great."

He leaned back, glowing with the excitement of recovery. I wanted to slap him. I knew his kid had been sober for almost three years. I didn't know why he and his wife were even at this weekend.

"I'm so glad you don't need to worry anymore," I said to him. "But how long did it take you to get there? How did you feel just a few months into it?"

His smile faltered. "Oh. Well, it didn't happen overnight, that's true. I—"

I turned to Supreet. "I know exactly what you mean. I feel that way a lot of the time too. I think it takes time."

Supreet smiled at me and then Carla took control of the conversation again. "We can never be completely sure our kids will be okay, unfortunately. But we need to trust that *we* can be okay, no matter what." She shared about losing her son to an overdose many years earlier; she was a living example of what she was talking about.

Later, as we waited for dinner to be served, Carla entertained us with inspiring stories about Gate Boys and recovery in action. Although she didn't use people's names, I immediately recognized Tristan in one of her stories.

She was telling us about a guy who struggled with low self-esteem, and how being surrounded by others in recovery helped him. This person, she said, had been a professional cook and decided to make dinner for the guys at Redstone, his first cooking experience since coming to Westgate. Suddenly, I could hear nothing but the blood pounding through my head. Tristan had told me, only weeks earlier, that he had cooked dinner at Redstone. He told me it went well. I knew I was about to hear another side of that story.

I missed what Carla said about what went wrong in the kitchen, but something did, and Tristan took off. One of the guys noticed he wasn't in the kitchen where he should be so they all spread out in pairs, calling him, searching the grounds. Eventually, they found him sitting under a tree, head in hands, with a tear-streaked face.

They wrapped him in love and understanding. They poured out stories of their own: "I've been there, man!" and "You wouldn't believe the time when I . . ." and "It's totally okay, that shit happens to me all the time." Then they shepherded him back to the kitchen where they wouldn't let him quit or throw everything out, as he wanted to, but worked with him, beside him, to finish up and get a good dinner ready. By the time dinner was on the table, an hour late, everyone was laughing and having a good time—including Tristan.

"And the supportive mood kept flowing through the entire evening," she finished.

Carla meant it as a tale of triumph, and the other parents were comforted by the solidarity of these guys in recovery, but I saw it as a reminder of Tristan's poor mental health.

"The guy in the story was Tristan, wasn't it?" I asked. Carla hesitated for a second and then nodded. "So, what happens if he's always so sensitive? If he always takes things too personally? What happens when he doesn't have all those guys around him anymore?"

"Well," she said, "recovery is about becoming less wrapped up in our own failings and learning to focus more on our progress forward, on building small successes over time that create a stronger foundation for a good sense of self."

She didn't get it. I sat forward in my chair and tried again. "But what if that person, like Tristan, struggles with depression? What if he's extremely sensitive by nature and it's just part of him and it doesn't go away?" I was desperate for her to understand how Tristan was not like everyone else. I was sure his issues ran deeper, that he was more troubled. Even after committing to my own recovery, I still found Tristan's needs much more urgent than my own. After all, *I* wasn't going to die if I messed up my recovery.

Carla took a breath, looked at me as if I were the only person in the room and said, "We have a saying in recovery. It's 'Live life on life's terms.' It means we don't get to call the shots on everything that happens in our life or choose the cards we're dealt." I felt the truth of that as a shiver ran through me. "A lot of us have mental health issues, trauma and other things that make life more difficult than it may be for others. It would be easier if those things could just go away, but they don't. They're part of us and wishing it were different doesn't help. Instead," she said pointedly, "we need to learn to live with them. To accept them, face them and understand them, but not let them defeat or define us. We learn to *live life on life's terms.*

"For Tristan, the terms of his life may be depression and extreme emotional sensitivity. Doctors can help him figure out when medication may be helpful. Recovery teaches him to recognize the signs and symptoms and learn to replace unhealthy behaviours and thoughts with healthier ones. I'm not saying it's quick or easy, but it *is* what recovery is about. And many, *many* of us are dealing with stuff like that. It is possible, Kathy."

I sat with that thought as the lasagna and salad were served, with garlic bread piled on a platter. I realized that a term of my life was that I had a son who struggled with addiction, low self-esteem, extreme sensitivity, depression and ADHD. And despite the many wonderful things about him and the joy he brought to the world, these were simply facts I needed to accept. These conditions were not separate from Tristan; they were not something he needed to get rid of. They were integral parts of what made him who he was and always would be. They just needed to be understood and managed.

From that place of acceptance, I didn't need to change him. He didn't need to be different in order to get well. He could learn to live his life and thrive despite his difficulties—and even, perhaps, *because* of them. Like working a muscle, he could develop strength and compassion unheard of in people who lived an easier life. Not right away, of course, but over time, as he learned to live his life on life's terms.

I needed to do the same. Whether he was sober or using drugs, Tristan had challenges that were difficult for me to accept. And while those were *his* challenges, not mine, they were unchangeable terms in my life, too. I needed to find a way to live with them. I could not let Tristan's addiction defeat or define me. If I was lucky and worked hard enough, perhaps I could become stronger and more compassionate because of these difficult terms of *my* life.

But for now, practicing acceptance was enough.

19

"MOM, YOU have to come get me." Tristan sounded distraught. I was instantly in crisis mode, my work in front of me forgotten.

"What's going on?" I asked, tempering my voice, trying to stay calm.

"Everybody hates me. I can't stay. I really, really can't. Please, Mom! You have to come get me, now." He was crying, maybe.

I wanted to save him, to let my mother's love wash away the world's hate, but I also wished I'd never answered the phone. I remembered stories I'd heard in Parents' Group of sons wanting to leave. *This was normal*, I told myself. *This could still be okay.*

"I hear you want to leave but you have to tell me why. Why do people hate you all of a sudden?"

"It's stupid, okay? I was stupid. I was smoking and now they're going to kick me out. So, we have to figure out what's next because they're not going to keep me. And everyone is really fucking mad at me. I was just fucking stupid."

I wondered if his admitting stupidity felt like taking responsibility to him.

"Hun, I can't do anything without talking to Ben."

"Mom," Tristan pleaded, "Ben isn't here today. He doesn't know anything about what's going on. You just have to come get me."

"Tristan, let me phone the office and I'll call you right back. Sit tight."

"Fuck, Mom!"

I hung up the phone and stared at it. My initial urge to rescue him had passed and I didn't want anything to do with this. Bringing him home in these circumstances would be a nightmare. I phoned Westgate and asked for Ben. The person who answered confirmed he wasn't in and asked if he could help. I began to explain the situation, but he stopped me.

"Tristan just called you?"

"Yeah, he just—"

"Right now? He was on the phone with you?"

"Yeah."

"Oh, that little bugger," he said. "Hold on a sec." I heard muffled talking for a few seconds and then he came back on the line.

"Sorry about that. I'm Antonio. I'm the caseworker who's been dealing with this, so I can fill you in. First of all, I'm really sorry he called you; he wasn't supposed to. He's back on restrictions while we review his case and figure out where we go from here. He was supposed to be in his room. But that's pretty common behaviour. First sign of trouble, an addict wants to get rescued. I take it he wanted you to come get him?"

"Yeah, he did. He said something about him smoking and everyone hating him and getting kicked out."

"Yeah, that's the gist of it, but we haven't made any decision about kicking him out yet. Apparently, he's been sneaking out at night for a while now to smoke. He's been encouraging other guys to go with him, which makes it worse. That's why the guys are pissed at him. He put their recovery and positions here at risk, and he denied it and kept lying about it when we confronted him. We had to get right up in his face, and he finally broke down and admitted it and had a good cry. I think he regrets it, but we do have to take this pretty seriously. That's not the behaviour of somebody in recovery."

I reminded myself to breathe in, breathe out, breathe in, breathe out.

"Okay, so what now?" I finally asked.

"Well, we need to talk it over tomorrow with Ben, his caseworker, and Dale, the director. I'll be honest, it could go either way. But for my part, I'd rather see him face the consequences and carry on here than run away. Running away is an addict's default. He has to learn to take responsibility and not run from the people he wronged. But we'll know more tomorrow, and we'll let you know." I saw a small ray of hope in that. "And you don't need to call Tristan back. I've already sent someone to fetch him and stay with him tonight."

"He'll be expecting my call though." I didn't want him to think I'd just left him hanging.

"I'll be sure to tell him you called and I told you we'll get back to you tomorrow. You did good, calling us and not rushing out to get him. Some moms do and that makes it really hard for us. As soon as we make a decision, we'll let you know. In the meantime, just know Tristan's on restrictions and shouldn't be calling you."

My mind went to worst-case scenario and I couldn't help asking one more question. "What happens if you kick him out? He's just out on the streets? Do I need to take him in?"

"Oh god no," Antonio said. "We'd work with him to figure out next steps. Try to get him into a different treatment centre that maybe he'd respond better to. It would be up to him, of course, but we don't dump guys out on the street."

There was nothing for me to do now but wait. They'd sort it out without me. I thanked him and hung up, then shut my laptop. I'd get no more work done.

I spent the next twenty-four hours working hard on my acceptance skills, reminding myself this situation was not mine to manage or to fix. Acceptance felt a lot like worry but without the responsibility—like sitting in a comfortable armchair, watching news coverage about a tsunami that was about to wash away a loved one.

In the end, Westgate decided to keep Tristan, in part because he had a strong reputation of helping new guys and had shown himself to be dedicated to his own recovery up to that point. But just as much, they told me, they kept him because of my involvement in Parents' Group and my support of him and his program. It seemed that even when I didn't help him, I was still helping.

Tristan was on restrictions indefinitely and would have his group sessions with the older men moving forward. Ben told me that many of the younger guys were angry with Tristan, but he could get a new start with men who'd been around a bit longer and understood more of the ups and downs of addiction without being judgemental.

Later, when Tristan was off restrictions and we were able to talk, he phoned to tell me that everyone still hated him, but he'd work as hard and as long as needed to regain their trust and make amends.

"Honestly, I can't believe I was given a second chance," he said. "I'm gonna prove those haters wrong with my ninja recovery skills! Nobody's going to regret their decision to let me stay, I promise you that." *Struggles can lead to strength*, I reminded myself as I hung up the phone, and Tristan typically excelled at whatever he put his mind to. This could all turn out for the best.

"DEAR MOM," Tristan read, "this letter is to show you how I am changing and for me to take responsibility for the harms I've caused. To be sitting here talking to you right now is such a blessing. I never planned on being an addict and all the damage I brought with it."

Tristan sat on my couch, holding his amends letter in both hands. I sat in the armchair across from him. His voice was shaky, his words peppered with the deep breaths he took to calm himself. This was a major milestone. I knew that the entire process from step four, when Tristan had created a moral inventory and identified the harms he'd caused people, to step nine, when he began to make amends, had been emotionally exhausting for him. He wasn't a naturally reflective person and hadn't liked what he'd seen in himself. It had been a rough couple of months but he'd stuck it out, stayed sober and kept working the program. I was so proud of him.

"... Thinking back on everything I've done, the worst thing would be the amount of worries and stress I put into your life. The number of times I've yelled at you for no reason are too many to count..." His words pushed on as he recounted the times he stole my car, my credit card, my cash. How he was toxic, "spreading misery" in my life.

But then he shared the successes he'd had, how his physical health and goal setting had improved. "I want to be a son again," he continued. "I will now be here for you. And I will have the ability to look after you all throughout your life. I'm also helping other suffering addicts by doing detox panels and am an active member in society and Narcotics Anonymous. I want to keep this positive momentum, so our lives keep getting better."

This was followed by a series of commitments: to be kind and respectful to me, to not use substances, to not steal, to pay me back the money he'd taken from me, and to remain an active member of NA. "And I commit to keeping constant contact with you, being a part of your life ... I love you so much, Mom. You won't have to go through that again ... None of these words mean anything unless I put action behind them. I'll always be there for you, clean and sober."

It was an important moment—surely, a heartfelt moment—but I couldn't feel it. Try as I might, I couldn't feel deep emotion or regret or a promise of anything within Tristan's words. His words just felt like words. I knew he'd worked hard on this, but it felt to me like a homework assignment he was glad to hand in and be done with.

I remembered the discussions from one recent Parents' Group when people shared their experiences of hearing their sons' amends. One of the dads said both he and his son ended up bawling together, it had been so emotional. One of the moms mentioned how her son had remembered even the tiniest harms he had caused her and came to her with a concrete plan of repayment for the money he'd stolen from her—and he'd stuck to that plan and paid it off over the next year.

I heard story after story of emotional connections and genuine commitments to make things better. The only exception was Paul's own story of reading his amends letter to his dad. "I read him my letter," he told us. "It was sincere, coming from deep within my soul. I poured my heart out to him and was proud to look him in the eye and tell him I was going to be different. Then I handed him the letter, so pleased. He just looked at me and said, 'Keep your letter. Your words aren't worth shit. Treat your mother well for a change. Do right by her. You do that for a few years, and I might begin to believe you.' Man, I was crushed!" Paul grinned, as if laughing at his younger self. "Crushed, and really pissed off. I went stomping back to Westgate cursing my dad. But you know what? He was right. It was just words. I had to work to regain his respect.

"So, I showed him I could be a good son. I talked to my mom regularly and asked about her day. I offered to help when she needed it and didn't ask anything from them. Then, literally when I was about ten years clean, my dad came to me and said, 'I guess you're going to stick to this recovery thing. I accept your amends now.' And that was that. Ten years later! But he didn't owe me immediate trust. I hadn't earned it."

Paul looked around the room, making eye contact with each parent. "It's okay if you need time to trust again. It's not your job to look after your kids' emotions anymore. Whatever way you feel about the amends you're getting, is just fine. And if it doesn't go as well as they'd hoped, *we're* here to support them."

I held onto Paul's words as Tristan finished reading his letter and looked up at me. He looked like he had when he was a small boy, uncertain and nervous, waiting for approval but steeling himself for disappointment. I realized that just because Tristan's words rang hollow didn't mean they were. He bonded through physical connection—through action, not words. He was out of his element. I couldn't, in good conscience, presume his heart was not in it.

"That was beautiful, honey," I said, hoping he wouldn't feel my emotional disconnection. "Thank you for that. I'm so proud of how far you've come." I smiled at him with all the warmth I could muster and gave him a tight hug. I felt our connection then, solid and eternal, and it had nothing to do with his amends.

Tristan relaxed and let out the breath he'd been holding. He'd done his part, as best he could, and I'd done mine. I hoped that was enough.

LATER THAT evening, Tanis joined us and we walked to an NA meeting Tristan had invited us to. To me, having him welcome us into his world was far more meaningful than hearing his amends letter. This was amends in action.

Just a week earlier, on Halloween day, I'd moved into a small apartment in New Westminster, a fifteen-minute walk from Westgate. I'd been planning to move for months, no longer needing my large place in Coquitlam. I'd been eyeing New Westminster as a perfect central location until Tristan ended up in treatment, and then it felt complicated. I fretted that I'd be too close if things went bad, or that maybe I was following him in an unconscious need to stay close. I mentioned my concerns to Ben one day as we were discussing payment for Tristan's medication. He said, "Kathy, where do *you* want to live? Leave Tristan completely out of it. It has nothing to do with him." The simplicity of his response floored me and made my decision much easier. Now, in New Westminster, I was enjoying the benefit of being close to my son and his recovery community.

Neither Tanis nor I had been to an NA meeting before, and we didn't know what to expect. "Matteo is taking his cake tonight," Tristan told us, referring to one of the senior staff at Westgate celebrating a sobriety anniversary. "The whole of New West is going to be there, so hopefully we'll get seats."

We approached the church and saw half a dozen groups of people standing around, and more moving toward the basement door. Tristan said hi to some of them on the way in, giving hugs or fist bumps to more than a few. On the cement stairway leading down was a metal coffee can filled with cigarette butts. Smokers stood nearby and I held my breath as we passed through their smog.

"Doesn't it bother you to smell cigarette smoke?" I asked Tristan, his own recent smoking fiasco in mind. "I thought nobody was allowed to smoke!" I added, outraged at all these people breaking the rules.

He shrugged his shoulders and smirked the way he did when he wanted to look nonchalant about something that bothered him. "No, it's fine. I'm used to it. And these meetings are public, Mom. Anybody can come, even smokers, even people who use drugs. All you need is 'the desire to not use.' It's just the Gate Boys and Manor Girls who can't smoke."

Tanis and I followed Tristan into the basement multipurpose room. As Tanis and I stood gaping at the crowd and Tristan scanned for open seats, a young guy approached us.

"Hey, Tristan. How's it going, bro? Is this your mom?"

"Good, good. Yeah, this's my mom, and my sister, Tanis." He pointed to the guy in front of us, "and this is Darren." Tristan's eyes still searched for empty seats. "Hey, are all the chairs out already? Are there any more in the back room?"

"Nah but come on. I'll get you front row seats." Darren turned and left us to follow him. When he got to where he was sitting with his two friends, he announced they were giving up their seats to Tristan, Tanis and "Mom" so we could all sit together. The other guys didn't hesitate. They grabbed their jackets off the backs of the chairs, said hi to Tristan and Tanis, said "Hi Mom, nice to meet you" to me, and went to stand against the back wall.

"Wow, that was really nice of them," I said.

"Yeah, they're good guys," said Tristan. "I'd do the same for them if they brought family."

It crossed my mind that people my age complain about the lack of manners in young people. I laughed to myself as I thought maybe they should spend more time around young addicts in recovery.

I'd been curious about NA meetings for months so I was happy to soak everything in. There were close to a hundred people in the room, some in seats, some standing against the wall. Some were talking and laughing and greeting each other, others were sitting silently, and a few were reading NA literature. At least half of them were mid-thirties or younger and I figured a good portion of these were clients of Westgate and Brook Manor—Westgate's sister facility for women. Some were dressed fashionably, most were not, but almost all were clean and presentable in jeans and T-shirts or something similar. A few people looked rough around the edges, as if they didn't have much clean time behind them, if any at all.

But generally, the people in the room just looked like people—everyday, garden-variety, run-of-the-mill people like me and my kids. They were a far cry from the sad-sack impressions I'd gathered about NA groups from movies and TV shows.

The meeting began with the chairperson announcing upcoming events and cakes, and then different people reading aloud the twelve steps, the twelve traditions and a short passage from the *Basic Text*. Out-of-towners, newcomers and people coming back into the program were welcomed, and white fobs and hugs were given to anyone celebrating one day of sobriety. Then, colourful fobs were handed out to people celebrating thirty, sixty and ninety days clean, then one year, and finally multiple years. These were also accompanied by hugs, clapping and an almost thunderous applause when Matteo took his fob to recognize six years of sobriety.

For the next hour, people stood to share personal stories of experience, strength and hope. The theme of the evening was responsibility, and one story caught my attention. The speaker was a young, clean-cut guy, about Tristan's age, who mentioned he had felt different from his classmates as a child because he had ADHD and was on medication for that. He believed, at the time, that it was the label and the meds that created distance between him and his classmates more than the ADHD itself. As a teen, he turned to drugs to fit in and now, in recovery, was finally taking responsibility for shaping his own life—for "living life on life's terms."

There was suddenly a lightness in my chest that felt like relief. I questioned the guilt I'd been carrying about not getting Tristan diagnosed and on meds earlier. Here was somebody whose parents did make that happen in childhood and he still turned to drugs. Perhaps it wasn't such a simple thing, after all.

As the next person walked to the podium, Tristan tapped my shoulder. "That's Matteo. Really good guy."

I focused my attention as Matteo shared his story about responsibility, his impish grin a permanent fixture under warm brown eyes. "I first came into these rooms about ten years ago—this isn't my first set of clean time. And taking responsibility for my actions wasn't something that came easy. I came in thinking NA was full of shit, full of rules and do-gooders. At one point, I even tried to sue NA because of a comment someone made about gay people. Got a lawyer and everything." He paused and laughed. "I'd been in and out of these rooms for a while and was pretty sure NA had ruined my life. In my mind, it was NA's fault I lost my job, my home and my relationship. Of course, it had nothing to do with the fact I was smoking crack all day! Nothing to do with me at all. It's crazy how crazy we become.

"Eventually, I came back. I knew I needed to do something different and I decided what I'd do differently is take responsibility. I started listening more and talking less—and for those who know me, you know how hard that is for me!" A chuckle spread around the room. "I stopped blaming others for what wasn't working in my life. I focused on 'doing the next right thing,'" he said, emphasizing another NA slogan.

"I couldn't wrap my head around the idea of living responsibly *all* the time, for years on end, so I didn't look far ahead," Matteo continued. "I only looked to the next decision in front of me. Do I pick up and use, or phone my sponsor? Do I do the kind thing, or the selfish thing? Just doing the next right thing. That's it. It took a while but my whole life changed. Today, I have the most amazing job that I love— probably spend way too much time at it, but I just can't help it. I have a great relationship. I love my life. And now, obviously, I love NA too and am pretty involved at all levels with that. It's amazing the things we can achieve by taking responsibility, one step at a time, one day at time, one decision at a time."

20

"I'M NOT having fun yet," I said at one Parents' Group in November.

"What did you do for fun before Tristan's addiction took over?" Paul asked.

I shook my head. "My kids used to call me 'the fun-sucker' when they were teenagers. I think that was pretty accurate."

Other parents laughed and nodded their heads. Some offered ideas.

One woman suggested I take up knitting. The woman beside me suggested I check out community centres for card nights; she enjoyed playing bridge with a bunch of seniors. Choir, yoga, golf, painting—none of the suggestions landed well. Something was missing. None of that sounded like *fun* to me.

Then Diedre, one of the more active members of the group, asked if I'd put any effort into discovering things I enjoyed doing. "Because it does take effort, at first," she said. "When I needed to bring more fun to my life, I made a commitment that I wouldn't say 'no' to new things that came my way. Even if I thought I wouldn't like it, I'd give it a try. You never know! I was just sitting there waiting for fun to find me until I realized I needed to get out there and make it happen."

It was true. I hadn't put any effort into having fun. Ever. It either just happened or it didn't. I enjoyed my work but it wasn't *fun*. I used to have fun with Leigha but couldn't remember the last time we got together and just laughed. Between Tristan's addiction, Jenn's drunken late-night calls, Tanis's worrisome diabetes, running my own business, and all of life's other stressors, I'd been too busy—and too exhausted.

I didn't know how I would do it, but I was determined to have more fun. Over the next few weeks, I began by simply noticing the things and people I enjoyed. I knew I needed to rekindle my relationship with Leigha but wasn't quite sure how to start. I loved spending time with Tanis and Jenn, but they were both busy living their lives and I rarely went out and did things with them. So, top of my list of enjoyable people was Emily, who always had more fun than she could manage on her own. And with Tristan so nearby, and once again having more freedom, I leaned in to having fun with him, as well.

Toward the end of November, I went with Tristan to a panto play of Red Riding Hood, tickets courtesy of Westgate. Arriving a few minutes early, we found a local craft coffee house and I ordered a London Fog. Tristan had a dark roast coffee.

"Mom, I think I should go into coffee tasting. That's a thing, right? Like wine tasting only with coffee? I love coffee." He was having a euphoric coffee moment. "And I can't exactly learn wine pairing anymore. Is there a job for a coffee pairing person? Never mind... I need to get my Red Seal first. But this is one damned fine coffee!" Who knew a two-dollar coffee could produce such a happy puppy-dog grin?

We walked into the theatre lobby, still sipping our drinks. It was packed with a whole lot of young male energy. It seemed like everyone from Westgate was there. The conversations were loud and full of happiness and innocent fun: some guys were talking about getting together with their families over Christmas, or going snowboarding, or doing their step work. Others talked about shovelling snow from neighbour's sidewalks or doing their first panel talk or looking for work. Tristan introduced me to a few people but we both were happy to stand back and observe.

The show itself was hilarious. I couldn't remember laughing so hard in such a long time; my cheeks ached to the point of cramping. Tristan and the rest of the guys laughed even harder.

Getting ready for bed that night, I decided that evening had been all the fun, and more, I'd been craving. I wanted to bottle those feelings with Tristan so I could quench my thirst with them whenever I got bored or lonely or tired of myself.

A few days later, Tristan joined me and Emily at the Discovery Centre by the Quay, a child-centred museum celebrating life on the Fraser River. The mighty sturgeon held a place of honour throughout the exhibits and activities. We cut out crafts and coloured pictures of fish and river animals. Tristan built a large arch of foam blocks, each with a picture of a river plant or creature, representing the fragile river ecosystem; Emily watched, fascinated. Their laughter lifted me, and I floated beside them as we moved through the museum, high on their smiles and loving chatter. Even their frequent bathroom humour didn't weigh me down. The slam-dunk winner activity, though, was the excavation sand box, where Tristan and Emily dug for buried treasure while I took a ridiculous number of photos of them, trying to capture their joy and playfulness forever. Emily squealed in excitement every time she unburied an object representing the history of the Fraser River basin, and Tristan yelled his enthusiastic congratulations even louder before burying the item in the sand again while Emily pretended not to look.

I *did* know how to have fun. I could have fun with my kids, and my granddaughter. And given the many years that my relationship with Tristan had been anything but fun, this was a blessing I intended to cherish. But I also knew I needed to stop relying on my children as my *only* source of fun. It was not their responsibility to provide me with the joy I so needed in my life. I needed to stretch my wings, make new friends, develop new hobbies. I needed to find my own joy.

STACKING MY chair at the end of Parents' Group, I overheard Diedre talking about starting a step group so parents could walk through a set of Nar-Anon steps together. She always struck me as constructive and kind, someone I'd be happy to spend time with. I'd been wanting to take a more proactive approach to my recovery and being part of a close-knit group of women intrigued me. I thought it might even be fun. I wanted in.

Before the wave of Christmas obligations washed over us, we held our first meeting. I brought Lucky's doughnuts—lemon meringue, apple bacon fritter, cinnamon sugar, crème brûlée and Earl Grey—which we cut into quarters so we could each sample multiple flavours. We met at Mary's house, where she had a selection of tea ready. Mary was the woman who'd shocked me months earlier with her resilience and commitment to self-care during her son's relapse. Diedre was there, of course, along with Kit from Parents' Group, who spoke rarely but with tremendous honesty and wisdom. The last member of our new group was Kelsey, Mary's close friend and next-door neighbour and a long-time Nar-Anon member. She was the only one of us who had worked a set of steps up to that point. A retired lawyer and current yogi, with blond hair to her waist, Kelsey had the most beautiful air of practical magic about her.

Just as we were about to settle in, Kelsey moved to the centre of the room and said, "I think we should start this gathering of good friends with a celebration through dance." She turned Mary's TV on to the Jukebox Music station as comfortably as if it were her own home. Cyndi Lauper was belting out "Girls Just Wanna Have Fun."

"Yes!" said Diedre, bouncing to the music.

All four women stood and started dancing any which way, as if nobody was watching. But I was. I was rooted to the couch, semi-panicked, watching as they lost themselves in the music, smiles wide across their faces, bodies going this way and that, regardless of the rhythm of the song.

I don't dance. I didn't want to dance. But I knew if I kept sitting there, alone, I'd look more stupid than if I danced stupidly.

I glanced at the doughnuts and tea, longingly.

Then I stood up and started awkwardly wiggling my body, desperately focused on my embarrassment without knowing why. Nobody was watching me. The music and the energy of those ladies cast their spell on me, so I decided to shut my eyes and just go with it. *Pretend it's tai chi*, I told myself. *Very fast tai chi. Relax. Just feel your way.* For a few long breaths, I was transported to a place of not caring, only feeling, and it felt good. A smile whispered its way onto my face, and I let it be. It felt good to smile.

I was having fun! *This is what fun is,* I thought. *It's dancing!* I let my face and shoulders relax just a bit more.

As suddenly as the music started, Kelsey turned it off again. "Whew! Nothing like free-form dancing to get trauma out of the body. Our nervous systems need us to laugh and smile, ladies!" she said, plopping herself onto the couch.

Certainly, there was a stronger, more positive energy in the room now. We were all grinning, still feeling the magic of that moment. I wondered if anybody noticed my eyes were suddenly teary. We had each danced individually, connected to our own bodies, but I felt so much more connected to these women than I had before. How did that happen? The connection felt unfamiliar, exciting and nerve-wracking. I blinked the tears away.

Eating doughnuts and drinking tea, we hashed out a plan for our monthly meetings. We decided to use Melody Beattie's *Codependents' Guide to the Twelve Steps*, because the language was easy and engaging, it was readily available, and she included a bunch of questions for us to work through at the end of each step. If we stuck to our plan, we'd complete our first set of steps in twelve months. I hugged each of the women goodbye and left Mary's house excited for the new year.

A new year focused on recovery.

My recovery.

21

"MOM, I got an interview!" Tristan told me during one of our regular evening phone calls. I put him on speaker phone so I could finish tossing dried cranberries into the batch of homemade granola I'd just taken out of the oven. I set it aside to cool before packaging it in festive containers to use as holiday gifts.

Tristan had been at Westgate for over four months, had completed all requirements for primary care, and was moving into the transition stage of his treatment. He had more independence. He could come and go on his own schedule, within reason, and get a phone again. He was encouraged to find work, though nobody was rushing him. He could live at Westgate as long as needed and use their support services at a reduced rate, which I'd continue to pay, his education funds having run out a month before. Of course, there were still rules to follow. He had to abstain from drugs, alcohol and cigarettes, work toward living independently, attend a certain number of NA meetings each week and meet with his sponsor regularly. He had to let Westgate know his schedule and general whereabouts, participate in their activities and be a good role model for the new guys, supporting them in their recovery journey. Basically, to get the privileges associated with being a "Gate Boy," he had to remain a Gate Boy, even out in the real world.

He was anxious to stop being a burden, to have his own place, his own job, his own money. And that worried me.

A few days earlier he'd applied for the position of *demi chef de partie* at Tramonto, a fine dining restaurant located in the River Rock Casino. Tristan had been offered every job he interviewed for, and I had no doubt he'd get this one too. I wasn't thrilled at that prospect.

"Do you think that's a good idea, hun?" I asked, taking one last taste of the buttery granola. "Working in a casino with all the drinking and gambling and partying?"

"I wouldn't be working *in* the casino, Mom," he explained. "I'd be in the restaurant. And whatever, casinos have never been my thing, so that's no biggie."

"What about the hours? You'd work long hours every evening; they're not even open in the daytime. So, you'd almost never get to meetings. *That's* a big deal." I moved to the bedroom and began packing my suitcase for an upcoming client meeting I had in Atlanta.

"Mom, it's not like I need to go to two meetings a day anymore. My plan is three a week, and I'll get days off work. There are morning and nooner meetings too, so that's totally fine."

"But those aren't the meetings your friends go to. How will you stay connected with your recovery friends if you're working every night?"

"Mom, you don't know anything about it." He was getting frustrated now. He wanted me to be excited for him. "My friends go to meetings any time of day. And sooner or later, people have to work. Lots of people work nights, and this job pays eighteen-fifty an hour, plus tips! It might even be going union soon and then I'd get more. There's extended health that would pay for my prescriptions so you wouldn't have to. You don't need to worry about me."

That part was true—his life was not mine to worry about—but I was also practicing speaking up more when I had something to say. I was trying to give my voice equal airtime to others', in all my relationships.

I tried a different tack. "What do Ben and the others at Westgate think about it?"

"They think it's a great opportunity." No hesitation. "They don't see a problem with it. But I'll make a plan and if things start to feel shaky I'll follow that plan. I can always quit if I have to, but I might as well give it a try."

Tristan would just have to play this out, it seemed, and I'd just hope for the best.

He started work in mid-December. We dug his chef's knives out of my closet where I'd been storing them, and I bought him a new whetstone as an early Christmas present.

Tristan loved being back in the kitchen again. "It's amazing how much better I am sober," he told me after his first shift. "And I hardly cut or burned myself at all," he laughed.

He made it sound wonderful, but I hadn't been wrong.

Within a week, he was kicked out of Westgate.

FOR OVER five months I'd listened to other parents talk about whether to have their children back home after treatment. Many of the kids were still minors, so there was little question they'd be coming home. But at twenty-one, Tristan was young enough to make coming home a reasonable option, but old enough to make it just that—an option, not a requirement. Westgate made it clear there was no expectation I'd take him home again. They felt that moving out with another guy from recovery would be a better choice for him.

It was a relief knowing I didn't need to live with him again, because the idea terrified me. I'd barely scratched the surface of my own recovery and knew how rapidly we could return to the dynamics we had before: me monitoring his moods, trying to solve his problems, tiptoeing around big issues; Tristan being rude and taking advantage. I was strong enough now to set the boundary that I didn't want Tristan at home with me, but I didn't think I was yet strong enough to stick to healthy boundaries if we lived together. Despite the massive progress Tristan had made, and the miraculous respect he'd begun to show me, I didn't think he'd be able to keep up with that if we were living together, either.

For months now, Tristan had been feeling me out on the idea of moving in with me after Westgate. I'd put him off by saying things like, "You don't need to focus on the future yet; just get through this next step" or "When the time's right, you can talk to Ben and the other guys and figure out a plan." But when he entered transition, got a job, and was actively thinking about new living arrangements, I needed to be blunt with him. I told him I liked living alone, I liked our relationship as it was now and I didn't want to go back to what we were like before.

"Mom," he said, "I'm different now. What do you think I've been doing the past five months? I know how to listen to rules. I can't afford to live on my own and I don't want to live with another guy. I've been living with so many people for so long and I hate having no privacy."

"Tristan, even your arguing with me shows you're not respecting my point of view."

He rolled his eyes and sighed dramatically. "I'm just trying to have a conversation," he said, but left it at that.

Progress, not perfection, I thought. Tristan allowing the subject to drop and moving on without shooting emotional daggers at me was huge progress for him, and me not caving in and saying he could come home was progress for me.

I was relieved that we'd already established he was not coming home by mid-December when I got the call.

"Hi, Kathy, it's Ben. Look, so, I need to tell you that Tristan is no longer at Westgate." He paused, briefly, to let that sink in. I held my breath as he continued. "Now, you don't need to worry. We've found him another placement at one of our partner centres, Purpose Recovery Centre—PRC. One of our guys is driving him there right now. It's in Burnaby, about fifteen minutes from here. Tristan hasn't been using drugs, he's still doing okay in that regard, but we feel he's no longer teachable here at Westgate and a new situation may be better for him."

I sunk down against the glass door that opened to my balcony, its coolness focusing me on the here and now. I felt sick, but not surprised. Tristan's recovery had been shaky at times and his new job hadn't felt good to me. But if Tristan wasn't using drugs, why would they kick him out?

"What happened?" I asked.

"Well, he's been taking things. Shampoo, conditioner, whatever, from the other guys. A bit of loose change. Nothing big, but that's not the point. He was stealing things, kind of compulsively, and lying about it. It's not like he needed shampoo or couldn't ask to borrow some if he did. Compulsion is part of addiction, we get that. But he doesn't seem to want our help anymore. We call that being 'unteachable.' It's a sign of relapsing behaviour he needs to address, but he's just not interested—at least not here, with us. We're hoping a new environment might help him recommit to his recovery. But," he paused, and then sighed, "to be honest, Kathy, I just don't know. He doesn't seem very interested in taking his own inventory or asking for help these days."

"No," I said. "No, he doesn't." I rested my head against the cold glass door. Then I had to ask. "Hey, what did you think of the idea of Tristan working at the casino? He told me that you, and everyone at Westgate, were supportive."

"He said that, hey?" Ben paused. "I told him he should keep looking for something closer to home, with less pressure and better hours so he could keep up with evening meetings. Certainly nothing inside a casino is a good place for a new guy in recovery. All the caseworkers here felt the same and told him so, but he also talked it through with the guys and they had mixed thoughts. Some thought he should go for it and those were the ones he chose to listen to. Let's just say they weren't guys with a lot of long-term success in recovery. But you know, people have to find their own way, make their own mistakes. We worked with him to make sure he'd recognize the early signs if he started to feel out of control, and he knew how to ask for help. But, like I said, he seems to have lost interest in our support."

As I hung up the phone, I became angry. Tristan hadn't even used drugs and Westgate kicked him out for showing signs that he was an addict, that he needed help. That's why he was there, for god's sake! At the first sign of him struggling, they took away his key, disowned him as a Gate Boy, rejected him. At least that's how Tristan would see it. Westgate passed him on like a hot potato so that when he failed, as it seemed he inevitably would, it wouldn't be on their watch. Tristan had loved Westgate. It was where he'd found his recovery family—it *was* his recovery family. If he relapsed and died, I thought, it would be on them.

But even though I was furious, I couldn't think of what they could have done differently if Tristan wasn't interested. Maybe instead of punishing him, they could have wrapped him in their loving arms and held him close until the crisis passed and then waved their magic recovery wand so he could live happily ever after.

I felt my son's pain, his shame, as if it were my own. I was so deeply sad for him, and scared. This was not heading anywhere good and there was nothing I could do about it.

Life on life's terms, I told myself, and turned my face to feel the cold glass door against my cheek. I closed my eyes and repeated this phrase, my new mantra for acceptance.

TRISTAN'S NEW caseworker, Danny, called the next day to introduce himself and tell me that Tristan was settling in. We talked about logistics: they'd honour the same pricing structure I had at Westgate and support Tristan through transition for as long as needed. I'd arrange payment for his medication through the pharmacy they used.

"When Westgate told us they had a guy who needed a fresh start, we wanted to help," Danny said. "The Gate Boys are a rare breed. They give their guys such a strong foundation that men who struggle for whatever reason over there often become leaders in recovery here. That helps to strengthen their self-esteem, give back to the community and connect them to their own recovery. Tristan has every opportunity to shine brightly here."

Tristan called me a few days later. He was pissed at Westgate, but optimistic about PRC.

"It's kinda weird because they didn't really think things through when they sent me here. I'm with a bunch of guys in primary care, not transition. So, I don't get home from work until after midnight, when most of the guys are in bed, and then I sleep through their morning sessions. It's kinda hard to get to know them, but they seem okay. One of the caseworkers, Aaron, is pretty cool. He's sometimes up late and we hang out after I get home. We went to the park last night and lay on the grass and watched the stars, even though it was freezing cold. And then we came home and made pancakes at one o'clock in the morning." Tristan laughed, sounding happy. "It'll be okay until I get a few paycheques behind me and get a place of my own. I'll be okay, Mom."

I hoped so but couldn't muster much optimism.

The next weekend I made lemon loaves, cherry loaves, shortbread, Russian tea cakes and chocolate-mint fudge and dropped Christmas packages off at both Westgate and PRC. Tristan made me tea and we visited in the kitchen while we ate my baking, receiving exuberant thanks from the guys who grabbed a cookie or piece of fudge on their way by.

I thought back to the time we were together in China, standing at the bottom of that long cement stairway, just before we began the exhausting climb up the mountain. I remembered how I held onto that moment as if it were all that mattered—as if it were infinity. I had the same feeling eating cookies with my son. It was just me and him and buttery shortbread having a Christmas party in our mouths. It was all that mattered.

22

ON CHRISTMAS EVE, my little apartment was festive and sparkling with a tree that Tristan and two of his recovery buddies had helped set up in front of the window. I was happily exhausted from spending the day celebrating Emily's third birthday, eating cake and watching her open presents wrapped in paper decorated with unicorns and rainbows and princesses. Even though it was Christmas Eve, it was still her birthday. No Christmas paper allowed.

Now, I relaxed and watched the lights on my tree. Through my window I could see the white glowing lights down Columbia Street as I nibbled on butter tarts and sipped jasmine tea, waiting for Tristan to arrive. King's College Choir sang quietly in the background.

I wasn't expecting him until after his work shift, around eleven o'clock, another couple of hours yet. I ran through my mental to-do list: I had eggnog in the fridge, and mandarin oranges, and chocolates, and baking already set out. My Christmas presents were wrapped and Tristan's stocking was stuffed and hidden away where he couldn't see it until I brought it out in the morning, before he woke up. This year I'd bought him a leather wallet, a purple sweatshirt with some weird psychedelic cat with lightning shooting from its paws, a Boos cutting board, and the obligatory socks and underwear. I'd made him a playlist of Chinese tai chi and meditation music. I knew he'd be happy. Together with the gifts I got for Jenn, Tanis,

Mom, Emily and a few others, including Balloo, they created a festive mountain under the tree.

As eleven o'clock came and went, I began to worry. What if he didn't show up? What if he showed up stoned? I tried to stop those thoughts. They were neither helpful nor fair—Tristan hadn't used drugs in almost six months—but they were persistent. By 11:30, I was pissed off. His shift had ended at 10 p.m. and I knew how long it took him to get here. If something legitimate had happened, if he wasn't using drugs, then why wouldn't he have called?

I watched the clock: 11:30, 11:40.

At 11:46 my phone rang. I didn't recognize the number.

"Hi! Mom, it's Tristan. I'm outside. Come down and let me in."

"Whose phone—?"

"Some dude, finally, I found someone who'd let me use their phone. I've been out in the rain for fifteen minutes. You really should get your buzzer set up! I'll tell you about it, but just come down."

Hearing his voice sober and clear relaxed my body, my mind, my heart. I gave myself a mental kick for giving in to worry and went down to let him in.

"Holy shit, what a night!" he said after I gave him a big hug, breathing in his smell of kitchen oil and cigarettes. He had started smoking again since leaving Westgate, as it wasn't forbidden at PRC. "There was a big table that just wouldn't go home, so we couldn't leave 'til almost 10:30. Then I realized I left my phone back at the house, so I've been outside waiting for someone to let me use their phone. I didn't realize how hard that was going to be at this time of night! Thank god for that dude, because I was just about to bus back to PRC." He scooped Balloo off the floor, flopped down on the couch and popped a Russian teacake in his mouth. "Mmmm, man, these are good!" He grinned happily, stuffing a second cookie in his mouth before he'd even swallowed the first. Then he bent his head and wiped the crumbs from his mouth onto Balloo's fur.

"Tristan!" I said, giving him the reaction that he was looking for. "That's disgusting. Have some manners."

"That's what she said!" He smiled as widely as he could through a mouthful of cookie. It was good to have him home.

TRISTAN HAD to work the dinner shift on Christmas Day. We met for Christmas brunch at Jenn and Alan's so they wouldn't have to cart Emily around to too many different places. Tristan wanted a break from cooking, so Mom and I brought everything needed to make breakfast. After the presents were happily given and happily received, Mom and I took charge of cooking bacon and French toast with fresh berries and maple syrup, topped with whipping cream and Christmas sprinkles. The kids visited and watched Emily play with her new toys.

Within five minutes, Tristan joined us. He couldn't help himself.

"Did you put vanilla in that?" he asked, pointing to the egg mixture I was beating for the French toast.

"Nope. I never do."

"Yeah, and that's the problem with the world these days," he said cheerfully as he began rooting through Jenn's cupboard to find vanilla.

He took the whisk out of my hand, added a capful of vanilla and said, "Alan's in a bit of a mood, huh? If I was Jenn, I'd want to punch him for talking to me that way. I almost wanted to punch him myself but," he looked at me, smiling, "that wouldn't be very spiritual of me."

"Ha! No, it wouldn't. And yeah, the tension between them is pretty high. I don't think they're doing too well." I opened the cutlery drawer and gathered knives and forks for the table.

Mom had been listening as she fried the bacon on a big electric griddle. "He sure likes to bark orders at Emily, doesn't he? Like he's a big man bossing around a three-year-old." She took off her glasses and wiped away some bacon splatter. "I wish I felt more happiness in this household."

We couldn't change the obvious tension between Jenn and Alan, but Emily seemed delightfully oblivious to it, and platefuls of good food with plenty of whipping cream brought their own special kind of joy.

I'D BEEN looking forward to babysitting Emily on New Year's Eve but, by mid-afternoon, I wanted to cancel. I'd just received a text from Tristan's counsellor, Danny, asking if I'd heard from Tristan or knew where he was. He hadn't come back after work the night before and was not answering his phone.

The idea of playing games with Emily, baking cookies and singing songs seemed trivial now compared to my worry over what Tristan was going through and the consequences coming his way. He was going to relapse. *No*, I corrected myself, *he has relapsed*. I knew I couldn't take him in, so he'd be homeless, I guessed.

I lay on my rumpled bed and envisioned the now-familiar imaginary horrors of how this would play out, of all he would lose, until there was nothing left. I wanted to throw up. Or crawl under the covers, curl into a ball and stay there forever. Or smash something. I wanted to scream. Hadn't I been through enough already? When would I stop needing to be so goddamned strong all the fucking time? And it wasn't even about me.

Poor Tristan. He had everything in his grasp and couldn't hold on to it, after he'd worked so hard to get there. He'd come so far; he'd be devastated inside—and it would be devastating for me to watch him tear apart the world he'd so carefully built these past months.

With effort, I stopped that line of thinking. I couldn't control Tristan. I didn't know what the outcome of this would be, but imagining catastrophe hurt me and helped nobody. *Let go and let God*, I told myself. I'd taken to saying that in my head over these past few weeks as I worried about Tristan relapsing. I'd written it on my bathroom mirror in green dry-erase marker, where I'd see it throughout the day. At first, I wasn't sure about the "let God" part, but I remembered the voice that rang through me that night in the bathtub so many years ago and how I'd heard the message of love, hope and peace just when I'd needed it. I liked the idea that I was handing my worries over to *something* rather than just letting them drop.

I told myself Tristan would find his way, or he wouldn't, but I couldn't help him now. I could only help myself, and help Emily have a fun New Year's Eve. My job was simply to do the next right thing for me. I'd been focusing on practicing gratitude lately and decided to replace my worries with ten things I was grateful for. I rolled over and looked at the ceiling.

I was grateful for Emily, for her joy and cheerful innocence.

Tristan would end up in the Downtown Eastside, sleeping in alleyways.

I was grateful for the moms in my step group and how they were such fantastic role models of recovery.

Tristan would hit a bad batch of something and overdose and die.

I was grateful for my Wednesday night Parents' Group, my sense of belonging there and the wisdom it provided.

Tristan would overdose and be brain damaged and require twenty-four-hour support for the rest of his life.

I was grateful for my daughters, whom I loved with all my heart and who were such amazing young women.

I was grateful for my cat, especially when he purred on my head.

I listed things I was grateful for until I couldn't think of anymore, then counted them. Only nine; I needed one more.

I was grateful for my business and how it provided me with a decent income and flexibility.

I took a deep breath; now I could move on. I *made* myself move on.

I stayed busy for the rest of the day cleaning my house, getting groceries and snacks that Emily would enjoy, buying a special bubble bath for bath time. I made cupcakes to have ready for Emily to help with the icing and sprinkles.

Thoughts of Tristan were with me constantly, a heavy lump in my chest, but I crawled over and around them. I didn't want them, couldn't do anything with them. I felt my heart ache and paused every now and again to take deep breaths, to restore calm. Then I'd keep moving. I was waiting for the call or text to say that he'd turned up, that there was some misunderstanding and he was just fine. Or he'd been found dead in a gutter somewhere. I just didn't know.

I pushed those thoughts away and kept moving.

My inner self was not where I wanted it to be. Try as I might, I was letting Tristan's actions hijack my emotions and paint a dark grey wash over my day—and it was *my* day, dammit! I was the only person responsible for my life, my emotions, my day. That was what I needed to focus on. I figured I'd better get good at it, and quickly by the looks of things, or I'd be pulled down into his darkness again.

At least I was trying. I praised myself for the strength it took to do that much.

When Jenn arrived with Emily, my mood lightened. Thoughts of Tristan were whirled aside by the flurry of Emily running toward me. "Cat-Gamma!" she called and hugged my knees. I bent to kiss her head but she was already gone in search of the cat.

The evening was busy with games where stuffed animals worked in an office made from an old crate with Tupperware containers for desks and Emily saved them from invisible monsters every now and again. We ate endless snacks and shook sprinkles over every kitchen surface including, fortunately, the cupcakes. We played Barbies in the bathtub and then Emily was clean, in pajamas and ready for a story before bed. She chose *The Book with No Pictures*, as she did every night she was with me, laughing at my feigned discomfort at reading such silliness, saying the words along with me, from memory.

She was asleep by 9:30, well past her regular bedtime. I gazed at my beautiful cherub, bundled in blankets, her tiny Christmas teddy bear clutched tightly in her sleeping hand. My heart overflowed with love and gratitude as I watched her sleep.

And then, with no more distractions, the truth of Tristan's situation kicked me in the stomach.

I tried to meditate, using a mish-mash of recovery slogans as mantras. I breathed in: *I didn't cause it, I can't control it, I can't cure it.* I held my breath for three seconds and breathed out: *Let go and let God.* Hold for three seconds. Again and again and again until my wandering mind was no longer filled with terrifying thoughts about Tristan, only how bored I was of the meditation.

My meditation was mediocre but I felt better. It helped to have concepts of recovery to hold on to instead of only worry.

I had a bubble bath with Emily's new bubbles. I had made it through the day, a day filled with the kind of fear that, not long before, would have consumed and paralyzed me or thrown me into an impossible frenzy of "fixing"; the kind of fear where you know something horrible is coming, surely, inevitably, moving closer to someone you love and you are powerless to stop its progress or alter its course. But I hadn't let Tristan's struggles defeat me; I had lived the day in fear but I'd spent time with Emily and felt joy in our precious time together. I was proud of myself for living my life, today, the way I wanted to.

I fell asleep, eventually, with love in my heart and a weight on my chest.

23

PREDICTABLY, TRISTAN got kicked out of PRC. I was not part of that discussion and didn't want to be. Danny told me they offered to move him back to primary care with them, or find him another placement, because primary care was where he needed to be. He needed to quit his job and refocus on strengthening his foundation in recovery.

Tristan was not prepared to do that. He was confident he could figure it out on his own. After all, according to him and confirmed by the drug tests PRC gave him, he hadn't used any hard drugs. He admitted to using weed, drinking a couple of beers, and hanging out with a girl until it got too late to come home. But he hadn't missed a work shift and he had come home to PRC, eventually. It was only one night. He couldn't figure out why everyone was so upset.

It was the old Tristan making excuses again. It was his addicted mind at work, blowing opportunities to the breeze while holding tightly to what made him feel good in the moment: drugs, drinking and girls. To hell with consequences.

I met him at a White Spot restaurant and he told me about his plan over lunch. He didn't ask to come home, and I didn't invite him. He said he had a friend in Coquitlam with an extra room. His Coquitlam friends were his old friends, his drug friends, but he assured me this guy knew he was in recovery and wanted to support him. He told me everyone was overreacting, that he'd go to meetings and stay connected with the recovery community. After he got his next paycheque, he'd find his own place to live.

His words meant nothing to me, but I didn't question them either. How could that help?

I believed Tristan was telling the truth, as much as he could. He thought he had a minor slip and had it under control. But it didn't matter what he thought because his mind was a mess. Regardless of what he had or hadn't done, or what he planned to do or not do, his addiction was king of the hill again. It had won this round.

I carried a boulder of worry because I had no choice. I reminded myself, again and again, that most people who use drugs, even most *addicts* who use drugs, don't die—even now, when reports of contaminated street drugs were everywhere. I'd been hearing of street drugs being cut with fentanyl, a sedative a hundred times more powerful than morphine. It was predominantly added to heroin, but increasingly to cocaine as well—Tristan's drug of choice. Nobody really knew what drugs they were taking when they bought from the street, and people *were* dying, in such record numbers that the government of British Columbia had recently declared it a public health emergency.

I knew that as long as Tristan stayed alive, he'd find his way back to recovery; that was where he'd found belonging and acceptance and fun. Recovery was his North Star now, not drugs. He may lose sight of it for a while, as many did, but sooner or later it would guide him home. I was certain of that. As long as he stayed alive.

I reminded myself of these things every minute of every hour of every day, just so I could keep breathing. And then I tried my best to continue to look after myself, to move my life forward in the direction I wanted it to go.

But goddamn, it hurt.

IT WAS the perfect time for me to begin working through the Nar-Anon steps, to more actively work my recovery program. The weekend following my son's relapse, I pulled out my copy of

Codependents' Guide to the Twelve Steps, nestled onto my couch with a cozy throw blanket and started reading.

I was working on step one: recognizing my powerlessness over others and admitting that by trying to control others, I made my own life unmanageable. The language didn't resonate with me. Words like "powerless" and "unmanageable" grated on my nerves. I argued silently with the author: *I am not powerless and I'm managing my life just fine, all things considered, thank you very much!* But as I read more, I understood that she was using these words in a way that was subtly different from the way I had thought about them before. They were not negative or judgemental, merely observant, and the more I accepted her use of these words, the more I could relate. For one thing, the "powerless" phrase applied only to the degree of control I had over *other* people. Still, I had a hard time accepting that one. I believed I had at least an important degree of influence, and influence had its own form of power. Didn't it?

Yet neither my power nor my influence had been enough to save Tristan from addiction or relapse. It wasn't enough to save Jenn, either, from the struggles she was continuing to have with overdrinking. Perhaps I was just comforting myself to think I had some control, because if I felt I had even an iota of control over their lives, their lives could not be completely out of control. I could always step in to save them—somehow. The thought that I couldn't was terrifying.

I also resented the author telling me my life was "unmanageable." It wasn't. Here I was, taking steps toward my own recovery. I'd recently restructured my work life so I could work and travel less. I practiced acceptance and gratitude. I bought a new scarf last month, for crying out loud, and learned how to wrap it in a way that didn't look like I was strangling myself. I was managing.

But these were all steps I'd taken in the last few months since attending Parents' Group. They *did* help to make my life more manageable, and I *was* heading in the right direction, but many aspects of my life were still out of control. I was not managing my money well. I was making Jenn's car payments, and resenting it, while living on my increasingly deep line of credit. I wasn't exercising or eating well. I wasn't dating and didn't feel worthy to date. And I still carried the emotional weight of my children's troubles. I had to admit there was room for improvement.

As I read, I highlighted passages that struck a chord with me; my heart beat faster with the simple excitement of knowing others had been where I was and moved beyond. The author's wisdom pierced me until words blurred on the page through my tears. She wrote about our need to meet the needs of others, as if that were our responsibility alone. And our need to solve other people's problems and fix their uncomfortable feelings, even if we were only guessing at what they might be.

It was as if that was written about me! The idea that I could step away from such responsibility for other people was dizzying. Knowing it was time to take responsibility and stop using my children as excuses for the areas of my life that were inadequate was frightening.

I'd lived my entire life in relation to someone else's dysfunction. As a child, I'd watched and learned as my mother maneuvered to earn my dad's attention while avoiding the lash of his tongue. A strong single mom, she'd sacrificed her wants and needs for the sake of her kids, finding her life's purpose by being useful to others. It felt natural to me to live for the men I chose to be with, and then for my children. I must have felt most useful around people with addictive and compulsive tendencies, because that was what I attracted and created.

The unifying thread of my life was trying to make people *feel* better so they could *be* better. In all my years of trying, I'd never saved a single one of them, yet it had never occurred to me to focus on myself instead. It was going to be a long, hard road to learn how to live for myself. It felt overwhelming.

Other pithy slogans I'd heard in Parents' Group popped into my head: "Easy does it" and "One day at a time." I laughed to myself and began to fully understand the importance and usefulness of these sayings.

Over the next few days, I decided to begin making two simple changes. First, if people wanted something from me, my kids in particular, I'd ask myself if this was something I *wanted* to do for them. Would doing it harm me in some way or make me feel resentful? Was it something they were capable of doing on their own? I committed to paying attention to how I answered these questions, but that was all. I'd still do as I wanted and be gentle with myself when I did something that may not be in my best interest. I just wanted to notice how it felt when I did things for others. Small steps at a time. Easy does it.

And secondly, I'd find small ways each month to take more responsibility for building the life I wanted for myself. I'd connect more with my friends and family. I'd start exercising. I'd speak kindly to myself.

It felt good to have a plan.

I HADN'T seen Tristan for a couple of weeks when I learned that Danny, Tristan's caseworker at PRC, had died of a drug overdose likely caused by fentanyl poisoning. I was horrified. I hadn't known Danny for long, but he had such a gentle energy and truly cared about Tristan. He had done so much, for so many, in recovery.

Danny's death terrified me. Sure, Tristan was struggling, but he was new at recovery. It could take time; I understood that now. But surely there comes a time when a recovering addict is safe. That's a fundamental promise of NA, straight from its *Basic Text*: Anybody can lose the desire to use drugs and create a new way to live. So, what the hell happened? How could someone with so much to live for, so much to offer and so much success in recovery go back to using drugs? Even knowing what I did about the insidiousness of addiction, Danny's death baffled and scared me.

After my next Parents' Group meeting, I approached Paul, who had known Danny, and asked him how somebody so well established in recovery could relapse. He paused before answering. "Kathy, for some of us, over time, the desire to use goes away. I've been clean for twenty-six years and don't feel the need to use anymore. But I also know that something could go wrong in my life at any time, or even *right* in my life, and I could rationalize my way to one little slip that would pull me straight down. I start every day with a prayer of gratitude for my sobriety and ask for the strength to make it through another twenty-four hours. You can't take it for granted. It's not an easy thing to do.

"Danny was certainly a force in the recovery community. He did a lot of good. But he struggled. It takes time. He didn't have years and years of consecutive clean time. It doesn't matter how much good people are doing in the world around them, you never know what's going on inside of them. And that inner world can be dangerous territory for addicts."

I thought of Tristan's inner world and shuddered.

WHEN I heard that Danny's celebration of life had been scheduled, I reached out to Tristan. If he knew about Danny, he'd be devastated and want to be there. He didn't have a phone, so I left him a message on Facebook and hoped he'd get it.

"Celebration of life." I hated that term. I didn't understand how people could come together to celebrate someone's life being so tragically, unnecessarily cut short. How could they feel anything other than rage? *I* was raging inside, and I barely knew Danny. If it were Tristan, I'd stand at the pulpit and shriek at the injustice. "Celebration of life" was a politically correct term that swaddled everything bad, anything remotely like addiction or death, in a gauze of sentimentality until you couldn't even recognize it. How could we do anything to stop the deaths—*so many deaths*—if we couldn't even recognize the tragedy of them? Perhaps the term was appropriate for older people, who'd lived a full life. That made sense, but not this.

Tristan messaged me back the next day letting me know he'd heard about Danny and, yes, he'd like to go. I was relieved. I knew Tristan would feel good about being there to pay his respects and say goodbye. It would bring him closure, I guessed, if that were possible. But I also saw it as a chance for him to reconnect with his friends in recovery, whom I doubted he'd seen in weeks. I imagined Tristan felt ashamed, embarrassed about relapsing and worried the guys would judge him. I didn't think they would and was grateful he was brave enough to find out.

On the day of the service, I picked him up from the house where he was staying and drove through McDonald's to feed him before the ceremony. He looked tidy, sober and tired. After we parked, it was a short walk up to the hall. Every ten feet or so, Tristan was stopped by someone he knew in recovery who wanted to say hi, give him a hug and tell him how great it was to see him.

I was still angry at the idea of "celebrating" this young man's death, and half expected somebody, at some point in the ceremony, to start ranting in outrage. I hadn't been to many funerals before and this was the first I'd attended for a younger person. The service turned out to be nothing like I expected.

Over the next hour or so, I was wrapped and held in so much love for Danny. I learned about his victories, saw the lives made better by simply knowing him, heard about the causes he'd championed and the good he'd done in this world. So many people shared stories of his kindness, his strength, his love. They shared stories of *Danny*.

Finally—*finally*—I understood that although Danny's death was tragic, his *life* was worth celebrating. It *had* to be celebrated. His family needed to share their sweet son because he was so much more than his addiction; he was so much more than his death. His friends and community needed to share how he brought light to their world on some very dark days. People who loved him needed to remember him, honour him and say goodbye to him. They needed to show gratitude for having had him in their lives, and that had nothing to do with his age or the circumstances of his death. Those details fell to the ground, irrelevant.

I glanced over at Tristan and said a silent prayer of thanks for his being alive.

Heading out was similarly slow going. Tristan was frequently stopped for hugs, fist bumps and well wishes. Many guys told him to come to a meeting sometime, and I heard at least two offers to drive him if he ever felt like going; all he needed to do was message them.

I dropped Tristan back at the house where he was staying. It hurt because I knew it was a bad place for him despite his assurances. *It's not my problem to solve*, I reminded myself for the thousandth time. I focused, instead, on the warmth in my heart that came from knowing the true friends Tristan still had in recovery, and the love and hope they held for him.

24

MY REVIEW of step one had gone well with the other moms in my group and I felt positive about tackling step two until I opened the book and started reading: To be restored to sanity, it told me, I needed to believe in a power greater than myself.

What a bunch of hogwash, I thought. I had barely wrapped my head around seeing my life as unmanageable and here she was calling me insane. I put the book down and started a load of laundry.

Sure, I *had* made crazy decisions in the past. I had spent a lifetime living with crazy people in crazy situations, accepting their craziness as normal and rarely considering my needs. I could see that as a bit insane, I supposed. But then, "a power greater than ourselves"? My first reaction was to distance myself from anything that sounded religious; that was how my staunchly atheist family had raised me. In spite of that, though, I did have a spiritual leaning and believed strongly in something greater than ourselves. I wasn't sure exactly what it was or how to define it. How could I be? But once again, I imagined a bridge of love, hope and peace that held us above life's troubles, that kept us from drowning in them. I could work with that.

Love, hope and peace could be a higher power—*my* higher power. They were part of me. I knew now that this heavenly bridge wasn't out there waiting for me to find it. It was inside of me, waiting to be built through my continual practice of love, hope and peace in turbulent times.

As I folded the laundry, I decided that when that seemed too slippery for me to grasp, I could use the wisdom of other parents in recovery as my higher power. There was no question they had collective experience and wisdom I could draw from.

Once I admitted my insanity and had my higher power sorted out, I sat back down with the book and step two was easy and uplifting. There was wisdom in the idea of owning my power in relationships, even if the other person was healthy and well-intentioned. I hadn't thought about my relationships with healthy people very much, and realized I was just as likely to defer to them as to get steamrolled by dysfunctional ones.

I felt such excitement knowing that something else was possible! My homework was simply to list the activities and people that brought me hope and strengthened my sense of self. It was easy: going to the Parents' Group and my step group; reading or hearing inspiring stories of recovery; taking small steps to look after myself by eating well, cleaning the house, exercising and wearing clothes that weren't ratty; and staying connected with my family and friends, sharing good times with them even in the midst of chaos around me—*especially* in the midst of chaos around me. Simple things, really, but I hadn't been doing them regularly. I would do more of those things.

Step two was exciting. Full of opportunity and promise yet without the uncomfortable work of changing my life. It was a step that prepared me for change, a simple shift of mindset that would give me a stronger foundation for the work I knew was coming.

FORTUNATELY FOR Tristan, there was a power greater than himself at work, as well. It turned out to be his recovery community.

Six weeks after Tristan relapsed, he came over to my place for dinner. He'd lost weight again and his skin was sallow but his eyes were clear, and he seemed excited about life. As we tucked into the beef stew I'd had simmering all day, he filled me in on his life over the past weeks and the surprising events of the past few days.

Tristan had been in a desperate situation: he had no money, had lost his job and was barely eating. His living situation was dire. There had been no extra bedroom in the house where he was staying, so he'd slept on a dirty mattress with no sheets on the floor of the living room. There was no other furniture—no TV for distraction or internet connection to help him figure out his options. His roommate used drugs constantly, partied all night and brought girls home. It was a crash pad for Tristan while he was using, and a depressing one at that. By early February, the roommate was tired of Tristan not contributing to the rent or food and said he had to leave.

Not knowing what else to do, Tristan found his way to a Friday night NA meeting. He said he had no thoughts beyond that, no plans. He was loaded at the time, but he went. It was all he could think of. Many of his friends were there and they gathered around him and asked how he was doing. Tristan was honest with them. They asked if he wanted to stop using, and Tristan said he did.

That was all it took.

Tina, a woman well known in the New Westminster recovery community, told him he couldn't go back to where he was staying; if he did, he likely wouldn't come back the next day. Truly, he might never come out of there alive. She told Tristan she was taking him home to her place to have a good meal and a safe place to sleep. A bunch of them would get together for brunch the next day to help him figure out his next steps. All Tristan needed to do was nod his head.

Over brunch on Saturday, they formed a plan. Doctor Hopkins, "Doc," was the medical doctor and addictions specialist for Westgate. He was at the brunch and suggested Tristan stay with him until Monday, when he'd call PRC about getting him back into treatment. Doc regularly provided transitional housing to three or four guys in early recovery. He was out of spare bedrooms, but told Tristan the couch in his media room was pretty comfortable. Doc was an older man, divorced with no kids, with almost thirty consecutive years of sobriety behind him. Helping guys who were struggling was part of what he did.

One of Tristan's friends picked up Tristan's things from where he'd been staying, so he didn't need to go back there again.

By the end of the weekend, Doc had agreed to be Tristan's sponsor and they decided together that what Tristan really needed was support navigating the world outside of treatment. He could do that from Doc's, under Doc's guidance. The deal was that Tristan would work a strong recovery program, be part of a step group and attend at least one NA meeting each day until he got a job, and then three a week. Once he was working, they'd agree on an amount he'd pay Doc for rent.

By the time we got together for dinner, almost a week after Tristan had wandered into that Friday night NA meeting, Doc had put him on his phone plan and given him a phone, bought him new running shoes and made sure his medications were sorted out. Tristan had updated his resumé and gone looking for a job again. He'd brought a book with him called *Living Clean*, which focused on how to live life while staying sober.

"This book has already changed my life, Mom. It's pretty amazing all the things it gets into. Like, listen to this: 'NA is all about love. When we are practicing Step Twelve to the best of our ability, love becomes central to all that we do—there is no more powerful antidote to the despair and self-destruction of addiction. The compassion that we feel for the newcomer is something we learn to extend to our families, to those around us, and eventually, to ourselves.'"

I was moved by those words and by my son sharing them with me. Certainly, the love and fellowship of his NA friends had saved Tristan's life this past week, but the message was universal. It occurred to me again that so many people could benefit from recovery literature.

Tristan was back. That boulder of worry I'd been lugging around with me for the past six weeks crumbled to dust and blew away. My son was safe again, for now.

After dropping him off at Doc's, I thought about what the recovery community had done for Tristan: Tina, taking him in so he wouldn't go back to a drug den; Doc giving him a home and guidance; his friends buying his meals and picking up his stuff. It filled me with gratitude and humility.

I knew they did this for each other because nobody else would. Nobody else would step in with love and generosity to save an addict when he wasn't able to save himself. Nobody else would hold space for the hope of recovery when a person felt themselves to be hopeless. Not the rehab centres, not the medical profession, certainly not law enforcement, just their own community. It was baked into their program. It was their twelfth step: to be of service, to give back, to help those still struggling. I thanked God for Tristan's recovery angels here on earth and wondered how I could ever begin to do as much good in this world as they do.

WITHIN TWO weeks of living at Doc's, Tristan began working at Linh Café, a French-Vietnamese restaurant in Kitsilano. The chef and food had a great reputation but it was a casual, family-style atmosphere rather than the fine dining that Tristan preferred. This was good for me because it meant I could afford to eat there.

Tristan had been working for about a week when Mom and I decided to go for dinner. Tristan said he loved working and his recovery was solid but I was too aware of his track record to count on him being there for long; we'd see how solid his recovery was after payday. In the meantime, Mom and I finally wanted to eat at a restaurant where he was cooking.

Tanis had to work that evening but Jenn came along. She had finally left Alan and rented a small basement suite close to Emily's daycare. Emily split her time between her parents, and I knew Jenn struggled on the days her little girl was not with her. I was glad she could come to dinner and have an evening where she could relax and feel taken care of.

We sat at a rustic wood table and ordered an assortment of appetizers: charcuterie, spring rolls, beet salad, lamb chops, mussels, fresh bread and, as an afterthought, a side of fries because they looked amazing. It was an odd assortment of food but we couldn't resist. Everything was delicious.

We had just finished our meal when Tristan got off shift and joined us at our table. He looked relaxed and confident in his white cook's jacket.

"So, what do you think?" he asked.

We raved about the food, the atmosphere. As we chatted, the server came to our table and placed an open bottle of beer and empty glass in front of Tristan. I stared at the beer like it might bite, and looked at my son, his eyes locked on the bottle. The server noticed our silence and explained to Tristan, "For after your shift. It's from the owner; you did a good job today."

Tristan continued to gaze at the beer with an odd, semi-amused smile on his face. My mind shut down, but another part of me took over and I saw myself pick up the bottle, give it back to the server and say, "Thanks, he doesn't drink."

She looked confused. "Oh. Can I get you something else?"

Tristan smiled at her and said no thanks, he didn't want anything right now, but to thank the owner.

My mom and Jenn went back to chatting as if nothing happened. Tristan was quiet for a while and then joined in with the small talk. My heart pounded and I felt sick. I'd been way out of line: managing that situation was Tristan's responsibility, not mine. I'd reacted on instinct; I saw my son in danger, and I got rid of the danger, as simple as that. But I knew better. *Clearly*, I thought, *knowing and doing are two different things*. I beat myself up for the rest of the evening.

Later, after I'd dropped everyone else off and was alone in the car with Tristan, I apologized.

"Yeah," he said, nodding his head in acknowledgement. "That was pretty embarrassing. What did you think I was going to do? Chug it down right there in front of you?"

"No. I wasn't thinking at all. Sorry," I said, but his phrasing worried me. I wondered what he'd have done if I wasn't in front of him.

"That's okay. Don't worry about it. It did look good though! It's pretty hard to imagine never having another beer again." He turned from me and looked out the window.

"I'm sure it is." I bit the inside of my cheek to stop myself from saying anything else, from yelling at him to think differently, to feel differently, to *be* different. I wanted him to hate alcohol and drugs as much as I did, to see them as dangerous and destructive—which, for him, they were. Instead, I reminded myself that his life was not my responsibility. Tristan's life was simply something I needed to accept, however it came.

The next day was Parents' Group and I confessed my lapse of judgement. Paul and Ben shook their heads and laughed at me. That reassured me. I figured they wouldn't be laughing if I was beyond all hope. Other parents related and shared similar stories of instinctively, thoughtlessly, *desperately* trying to save their kids when it clearly wasn't their place to do so.

I hadn't shared my failure because I was looking for wisdom, or learnings. I wasn't struggling to figure out what I should have done differently. I knew that already. I wasn't even wanting to be told it was okay, we all slip up at times. I just needed to surround myself with people who understood how complex and difficult and fraught with peril something like a bottle of beer could be for me—for *me*, not Tristan.

25

BY THE time our step group could meet to go over our step three work, cherry trees were in blossom. A few days before our meeting, I pulled Balloo onto my lap and opened my workbook. Step three was about to choosing to turn ourselves over to the care of God. The word "God" grated on me, but I knew from my previous work that I could get past it and dove right in.

Step three challenged me to use acceptance and gratitude as tools to build the life I wanted. It felt uplifting and validating. Reading the chapter, I realized I already had a good handle on gratitude and was practicing acceptance, but when I delved into the homework, there were a few revelations.

I was becoming increasingly resentful about making Jenn's car payments, which I had cosigned on. Since leaving Alan, she could no longer afford any payments herself, and because I refused to pay for insurance, her car was sitting uninsured in my mom's carport, and she was driving *my* car. So, I was paying for two cars, yet rarely had one to drive. How did that happen? It happened because I wanted Jenn to have a car so her life would be easier and more manageable for herself and Emily; I wasn't thinking about what worked best for my life.

For the final activity of step three, I was supposed to write about what I felt, wanted and needed, then to share that with someone safe and ask them to listen and accept me as I was, not to rescue me or fix anything.

My biggest fear was that my family wouldn't understand my recovery process, or they'd misinterpret it as being too woo-woo, silly or sad. I feared that, instead of seeing me as strong and proactive and inspiring, they'd see me as broken, floundering and grasping. I wasn't sure, exactly, where this fear came from, but I'd been raised in a family that never spoke deeply about personal struggles or emotions. We'd valued success more than exploration, science more than spirituality, the arrival more than the journey. And I was bumping my way through a spiritual journey with no known destination, where my successes would be internal and not easily recognized by others.

What I wanted was for my family to know that I was trying to set boundaries and make changes. I wanted them to accept that I would make mistakes and get lost along the way; the beer bottle incident was a glaring reminder of that. I wanted them to know it was a process and it might take a long time to get there, wherever "there" was, but that didn't mean any progress I made along the way was invalid or shouldn't be celebrated.

I needed my family to respect this process and support me by not asking for material help and by looking after their own financial affairs. I needed them to understand how hard I'd struggled in these areas, not from weakness but from a misplaced strength and willpower that put other people's needs above my own. I didn't want to be strong for others anymore; I wanted to be strong for myself.

As I reflected on this, it became clear that I should choose a family member to share this with. Tristan would understand what I was trying to do, because he worked a program of recovery himself, and he'd often told me how proud he was of me for embracing my own recovery. But Tristan had enough to deal with just trying to live his own life sober. And it was all too possible he'd misconstrue what I said to make it about him.

I could tell Mom. She'd listen, but she had a tremendous capacity to feel my pain as if it were her own and a soul-deep need to take my pain away. Sharing my problems with Mom created an echo chamber of caretaking, where I felt the need to look after her feelings while she tried to look after mine.

I probably *should* tell Jenn because she was the one most likely to bury me under her own wants and needs. She was the one who was using my car and who turned to me to pay her rent and fix her problems; she was the one with whom I had the hardest time setting limits right now. But Jenn was living in crisis; I wasn't sure she'd even hear me and, if she did, I could imagine her responding from a place of guilt, fear and anger: "Fine Mom, just take your car back and don't give me money then. I can quit my job, go on welfare and take Emily to the food bank on the bus!"

Then there was Tanis. Tanis felt safe. I knew I could ask her to listen, and she would. I knew she wouldn't make it about herself, feel my hurt as her own or feel threatened by my desire to set limits. She relied on me for little and there was nothing for her to lose. The idea of showing vulnerability to one of my children was uncomfortable, but I could do it. Tanis might think it was weird and awkward, but neither of us would be any worse for it.

I phoned Tanis and told her my fears and wants and needs. It *was* weird and awkward, but she accepted what I had to say. She accepted me just the way I was.

IN AN attempt to look after my physical self, I signed up for a Walk to Run program. I bought new running shoes, sports socks, cold-weather leggings and a runner's toque. The people seemed lovely and the effort was reasonable, but after the first week, I came down with a cold and missed the second week. The third week was cancelled because of ice. I never went back.

Disappointed in myself but determined to keep working on self-care, I thought there might be easier ways to start.

I hated how I looked. Not physically, but my overall image. I felt like an old sloppy-slop. My everyday clothing consisted of old jeans and T-shirts, long-sleeved in cold weather and short-sleeved in warm, which I pulled from my "clean" pile on my floor (although sometimes I decided my favourite grey T-shirt was still acceptable to wear even if it was in my "dirty" pile and sometimes the piles blended). I had a small handful of business-appropriate clothes on hangers, but they were my work armour; they weren't day-to-day me.

I longed for colour, for nice shoes and breezy scarves, for blouses and trousers and handbags and accessories. I longed to feel like a woman, to feel like I fit in among women, but I hated clothes shopping and had no idea how to go about it. I splurged and hired Dana, a personal shopper and stylist, to help me choose a selection of clothes I could wear in both personal and casual-work situations.

After a colour consultation, where I discovered many colours that looked great on me—beautiful teals and warm reds, soft coral and deep orange, spice and saffron, plum and lime—Dana and I went shopping. I felt like a TV star, pampered and spoiled and ready to spend the money I'd withdrawn from my work account for the purpose; a uniform allowance, I called it. The day was a whirlwind of blouses and blazers, pants and skirts, dresses and scarves, jeans and necklaces, shoes and shirts.

The next Wednesday, I went to Parents' Group wearing new café-coloured jeans, a plain ivory T-shirt, an intricately patterned red scarf and brown leather ankle boots. I even put on lip gloss. I smiled and looked people in the eye. Nobody commented on my clothes or my new look. They probably didn't notice. But I did, and it felt good— so much better than wearing my old jeans, running shoes and grey long-sleeved tee. It felt more like me, less like I was hiding.

Once I felt good *about* my clothes, it was time to start feeling good *in* my clothes. I needed to buckle down and focus on fitness. Tristan's recovery inspired me. If he could work hard to give up drugs and build a life focused on wellness, I should be able to do a few squats or jog a couple kilometres now and then. But with my track record, I knew I needed help. Toward the end of March, I hired a personal trainer to come to my home three times a week. The investment was scary, but I wasn't paying for Tristan's rehab anymore. It was time to prioritize myself.

I was beginning to get the hang of self-care. I wasn't sure I was having regular *fun* yet, but I was certainly enjoying myself more than

I had in a long while, maybe ever. But between work and exercise and shopping and step work and Parents' Group and spending time with my family, it felt like I was still running at full speed, and the world around me still felt complicated.

While Tristan continued to embrace recovery, Jenn's life was becoming increasingly chaotic. I had hoped when she left Alan in January the drama in her life would settle down but it had only gotten worse. She rarely made her rent without my help, still couldn't pay for her car and was increasingly unreliable unless it involved Emily. Thankfully, she continued to be an involved, dedicated mother.

I was helping Jenn more than I wanted to—for Emily's sake, I told myself, knowing it wasn't sustainable or in anyone's long-term interests. I needed to step away from taking responsibility for Jenn's problems, but I had to think that through first. There would be repercussions beyond Jenn: Emily would feel the impact. I needed time to consider all angles.

I hadn't travelled much outside of work since I'd visited Tristan in China five years earlier. I wanted a vacation where I could just sit and be with myself.

WARM CARIBBEAN air washed over me as I stepped down the stairs from the tiny eight-seat plane to the tarmac in Isla de Culebra. Surrounded by rolling hills, palm trees and blue sky, I was eager to see the turquoise ocean that surrounded this tiny island in the Puerto Rican archipelago. I picked up my Jeep, the only vehicle the rental company offered other than golf carts, which were great for getting to the beaches but couldn't be used to navigate the steep island hills. *Watch out Culebra, here I come!* I said to myself, as I turned onto the main road—only to be stopped by a flock of chickens that looked at me with beady eyes and bobbing heads as they made their way slowly to the side of the dusty road.

The one-room hilltop *casita* I'd rented was a magical little taste of the Caribbean, with a hammock on the patio overlooking the ocean. Geckos skittered on my walls, and the songs and screeches of forest creatures entertained me through the nights. I spent the next week exploring the island in my white Jeep, feeling powerful and oddly feminine, like a heroine in an action movie. My days were filled with white-sand beaches where I snorkelled and sunbathed and swam beside giant green sea turtles. In the evenings, I drove to hilltop viewpoints to watch the crimson sun set across the vast expanse of water, no longer turquoise but a rich midnight blue scattered with silhouettes of other islands.

I stayed in touch with my family every few days by Messenger or Facetime. Everything was gloriously uneventful back home until a week into my vacation when I got a message from Jenn, asking me to call her. She spoke rapidly and I couldn't quite make sense of the details, but she'd fallen and hit her head and had a concussion. She said something about having a mini stroke and ending up in hospital. But that wasn't the problem, she said, as my mind swam over the many ways these were, in fact, problems. Alan had heard about this and was threatening to sue for full custody of Emily, even though Emily had not been with Jenn the night this happened.

"Are you okay?" I asked. I was still way behind her in this conversation.

"Yes, I'm fine," she said. "Alan's just being a dick and I need a lawyer."

"I don't understand what happened. What's this about a stroke? Were you drinking?"

"Of course I was drinking. Too much. And it wasn't a stroke, it was a *mini* stroke. That's different, apparently. Anyway, I'm fine, but that's not what this is about."

"How did you get to the hospital?"

"I called Grandma and she took me."

Oh god, my poor mother.

I told Jenn there was nothing I could do until I got home, but that Alan was not going to take Emily from her. If she needed a lawyer, we'd get one. As much as Alan loved Emily, I knew he was not a stable father: he was angry, emotionally abusive and often unemployed. He abused drugs and alcohol just as much as Jenn did, possibly more. He showed no interest in helping to pay for Emily's dance classes or taking her to playdates or birthday parties. This may not be my problem to solve, I realized, but I'd turn my life and my finances inside out if it helped keep Emily with her mom. I'd sworn I was done saving Jenn but I was wrong. For this, I'd jump in the deep end again, without hesitation or regret, because Emily needed Jenn to fight for her and Jenn needed me to help her fight. The only question was, how would I protect myself in the process?

I lay in my hammock, looked out at the ocean and felt that I was exactly where I wanted to be—close enough to hear about what was happening back home and express my support, but too far away to be pulled immediately into the urgency of it all.

I committed to enjoying the rest of my vacation even though I was carrying a new weight at the thought of Jenn in pain, and a new fire in my belly at the thought of being needed, of making a difference. I was weirdly comforted by the idea of returning to a child in crisis. It felt familiar and purposeful, and I slipped into it easily, comfortably, like my old grey T-shirt.

26

BACK HOME, I wanted to know every detail of what happened to Jenn that night. Where was she when she fell down? Who was she with? Why was she so drunk? And a stroke, even a *mini* stroke—what did that mean for her future? What did the doctors say? For god's sake, what happened?

But I didn't ask. As loud as those questions were in my head, I had another voice even louder, stronger, more in control. It simply said: *Leave it be. It doesn't matter. It's not your drama.* And that voice was right. The only thing I needed to concern myself with was the present moment: *my* actions and reactions, *my* thoughts and feelings. I needed to figure out what *I* wanted to do, and not do. I recognized that as progress, even as I assumed responsibilities that I knew weren't mine. At least I was thoughtfully choosing the responsibilities I took on.

I committed to paying for Jenn's lawyer, if needed. I decided this was not the time to give Jenn any ultimatums about living within her budget. I knew how difficult balancing finances could be as a newly single mom even at the best of times and was still grateful for the help my mother had once given me.

But Jenn was going through an emotional crisis beyond anything I'd experienced, and alcohol was fuelling the crisis. Left unchecked, I was pretty sure Jenn's life would explode and Emily would be collateral damage. Again, not my problem but very much my concern. I didn't know what I could do to prevent that but I would do anything I could to help.

I began to spend more time with Jenn and Emily. I bought groceries, helped make dinners and drove Emily to school in the mornings as Jenn rushed to get ready for her workday. Their tiny, tidy basement suite became my second home. Jenn continued to be a great mom, attentive and loving, but when Emily left the room it was like Jenn's spirit went with her. Without Emily around, Jenn was deflated, fragile, emotional. I held her in my arms as she cried that her life was a wreck, she was a disaster and Emily was the only reason in the world for her to stay alive.

My heart broke for her and my mind screamed at me to spew out solutions to her problems, the most urgent of which was: *Stop drinking!* But I just held her, stayed silent and continued to find ways to help. I looked for opportunities to share recovery stories and talked about the strides Tristan was making. Then one evening I invited her to come to a meeting with me.

"Jenn, I'm going to Diedre's daughter's one-year cake this week. Why don't you come along, see what it's like? It's been working for Tristan."

"Oh my god, celebrating a year without alcohol—that sounds so depressing. I'd rather kill myself. No thanks. And I'm not Tristan. Obviously, I'm stressed right now because Alan's being King Dick and being a single mom sucks, but I don't *need* to drink. I'm not an alcoholic. I'll get my shit together." I'd heard that so many times from Tristan, usually just before he totally lost his shit. I took a deep breath and prepared myself mentally to catch Emily in case Jenn fell so hard she lost hold of her.

TRISTAN HAD lost his job at Linh Café after his first paycheque, but his slip back into drug use had lasted only one day before he'd confessed to Doc. They agreed he was not yet ready to manage the pressures of a job and paycheque. Tristan's compulsive need to spend, and spend on drugs, took him out every time. Doc wrote a note stating Tristan was medically unable to work, so he could apply for welfare and practice managing his money that way. Managing his financial life was not something Tristan had done before, and he wouldn't get help with that in a treatment centre. So, Doc gave him a pass and let him continue to stay with him, where he could get supportive living experience. But he was back to at least one meeting a day and more often two.

One afternoon a few weeks after Jenn refused to come to a meeting with me, Tristan drove me home so he could borrow my car for a few days. He told me Jenn had started going to NA meetings with him.

"How come she goes with you when she wouldn't go with me?" I asked. "She told me she doesn't have a problem."

"I guess I'm just cooler than you," he laughed. "But seriously, I get it, Mom. I know where she's at. She has no idea how to have fun without drinking or drugs. She needs to see you can have good friends, fun times, sober. It's what she's missing right now. We went out for pho with a bunch of my friends before home group last week and she had a great time. She saw *us* having a great time, sober. It makes a difference."

"Did she admit she has a problem?" I probed. "Because she keeps telling me she's fine. And I know she's still drinking."

"Mom, Jenn's an addict," he said. "Addicts are the last people to admit they have a problem. She *wants* to stop drinking, though, if only for Emily's sake. So, I'll keep bringing her and see what happens."

ON A Sunday evening in early June, Jenn called me. "Mom, what do you think about the idea of me going to rehab?"

My mind raced. What about Emily? I wanted to tell her that her drinking problem wasn't *that* bad, that she could go to meetings, or get a counsellor, or get whatever other help she needed. My mind was yelling for her to keep her job, keep her home, *keep her daughter close*. Those thoughts flashed through my mind in microseconds. But I knew Jenn's problems *were* that bad, and she shouldn't need to lose everything before she asked for help. Her life shouldn't need to get any worse than it already was.

Still, it was a big decision and it had to be hers.

"Why do you think it's a good idea for you?" I asked, not wanting to sway her.

"Well, I can't stop drinking." She took a few deep, shaky breaths and I knew she was crying. "I've tried and I really can't. I go to those meetings with Tristan, I get all inspired and decide to stop, but instead of pouring my wine out when I get home, I pour it into my glass. I don't even know why. I don't want to lose Emily. I want to have a good life and be a good mom for her."

"You deserve that, honey. You and Emily both deserve that. Why do you think rehab is the best option, though, rather than counselling?" I asked, keeping my voice neutral.

"I can't make the changes I need to in the middle of my life right now. There are too many pressures with work and parenting and Alan being an asshole. There's just too much stress. I've tried on my own, I've tried going to meetings, but I keep on drinking. And rehab was good for Tristan. Even though he's still . . . well, working on things, he's so much happier since he went into treatment. I need to get away from everything and focus on myself."

She hadn't needed my opinion at all, just someone to hear her.

"Good for you, hun. You're being very brave."

I hung up the phone and sat with so many mixed emotions—pride and sorrow, exhaustion and excitement, love and shame. I didn't even try to sort them out.

It turned out that Brook Manor had a spot available right away and Jenn qualified for government funding so there'd be no cost to her. She had one week to quit her job, find a place to store her stuff, move out of her suite, let Alan know she couldn't have Emily for the next three months and deal with any complications that arose.

We'd both have a busy week. I looked at my calendar to see which work meetings I could reschedule.

I KNEW Tristan was relapsing again, maybe before he did. It was just a simple lie and a sketchy look in his eye that gave it away. I'd let him borrow my car over the past weeks to run errands and go to meetings. He and Jenn were basically sharing my car now, and I'd borrow Mom's if I needed to get somewhere that transit wouldn't take me.

Tristan had happily agreed to help us move Jenn's things out of her basement suite and into Mom's spare room the day before Jenn was scheduled to go into Brook Manor. The day before the move, I phoned Tristan to remind him to drop off some boxes I had in the back of the car to Value Village before he came over in the morning.

"Yup, already done," he said without hesitation. But when he showed up the next morning, on time, ready to work, the boxes were still there.

"What happened? You said you dropped them off already."

"Oh, yeah, well I was going to but then I got busy with our step group. I forgot I had it last night. But I can go do it now if you want."

"No, we don't have time. Just put them in the carport." Tristan's lying and casual explanation were worrisome; this wasn't how he behaved in recovery.

We drove to pick up the moving truck I'd rented. After loading the dollies into my car, I rode with Jenn in the truck back to her house while Tristan followed in my car. Jenn and I organized boxes as we waited for Tristan to arrive with the moving dollies and his muscles. When we'd done all we could by ourselves, and Tristan was still not there, I began to get nervous.

"Do you think Tristan got lost?" I asked Jenn. "He would have called us, right?" I didn't wait for her response but tried calling him. No answer. "Maybe his phone's dead, and he didn't remember which road you're on. Let's watch for him at the corner." We went to the end of the road and sat on a large boulder. If he was coming, he'd drive past this spot and I'd see him. We watched the cars come and go for some time. "Maybe he was in an accident," I said hopefully.

Jenn laughed. "It's pretty twisted when we're hoping Tristan was in an accident."

"Not one where's he's hurt," I said. "Just one that's prevented him from getting here or calling us." Anything seemed better than him ditching us to get loaded.

"Mom, I don't think he's coming. We should get started."

"Let's give it a few more minutes. I hate to think of him driving around not being able to find us."

"Mom, he's not coming. If he was lost, and his phone was dead, he would go back to Grandma's and call us. It's not that complicated. Besides, he knows where I live. The fucker's not showing up." She was worried, but she was also angry. We both were; we'd counted on him being there. We'd counted on him being sober.

BROOK MANOR consisted of three houses on a quiet residential street in New Westminster. They were older but well kept, like all houses in that area. Tidy, neat, nothing fancy. We went around the side gate to the backyard, which opened onto a large cement patio with four picnic tables and plenty of room for kids to run around when they visited their moms. A little brown-haired girl about seven years old kicked a large blue bouncy ball like she was a soccer super-star. Four women sat at a picnic table talking.

"Hi, are you a new girl?" one of them asked Jenn.

"Yeah, I am. I'm Jenn."

As Jenn introduced herself to the others, one went inside to get the intake worker, who came out and eyed Jenn up and down.

"First thing, you need a shower. Then, put all your belongings through the high-heat drier to make sure there's no lice or bed bugs or anybody else hitching a ride with you. We only have room for you, not for any little critters." She laughed at her own joke while Jenn stood stunned.

"Um . . . I don't have lice," she said.

"Doesn't matter. Policy. Come on, I'll show you where to go."

We both started down the cement stairs to the basement door, Jenn bumping her heavy suitcase down each step. The intake worker turned around when she got to the door. "Not you, Mom. You're welcome to visit once your daughter is all settled and off restrictions. We'll take it from here." She went inside without waiting for a response.

Jenn looked scared and uncertain. I gave her a long, deep hug and told her I was proud of her.

"Mom, I don't think this is a good idea," she said, looking like she wanted to run, far and fast.

"You're here now, honey," I said. "You chose this. And you had really, really good reasons. It was a brave decision. Do it for you and do it for Emily. Don't question it now. Just do what they ask."

"Even if they ask me to take a stupid shower after I spent an hour this morning doing my hair? Oh god, this is going to be hell," she said, then hugged me back. "Love you, Mom."

"Love you too, baby girl. So much!" I gave her another tight squeeze. "Call me when you can."

I SPENT the rest of that day and the next trying to reach Tristan, calling every few hours, but he didn't answer. Until finally he did.

"Hi, Mom, what's up?" He sounded cheerful, chirpy even.

"Um, you have my car? After ditching us when you were supposed to help Jenn move? Sound familiar? I need my car back, Tristan." I was pissed—by everything. By his pretending he hadn't abandoned us. But most of all, by his chirpiness.

"Yeah, sure. I just need to take a friend to a meeting tonight but can drop it off after that if I can get a ride back?"

"Sure, just get it back. Tonight." I hung up and tried to distract myself by catching up on work.

He didn't show up that night. He didn't answer his phone again, and again, and again.

I thought about what I should do—for myself. How would somebody who's not a doormat act? How would a mother in recovery act once she's made the decision to let her addicted son take responsibility for his actions?

After another morning of phoning Tristan and mulling my options, I phoned the police and explained that my son had stolen my car, it wasn't the first time and it needed to end. I mentioned he had a history of drug issues and had been doing so well for so long, but he clearly wasn't anymore.

"So, you'd like to report your car stolen?" the officer clarified. "You do understand if you do that, it will likely end with your son having a criminal record."

"I don't know what else to do. He can't keep stealing my car. He's probably using drugs again and driving impaired. I'd feel responsible if something happened. Can you just look for the car and return it to me and give him a good scare?"

"Unfortunately, no. We can't return the car to you unless you report it stolen. Once you do that, charges *will* be pressed if we find your son; it won't be up to you. It will be in the system, and we'll need to charge him with auto theft."

"Oh god," I said, and sighed. "But he can't keep doing this. Honestly, what would you do if it were your son?"

The officer paused, and then said, "I'm not supposed to offer advice, but if it were my son and he had a drug problem, I'd do everything in my power to get him the help he needed without a criminal record attached. If your son is found guilty of auto theft, it won't make life easier for him. It won't get him help and will cause problems for the rest of his life with getting jobs, travelling, all sorts of things. If your son isn't a criminal, I wouldn't report this. I'd do whatever I could to find the car myself. Hang out at his house, or at his friends', or wherever he's likely to be."

I thanked him and hung up. He was right. It was good advice; I didn't want to be responsible for Tristan having a criminal record. He didn't need that. I was just so fucking tired of it all.

Tristan, it seemed, was still pretending his life was just fine. He was, as far as I knew, still staying at Doc's. I decided to borrow Mom's car and do regular drive-bys until I spotted my car, and then steal it back with my spare key.

It took me two days and five drive-bys before I saw my car parked on the street out front of Doc's house. My heart raced. What would I do if Tristan saw me getting into the car and confronted me? The fact that it was *my* car didn't ease my anxiety. I didn't want to create a scene; I didn't want Tristan angry with me. I knew these were dysfunctional thoughts but they were my thoughts just the same.

I parked Mom's car a dozen feet ahead of mine and ran to my car, fumbling to get my spare key out, and then sped away. Success! I was thrilled. I felt like *I'd* stolen a car and my heart beat a hip-hop rhythm in my chest. I drove the five minutes to Mom's house, picked her up and dropped her back at her car. Still no sign of Tristan.

I was relieved to finally have my car again, but it was a disgusting mess. Fast food garbage everywhere, tiny plastic baggies with white power residue, wadded-up tinfoil, and tissues with blood on them, either from bloody noses that Tristan got when snorting cocaine or from picking at his scabs when it felt like coke bugs were crawling beneath his skin. Nothing new or unexpected but it made me sick. Worst of all, Tristan still had a key so there was nothing stopping him from coming and stealing the car back again. I had to get that key.

Just after I walked into my apartment and put the kettle on, Tristan called. "You took the car."

"Yup, I did. It's my car."

He didn't say anything, so I pressed on. "You have the other key. I need it. Are you at Doc's now?"

"Yeah, of course."

"I'll be there in fifteen," I said and hung up. I was deep-down, bone-weary exhausted and the last thing I wanted to do was get back in that drug-infested car and confront my drug-infested son. But I needed that key before I could rest.

I pulled up in front of Doc's house and texted Tristan that I was there. He came out almost immediately and gave me the key. I took it and said, "Thanks," because I couldn't trust myself to say anything else. I didn't meet his eyes. I could not look at him. I drove home and slept soundly that night, knowing he couldn't take my car, knowing, at the very least, that my car would not aid him in his drug deals, that he would not kill himself or anyone else by crashing it while under the influence.

I was proud of myself, a warrior woman who'd won a pivotal battle in a war that continued to rage within me—a war that pitted my needs against my kids' wants.

27

"I WAS so tired of my son telling me he was going to kill himself *all the time*," said an older mom sitting a few chairs down from me in Parents' Group. "The last time he phoned to tell me that, I said to him, 'For god's sake, stop talking about it and do it already!' And I hung up on him. I just couldn't go through that anymore. Seventeen years was enough." The topic in Parents' Group had turned to how our children frequently threatened suicide. Sometimes as a call for help, but many times to manipulate.

She continued her story, her voice rich and dramatic, with a hint of an English accent. "My husband looked at me with these pussycat eyes and called me Ice Queen. Fine, I'll be the Ice Queen." She glanced to her left where her husband sat, looking both amused and bashful. "Of course, he called our son back, took him to the hospital and sat with him through the night. So, the next day, my husband had to go out, and he calls and tells me that I need to go sit with my son. Now it's his pussycat *voice* on the phone. So, fine. I go.

"I sit beside my son, who's detoxing now. That's something no mother should have to see. It's terrible. And I look at him and I think to myself, 'What did I create?' You just get so confused and feel so helpless and small at times. You want it all to stop. But it doesn't, and I'm so damn tired of it. So, I just don't engage with my son when he says he wants to kill himself anymore. 'Go do it, if you're going to,' I say. 'Just leave me out of it.' But he won't. It's all manipulation."

This conversation started because one of the guys currently at Westgate was hospitalized the night before after talking about suicide. "We err on the side of caution when one of our guys disclose that they want to self-harm," Paul said. "We're experts in recovery, and we stick to that, so we make sure doctors or psychiatrists and people who specialize in mental health are there for the guys when they need them."

Paul leaned forward, resting his elbows on his knees. "I remember this one kid who came for intake with his dad, a fifteen-year-old punk with a lot of attitude, a lot like me at his age, and halfway through his intake he stands up, says he's going to kill himself and runs out the door! Whoosh, he's gone! His dad and I are left staring at each other." Paul pauses, eyes wide, mimicking an astonished stare.

"So, I pick up the phone and dial 911. The dad says to me, 'Do you really think he's going to kill himself?' By this time, we're both at the door watching his kid run up to the corner, where we see him press the button and wait for the walk sign to come on before looking both ways and crossing the street. I say to the dad, 'In my experience, people who really want to kill themselves aren't so concerned about traffic safety, but he's not ready to come here and he's clearly in distress. He needs some sort of help.' Then I turned to the dad, and said, 'This isn't easy for you. What kind of help do *you* need?' And we talked through options like Nar-Anon, and reading literature about detaching with love, and counselling. Because as parents, that's what we can control: our own well-being."

I listened to more stories about suicide threats that, for some reason, had us all laughing. Like the one where a teenager had stolen his dad's car and then, when caught, told his dad he felt so bad about it, he was going to kill himself.

"Oh no, you aren't," said the dad. "At least not 'til I'm done whipping your ass!"

Or the mom who said she told her son, "You're taking a very long and painful route to it, with your drinking. Better you just take a gun and save yourself years of pain."

It was dark humour, to be sure, but cathartic. Everyone in the room had felt these things, at one point or another. Here, we could say them out loud and be understood.

There were also heartbreaking stories of suicide attempts. One mom found her teenage son on the floor of their bathroom in a pool of blood and another found her boy unresponsive after an overdose. But both of those boys were now over two years sober, living their lives in recovery, one going to school and the other working—and no more talk of suicide.

That's what recovery can do, I thought. If recovery worked for kids who were suicidal, it gave me hope that it could work for my kids. I walked home from that Parents' Group session with much on my mind. By this time, Tristan had been back at PRC for two weeks, having checked himself in two days after the car fiasco; Jenn had been at Brook Manor for almost three weeks.

Jenn had always been dramatic but had never expressed a real desire to kill herself. With her, I was more concerned about what she *didn't* tell me than what she did. But Tristan? I couldn't count the times I'd heard him say he was going to kill himself. It always felt like manipulation to me—a cry for help, for sure, but what kind of help I had no way of knowing or providing. I had spent a long time living in fear, thinking, *What if I was wrong? What if he did try to kill himself?*

I hadn't heard Tristan threaten suicide since he'd first come into treatment the previous year, even through all his ups and downs. I wondered, vaguely, what I'd do if he told me he was going to kill himself now. Would I shrug it off as manipulation, as I used to? Or would I call 911 and report him as someone having a mental health crisis?

ONCE A week through the summer months, Westgate held outside speaker meetings at their Redstone retreat in Mission. Men from Westgate, women from Brook Manor, alumni, family and friends were welcome. Jenn called to let me know that she and some of the girls were allowed to go to an upcoming speaker meeting, if they could find a ride. She asked if I could drive a carload of them. I jumped at the opportunity.

It was the first chance I had to spend time with some of the women Jenn was sharing her life with, and the first time we could visit away from Brook Manor. I loved going to speaker meetings—they lifted me. This evening would be an opportunity to reconnect with Jenn and hear inspiring stories of recovery.

Jenn introduced me to her friends as they piled into my car. I had met Anna on a previous visit. Jenn's best friend in recovery, Anna was all heart and soul; she exuded warmth through every strand of her waist-length platinum blond hair and two-inch mani-cured nails.

Barb was Jenn's other close friend and roommate. Like Anna, Barb was in her early thirties. She was a tiny, energetic woman with sharp eyes and a sharper wit. A natural entertainer, she saw every interaction as an opportunity for laughter.

And then there was Denise. She was brand new at Brook Manor and, so far, Jenn found her annoying. Denise was eighteen years old but spoke and acted like someone closer to thirteen. Although she'd been living rough in the last few months of her heroin addiction, she seemed sweet and naïve and trusting. I wanted to take her home, feed her chicken soup and keep her safe.

Just as I was about to start the car, my phone rang. It was Tristan's dad. "Do you know where Tristan is?" Brad's voice was shaking, and I could hear his quick breaths.

"He's not at PRC?"

"No, I haven't been able to reach him all day yesterday or today, so I called Aaron at PRC to see if he knew where he was. He said Tristan never came home last night. He's been out since yesterday morning. I was hoping he was with you."

"I wouldn't have kept him when he was supposed to be in treat-ment," I said. Brad knew that but was grasping. The girls had been goofing around and laughing but had quieted down and were waiting for me to go.

"I'm with Jenn and some of the Manor Girls right now and I can't talk. But let me know if you hear from him. I'll call you later tonight when I'm home again."

I hung up the phone and took a moment to feel; to acknowledge my pain and worry and sorrow; to feel the tears burning my eyes and my heart aching for my boy. My instinct was to push these painful feelings away, to disassociate through distractions or numbness, but that wasn't how I wanted to live my life anymore. I allowed myself to feel those feelings, for me, and then I refocused my thoughts and feelings on what I could control: this evening of recovery and connection with my daughter and her friends. I got in the car.

We spent the hour-long drive laughing about god-knows-what and singing badly and out of tune. Denise, with only a few days of sobriety, was planning her next career and Barb was razzing her about not being present in the moment in a way that seemed hysterically funny to all of us. I could feel the stone of fear in the pit of my stomach as I worried about Tristan, but there was nothing I could do for him right now, so I let it be. I focused, instead, on the joy of these girls and their laughter.

"No, seriously, though," Denise said. "I can dance. I took dance lessons for years, and there are always clubs hiring. I could make enough money to pay rent and buy a car."

That sent Barb off on a whole new tangent of hilarity, as Denise seemed genuinely confused about why dancing in a club may not be the best thing for her long-term recovery.

"You do know that dirty old pervs will be watching you dance in your next-to-nothings?" Barb said.

"Well, I guess, but it's not really about that," Denise said.

"Yes, it is. It's *exactly* about that!" Barb laughed, and even Denise started laughing at her own messed-up perceptions. "That's why you're in treatment, Denise. Because your thinking sucks. Maybe don't plan beyond completing your first set of steps right now."

"Yeah, you might be right," Denise agreed cheerfully in a way that cracked us all up again.

By the time we pulled into Redstone my sides hurt from laughing so hard. The girls tumbled out and I followed them into the open courtyard where they held the meetings. Blue Adirondack chairs were arranged in a large circle. I left my bag on a chair next to Jenn's and went to say hi to some of the parents and staff I recognized. As I was chatting, my phone rang. It was Brad. "He's here and I don't know what to do!"

"Tristan's at your house?"

"Yes. No. He's sitting outside on the curb about a block away. He didn't call or knock or anything, said his phone is dead. He refused to even come into my place. I was just coming back from a walk and saw him sitting there. He looks horrible. His face, Kathy, it's just... horrible. He keeps saying his life's over and he's going to kill himself. What do I do?" I could hear his panic.

I took a deep breath to calm myself, but Brad jumped in again. "I made him a sandwich. All I could think of was to take our son a sandwich. On the street corner. He won't even come inside! A god-damned *sandwich*!"

"Okay, well," I said, interrupting him before he went completely hysterical. "If he's threatening to kill himself, you need to dial 911."

"Really? Is that what you'd do?"

"I just had this conversation with other parents. Clearly, Tristan is in crisis and needs help. Even if he *isn't* going to kill himself, he needs help. If he's serious, it could save his life. And if he's just saying it to get attention, then maybe he'll think twice before he makes threats like that next time."

"I don't know. Is that what you'd do?" he repeated.

"I hope so," I said. The truth was I had no idea and I was glad Tristan hadn't sat on the street corner outside of my house. "The meeting's about to start, but I'll leave my phone on. Let me know if anything happens."

I sat through the next hour of speakers in a state of intense gratitude. I was acutely aware of every word they spoke, every piece of wisdom they shared. I held tightly to one guy's story of spending years in the recovery/relapse cycle before finding solid ground in long-term recovery. As I listened, I couldn't help but worry about Tristan. How long would he be out before he went back to recovery? Would he survive? But I stopped that train of thought immediately. Even in this fentanyl crisis, the vast majority of people who used survived. The odds were still in his favour. There was more reason to hope than not.

I brought myself back to the present. I was grateful that on this night of worry, I was sitting beside Jenn, surrounded by people in recovery, talking about recovery. It was exactly what I needed. It didn't lessen my worry, but it lessened the power it had to bring me to my knees. Here, I could lean on the love and hope I had for Jenn, the joy of friendships she was forming, the connection I felt with other parents, and the strength of those who had walked in Tristan's shoes and found their way to wellness. Here, I was living in the solution and not the problem; here, Tristan's relapse was just one more step on his recovery journey and I wasn't going to let his misstep pull me from *my* recovery path.

With conscious effort, I stayed engaged in the conversations on the way home and felt the warm glow of happiness wash over me, even as worry gnawed at my bones. When I was finally home, my pajamas on and a cup of tea in hand, I phoned Brad for an update.

"I ended up phoning Aaron," he told me, "and he came with another guy and took him back."

"Back to PRC? They're letting him stay?"

"For now, but I don't know," Brad said. "Aaron thinks maybe he can make a case for him. They never should have given Tristan his phone so soon, he was nowhere near stable enough. They should have known. But it's not just up to Aaron. We'll have to see."

"Does Tristan want to go back?"

"He said he does. He was crying, really upset. But, yeah, he said he definitely wanted to go back."

Well, that's something, I thought. *Maybe a big thing.*

I went to bed feeling the joy and heartache of recovery intertwined. Recovery was never easy and rarely a straight line, but I reminded myself that it was possible, even probable, if Tristan just kept coming back.

And he always seemed to keep coming back.

A FEW days later, I walked into the church hall, excited to see Jenn take her thirty-day sobriety fob. I blinked my eyes to adjust to the sudden dimness and then saw Jenn and her friends waving me over. "Tristan's over there, with Aaron," Jenn said, jutting out her chin to point across the hall unobtrusively.

He was not in good shape, but he'd showed up. In the midst of his pain, shame and batshit-crazy-brain, he was there because, I knew, he was so, *so* proud of his sister and needed to be here for her. To support her, to love her, he showed up.

PRC had deliberated for a day before allowing Tristan to stay and continue treatment. They recognized they had given him too much freedom, too soon. This was his first outing since his slip two days earlier and, thankfully, he was accompanied.

My son stared at his feet, Aaron somber beside him. In the dim light, I could just make out the side of Tristan's face and the new red scabby splotch on his chin. My stomach rolled. I hated seeing him unwell and clearly ashamed to be back in these rooms after yet another Day One, but I was so happy he was here, again, and stunningly proud that he made the effort to show up for Jenn. It didn't look like he wanted company, so I let him be. This was Jenn's night and I wanted to focus on her successes and accomplishments.

The topic for the evening was gratitude. A number of people spoke about gratitude for their sobriety, family connections, friends and food, gratitude for second chances and new beginnings. One buff, tattooed man in his thirties stood to share. "Welcome to all the newcomers, congrats on being here," he began. "And congrats to everyone who's taking clean time. As many of you know, this isn't my first-time round in these rooms but, you know, I'm coming up on two years now and feel so much love and gratitude for Narcotics Anonymous. My entire life has changed. I don't want to share too much about the mess I was in before, but I was not a good person." He shifted his weight and took a deep breath. "I was a bad dad. I fought with my daughter's mom, in front of her. I didn't care. I couldn't see past my own sick wants and needs. So, I wasn't allowed around my daughter. That's why I got into treatment this last time, why I work so hard to make it work. I want to be there for her.

"So, yeah . . . gratitude," he continued. "I remember the first time I saw my daughter after getting clean. I was thirty days in and walked up the steps to their house and knocked on the door. I was so fucking nervous, man! I thought she wouldn't want to see me, that she'd hate me. I'd totally understand if she did; I deserved it. My crazy mind was telling me horror stories, telling me to run. But the door opened, and she ran straight to me and gave me a big hug, saying, 'Daddy, Daddy, Daddy!' and I just about died from love and gratitude right then." He paused to wipe away a tear. "It was the first time I could accept her love without guilt. Like maybe I *could* be a good father and be worthy of her love. Recovery brought me back to my daughter. She's in my life now; we have a great relationship. So, yeah, I'm forever grateful. To any of you newcomers who think it won't happen, just keep coming back, man. And with that, I'll take another twenty-four."

Then it was Jenn's turn to share her message of gratitude for her new-found sobriety. She concluded with a special message. "Mostly, I'm so grateful for my brother, Tristan, for being there for me." She looked to where he sat, eyes still on his shoes. "If it wasn't for you, Tristan, I wouldn't be here today. You shared your recovery with me when I needed it, you believed in me when I didn't believe in myself and you loved me when I couldn't love myself. That carried me through a really dark time.

"You showed me there was a different way to be. If it wasn't for your example and support, I wouldn't be here today taking my thirty days. I wouldn't have made such progress working on myself, my life, my relationships and being a good mom for Emily." She paused and took a deep breath, but her voice still broke with emotion. "I'm *so* grateful that you're here today, Tristan."

I watched Tristan through my tears. He was still looking at the floor, but he nodded a little bit. He heard her.

After the meeting, I gave my daughter a big, proud-mama hug and then wound through the crowd to my son. "Hey, Tristan. I'm glad you made it tonight. It's good to see you." I tried to convey my love and belief in him in those few, acceptably neutral phrases. I reached out to give him a hug but he didn't join me; my arm just landed on his back. I gave him a pat of support, instead.

"Yeah, of course," he said, nodding. "I had to be here." Eyes down. He didn't want me to see his scabby face. I looked at Aaron, who had one arm around Tristan's shoulder, ready to escort him through a minefield of people and emotions. His focus was on Tristan.

"Thanks, Aaron," I said, with sincere gratitude and an awkward half-hug. "Thanks for bringing him."

"You're welcome," he said. "I'm happy to. He's been there for me. It's what we do." Aaron gave me a small smile and wove Tristan through the crowd and out the door.

Walking home, I basked in the silence of twilight, relishing the silken breeze on my face. I thought about the importance of community, of having people who step up for us and inspire us to step up for others. I didn't want to imagine where my kids might be without their recovery community. Or where I might be without mine.

28

JENN HAD been at Brook Manor for almost two months when she turned twenty-five. I ordered a massive red velvet layer cake from a local bakery, decorated with swirls of whipping cream, plump local strawberries and a chocolate plaque that read "Happy 25th Birthday, Jenn!" It was big enough for all the women at Brook Manor to have a piece—or two. Today, I wanted Jenn to feel our love as we celebrated her life in all its messy wonder.

I picked Emily up early from daycare, so we had time to buy a birthday gift. She raced to the car and scrambled into her car seat, insisting she didn't need my help to buckle herself in. "I made Mommy a card, see?" She pulled a folded-up piece of construction paper from her backpack. It was covered in glitter and stickers and random crayon squiggles. "This is me, and this is Mommy." Her chubby fingers pointed to some squiggles with lines coming out of them. She'd recently learned to draw arms and legs.

"That's so beautiful!" I exclaimed. "Your mommy's going to love that. I thought we could buy her a birthday present from you, too. Do you want to go to the Dollar Store or Walmart?"

"Oh, oh, oh, I want to go to the toy store Gae-Gamma takes me to, by the chicken place!" She was talking about the specialty toy store beside Nando's Chicken that my mom, her Great-Gramma, took her to.

"Hmm," I said. "Yeah, that's a great store. But it's more for kids than for adults I think."

"No, Mommy *loves* that store too. It's her favourite. I can find something perfect. They have *Frozen* things!" Emily's favourite movie was *Frozen*. She wanted everything to have a picture of her favourite character, Elsa, on it, including, apparently, her mother's birthday present. She continued to bump up and down in excitement until I told her we could go.

In the store, I practiced patience and the art of redirection.

"Mommy would love this!" Emily said, holding up a Shopkins rainbow camper van.

"Hmm. That one is a bit big. Let's look for something smaller." Emily reluctantly put the toy back on the shelf.

"This is small!" Emily said, jumping up and down holding a clear skipping rope filled with pink glitter.

"It is, you're right. It's a good idea. Let's hold on to it but keep looking to make sure it's the best present in the store."

Emily kept finding new exciting presents for another fifteen minutes, until I was able to direct her to some cute little beaded bracelets I thought Jenn might actually wear—at least for a little while, and at least when Emily was around.

"I *love* them!" Emily said, sifting through a tub of them, choosing a purple one with little hearts on it. "I love it *so* much! Mommy is going to love it so much too."

I was just thinking how successful this turned out to be, when Emily caught sight of the musical jewellery boxes next to the bracelets.

"Oh, Gamma, look! Look at this!" She was holding a small pink heart-shaped box, edged in ribbon and sequins, which opened to show a rainbow unicorn turning in circles to a tinny melody. "It's perfect. Please? I don't want the bracelet anymore." She threw the bracelet back in the bin and hugged the music box close to her heart, looking up at me.

I checked the price. Seventeen dollars and ninety-nine cents for the music box, as opposed to four-ninety-nine for the bracelet. But she was too darn cute, and too damn adamant.

"Okay, fine. But I think you need to get the bracelet too, so your mom has something to put in her jewellery box." Emily yipped happily and retrieved the bracelet from the bin.

Standing in the checkout line, Emily tugged on my shirt. "So, these are for Mommy, but I can keep them while she's in daycare, right?" The counsellor at Brook Manor had suggested that Jenn tell Emily she was going away to school for a while, to learn new things. It was all Emily needed to know. In her three-year-old mind, she considered school to be like daycare, so that's how she referred to Jenn's treatment centre.

"Well, you're already keeping the artwork you made for her on Canada Day, remember? Usually, when you give a gift to somebody, you give it to *them* to keep. Your mommy can wear the bracelet and keep the music box by her bed, and they'll remind her how much you love her, and how much she loves you."

"But . . . but I want to wear the bracelet too, and remind me how much she loves me." Emily's eyes were tearing up now as she held her treasures tightly.

I squatted down to her level and looked into her big blue eyes. "I have an idea. How about you run back and find another bracelet and music box for yourself. Then you and your mommy can have matching bracelets and matching music boxes. And you can both remember how much you love each other."

I watched Emily skip down the aisle. I'd totally blown the budget I set for myself on things not likely to have long-lasting value to either of them. But boy oh boy, they had a whole lot of value in the short term.

I SAT at one of the picnic tables in Brook Manor's backyard. Jenn and Emily wore their matching bracelets as they played hide-and-go-seek with Tanis. Emily wasn't good at hiding. She couldn't help running around, high on cake and excitement.

Tristan sat on a plastic deck chair, chatting with Kimmi, a young woman who'd recently come back into treatment. Kimmi's father, Sam, sat beside her, with a few other Brook Manor clients filling out a circle. I was close enough to hear their voices over the general chatter and Emily's frequent shrieks, though not what they were saying. They seemed to be in their own little world. Tristan was making Kimmi laugh, and Kimmi was giving him her full attention.

Was Tristan flirting? I wondered. I felt my shoulders tighten as I watched. He had no business flirting with girls at this stage of his recovery, I thought, especially at his sister's birthday when he was supposed to be spending time with us.

Then again, what did I expect—that he'd bring out the *Basic Text* and start reading it aloud every time he saw a pretty girl? Maybe it felt strange because I wasn't used to seeing him around girls; I still thought of him as shy and awkward, and this version of him proved me wrong. He was smooth, charming and attentive. I realized I was watching a more grown-up version of Tristan than I'd seen before.

Jenn had special permission to miss the evening's NA meeting so she could spend more time with Emily on her birthday. PRC let Tristan determine his own schedule for community meetings, so he could have stayed with us through the evening if he wanted to. But when it was time for the Manor Girls to go to their meeting, Tristan said he'd go as well, so he could walk with Kimmi.

Fine, I huffed to myself. If Tristan wanted to prioritize a girl over his family, what could I do? It was his life to figure out. I gave him a hug and said I'd talk to him the next day. As Jenn and Tanis and I began colouring with Emily, Sam approached us. We knew each other, slightly, from the Friday family barbecues at Brook Manor. He was a middle-aged hippie, with eyes showing a heart of gold.

"Hey, Kathy, I'm heading out but just wanted to thank you for raising such a wonderful son. It's Kimmi's third day back and she's struggling. I wasn't sure she'd make it through the day, to be honest. But talking with Tristan helped, I could tell. He's so generous with his story, so encouraging of hers. He's an inspiring young man; you should be proud of him."

My eyes welled up. Here was a person who completely understood the ups and downs of addiction and recovery, telling me I had an awesome kid—a kid who, he knew, had less than thirty days sober.

But Sam also had an awesome kid, less than a week sober. He could see a person's awesomeness where others saw only the veil of addiction or the fragility of early recovery.

"Thank you. Thank you so much," I said.

He smiled at me, said "happy birthday" to Jenn, goodbye to everyone else, and went on his way.

Later that evening, I phoned Tristan to share with him what Sam had told me.

"Yeah, Kimmi was feeling low. She was planning on booking it. Her sister's still out and she wanted to go back to her. That's why I was talking with her and went to the meeting with her. I hope you didn't mind me cutting out early. She just needed someone to keep her moving in the right direction. She felt better after the meeting, though, so that's good. Hopefully, she'll stay."

All that time I was upset that Tristan chose to flirt rather than spend time with family, he was in fact being of service to someone in recovery who needed him. He was making a difference in someone's life—possibly a life-saving difference.

I realized how narrow my thinking had been, how limited my perspective. I wished I could see Tristan as he truly was, as other people saw him, without my mom-filter colouring his actions with judgement and expectation, no matter how hard I tried.

I went to bed grateful for the day with my family, for another year of Jenn's life, for having all my children and grandchild together for the evening. I thought of how the recovery community had changed my world and given two of my children a new chance at life. And I was proud and a bit humbled to have seen Tristan practicing recovery by sharing recovery.

29

A WEEK or so after Jenn's birthday, Tristan came for dinner. I shucked corn and made a Caesar salad while he grilled the steaks. After eating and tidying up, he took Balloo out for a walk in the hallway of my apartment building—it was Balloo's greatest pleasure, and Tristan had much more patience than I did for the endless walking back and forth and sniffing at every door. Then we found an episode of *Chef's Table* on Netflix and settled onto the couch to watch an ambitious chef reclaim his country's cultural roots and turn them into a modern culinary empire.

"Wanna give me a shoulder rub?" I asked Tristan, hopefully. "My neck is killing me from lugging around my laptop all day."

"Yeah, sure," he said. "Just sit down here, it's easier."

I pushed the coffee table aside to make room for my stretched-out legs and sat on the floor leaning back against the couch. Tristan sat above me, legs to either side, hands on my shoulders.

It felt good to connect again. I remembered the "birthday back rubs" I gave the kids when they were little. Once a year, they could count on getting a full-body massage with lotion. When they were old enough, they gave me a birthday back rub once a year, too. Six tiny hands pitter-pattered randomly over my back, earning an "A" for effort if not effectiveness. I'd been enthralled by how cute they were.

As he got older, Tristan and I had some of our best conversations during a back rub, either one of us on the receiving end. With Tristan in recovery, I tried to avoid talking to him about his plans, hopes and dreams, to keep things in the moment. He had to take one day at a time and futurizing was not helpful. But it wasn't easy for me. My conversations with *everybody* tended toward future thinking. Staying in the present was hard work for me, requiring constant vigilance.

Watching *Chef's Table* with Tristan, his fingers kneading the knots in my shoulders, I couldn't help thinking that he must be upset that cooking in fine-dining restaurants—becoming a chef—may not work out for him. The intense atmosphere wasn't good for his recovery, he'd realized.

"You know, you could always become a certified masseuse while you're figuring out what else to do. You're good at giving massages, and you seem to like it." As I spoke, I recognized that my unstoppable need to find solutions to Tristan's problems had stepped onto centre stage again. He paused, his fingers stopping their kneading and pounding briefly, then said, "Nope. I can't. That's a big trigger for me."

"Really?" I was nervous for some reason. I wasn't sure I wanted to hear what he was about to say, but I needed to. I needed to know him.

"Yeah, I can't touch girls like that. It gives me fucked-up thoughts. It's all part of my addiction." He sighed and then carried on. "There's a new group starting in September that I've been invited to join. One of my friends is starting it up. He's a good guy, got a decade of clean time. It's for guys who have a sex addiction. Like a step group, but with that focus. I dunno. We were talking after a meeting last week and he thought it might be good for me. So, yeah. I think I'll do that."

A crazy mix of emotions filled me: shock, of course; gratitude that he trusted me with this; but predominantly grief over this one more thing he had to struggle with. Nothing was simple for Tristan. Something as fundamental as having a girlfriend, something meant to bring joy and comfort, was a minefield for him. At twenty-one, the possibility of him having a loving, romantic relationship was already complicated by his addictive behaviours and perspectives.

Thoughts of what Tristan might have done, *must* have done, in his addiction suddenly nauseated me. When did this start? How did it start? What did he do in China that I didn't know about? Certainly, he'd crossed a line in Thailand. I thought back to some of his Facebook messages that I'd seen—spied on—when he was a teenager, offering girls cocaine if they'd hang out with him.

My sweet little boy. Sex addiction didn't surprise me; not really. If I was being honest with myself, I already knew.

Somehow, his addiction to women and sex seemed worse to me than his addiction to drugs. It involved another person, for one thing. I wept inside for the girls he used, without loving them properly, each one deserving so much more. And I wept for his inability to feel truly, deeply loved for himself—to feel a real partnership with a woman.

But I was also proud of Tristan for being open about it, for acknowledging it and making it part of his recovery, for giving himself a chance to heal. It couldn't have been easy for him.

"Well," I said, "good for you for knowing that." I took his hand from my shoulder and gave it a squeeze of love and acknowledgement.

MY STEP four work stretched out for months. It was now my turn to make a fearless inventory of my character traits. I thought back to when Tristan had procrastinated doing his step four, saying he had to "make a list of all the bad shit I did." But it wasn't that; it was harder. It was making a list of *all* the shit I did, good and bad. It required deep reflection and honesty with myself.

It was slow going in part because it was a busy time for the other moms in my step group, and we'd skipped two of our monthly sessions; and partly because step four was one big beast to wrap our heads around. In mid-August, we met to review our work for the second time; still none of us had completed the comprehensive workbook we got just for the occasion. We agreed to wrap it up in September, no matter what; to focus on priority areas and leave the rest to another round of steps. We didn't need to tackle everything on our first round.

Step four was eye-opening in many ways, but one big takeaway was particularly illuminating. I'd always prided myself on being honest but I realized for the first time that I was not very *truthful*. While the words I spoke were typically true, the words I kept inside of me told a story others could not fathom. I withheld the full truth, especially *my* truth—my thoughts, feelings, needs, hopes, dreams—more often than I shared it, and almost always when I felt it wouldn't align with what another person wanted or needed from me, or when it made me vulnerable in some way.

I thought about the imaginary invisibility cloak that had protected me from being seen as a teenager. That invisibility cloak was worn ragged, now, but I still wrapped myself in its tatters more often than was good for me. It was time to cast it off, to let the shy, anxious girl—now woman—show herself. I could not be honest with others or true to myself while I was hiding, especially since I no longer knew what I was hiding from.

It was time for me to step into the world, proudly, with all my faults and imperfections; to have my opinions, to speak my mind and, if others didn't like it, that was their problem, not mine. It was time to tell people I loved them, I was grateful for them and I was a better person for knowing them. And if they stared blankly back at me, and I ended up feeling awkward or embarrassed, well . . . too bad.

I knew this wouldn't happen overnight—it might take a lifetime, or longer—but it would be my mission. All I needed to do was pay attention, try my best and trust the process. One day at a time.

TRISTAN AND I got together once or twice a week through the summer and were increasingly relaxed and easy with each other. My son was once again becoming himself. We'd cook together and he'd help me clean up. He came to play with Emily when she visited. He made a point of visiting my mom, checking in with her and being a good grandson.

Until, suddenly, things shifted.

In mid-August, Tristan and I met at New Westminster Quay to walk together to the beach volleyball courts, where Brook Manor and Westgate were having a tournament. Tristan had been invited to participate but chose to watch instead.

"Hey, Tristan. How're you doing?" I asked when I saw him, giving him a quick hug.

"I'm good," he said, then looked at me.

I looked back. It seemed like he wanted to say more, so I waited.

"What?" He was suddenly agitated. "Why are you looking at me like that?"

I'd been relaxed, expecting another enjoyable day with Tristan, but his reaction, the way his thoughts jumped, did not bode well. I opened my mouth to respond but he cut me off.

"Why do you keep asking how I'm doing if you've already made up your mind? You never believe me, anyway. You always think I'm using so why should I even bother?"

I looked at the river behind Tristan and felt like I'd just been thrown in. I imagined hopping on a raft that would take me away from this moment, then looked back at him. "What are you going on about, Tristan? I never said I think you're using."

"Right now, when I told you I was doing good, and you just stared at me. Who does that? It's pretty clear what you were thinking."

Details began to settle in my head like jigsaw puzzle pieces. I'd had my doubts over the past few days after seeing Tristan's Facebook status change to "in a relationship." I grew even more concerned when I realized the woman he was in a relationship with was Denise—the young girl I'd driven to the speaker's meeting at Redstone the night of Tristan's last relapse, the one who'd been planning her next career as an exotic dancer. In her Facebook profile picture she was dressed in provocative clothing, but her face still managed to look innocent under the make-up. She'd be dangerous for Tristan.

I'd phoned Jenn the day before to ask if she knew anything.

"Yeah, I just saw his status change too. The fucking guy. She's not good news. She only lasted here a couple of weeks. Now she's a hostess at the strip club down on Columbia Street. She still goes to meetings and says she's clean, but no way. I'm going to tear her fucking head off next time I see her if she doesn't leave Tristan alone!"

So, I had my doubts about Tristan's sobriety but his attitude now confirmed my fear. Whether he had used or not, at this point, was irrelevant. He was heading in that direction.

"Look, Tristan, it doesn't matter what I think. I just want to have a good day with you and Jenn. If you're pleasant to be around, I'm happy."

"Well, if you don't think I'm clean then you clearly think I'm using. Why don't you just admit it?"

We had stopped walking, and I sighed. "I try hard to have no expectations, Tristan. I'm happy when you're solid in recovery and I'm scared when you aren't. But there's a huge grey area in between when I have no idea what's going on with you and it's not my job to figure it out. That just takes me to crazy places. So, no, I don't think you're using, and I don't think you're *not* using. Truly, I try hard not to think about it."

"Great. You'll win 'Best Mom of the Year Award' with that one. Not even believing in your kid. Good job, Mom," he said sarcastically.

He was planted in place, ready for a good argument. I glanced to my left, where the happy energy of crowds at the volleyball courts called to me. Jenn was there somewhere and I resented being stuck on the hot concrete with Tristan.

"Your recovery is yours to take care of, Tristan, don't make it about me." I started walking again, creating space between us. He swiftly passed me, taking long angry strides, and I walked more leisurely the rest of the way. Well, I thought, I spoke my mind. I expressed myself. It didn't exactly go over well—it would have been much easier if I'd simply told Tristan that, of course, I knew he was clean and sober. But I had been true to myself, and that felt good.

I strolled down the boardwalk slowly, focusing on my breath and the sunshine. I watched as Jenn and her friends played volleyball, badly, but with much enthusiasm and laughter. Tristan sat with his friends and cheered loudly for both sides. As the games wrapped up, he came and sat beside me.

"Sorry, Mom, for earlier. I shouldn't have been so snarly with you." He held eye contact, looked sincere.

"Thanks, sweetheart. I appreciate that."

"I'm going to go grab a coffee with some of the guys, but maybe I can come for dinner soon?"

"Absolutely. Just let me know when," I said, and gave him a hug goodbye.

30

THE NEXT Saturday Tristan called me, but it wasn't to arrange dinner plans.

"PRC kicked me out, Mom. I know I screwed up by not coming home the other night, and I did smoke weed. But I swear I haven't used any drugs!"

I said nothing. There was a time for speaking my mind, but also a time for listening before launching grenades of opinion and judgement. Tristan told me he was going to an NA meeting and would then try to arrange a meeting with Doc. He asked if I could give him a place to stay just for one night until he figured out his next steps.

"Sure," I said, "but only tonight. You'll have to figure out a longer-term plan."

I hung up the phone and scooped Balloo into my lap, the wind knocked out of me. I was exhausted. I was sad for Tristan and his continuing struggles. It was beyond tragic. My sweet, sweet boy living inside that troubled head that just kept knocking him down, no matter how hard he tried.

It reminded me of a series of stories called "The Busted Brain" that he wrote when he was in Grade 4. They were about a boy whose brain was broken in such a way as to cripple him in certain situations and turn him into a superhero in others. I had been impressed by the creativity and energy he'd poured into those stories. On the front of one of his writing journals, he had drawn a boy with his head separated down the middle, the two halves rising up from his neck, each side of his mouth smiling. Those stories now struck me as prophetic.

But along with heartbreak for my son was also anger. I knew too well the amount of strength it took to focus on self-care and connection while navigating the impossible currents of his relapse. I knew the constant ache, deep in my soul, that I could work around and ignore but that would stay with me just the same—a familiar, deep-seated fear. And here it was already, like a homing pigeon returning to roost.

I didn't want this. I was so goddamned tired of it. I'd been moving forward, and I was determined to keep moving on. Tristan had other people in his life now, much better equipped to help him than I was. I knew this for a fact, had seen it in action time and time again. So why did I still feel so responsible? Like something important was missing and only I could find it?

I'd had those thoughts before, many times, and they did no good. I acknowledged my fear and grief but told myself that Tristan's relapse was just another spin cycle that would help him understand himself better and commit more deeply to getting the help he needed and sticking to it. He'd survive, he always had. Why think about the slim possibility of something tragic happening when it was much more likely this would move him forward in his recovery?

Eventually.

And there was nothing I could do about it anyway. I cried a few more tears and then turned on Netflix.

JUST BEFORE dinner, I let Tristan into the apartment. He looked good—clear-eyed and healthy. I was determined to enjoy my time with him and tried to find positive things to focus on.

"Hey, the movie It is coming out in a couple of weeks," I told him. "On September 8, the day after my birthday. I thought we all could go together: you, me, Tanis and Jenn."

"The one with the creepy clown and red balloon?" Tristan asked. When they were young, the kids had loved being terrified by the

1990 version of the Stephen King classic. It would be the perfect thing to do together for my birthday. "For sure. Clowns still freak me out because of that show! I'd love to see that with you."

Cooking dinner, we soon ran out of chatter and worked quietly together. It was a hot August evening and my open patio doors did little to cool the room. But it was the weight of my worry and his shame at getting kicked out of treatment, again, that sat heavy between us.

After dinner we watched *Stranger Things*, but it didn't hold our interest and we went to bed early. On Sunday morning, I woke Tristan with a cup of tea.

"Do you want bacon and French toast in a bit?" I asked.

"Thanks, Mom," he said, "but I gotta go to a morning meeting and then I'm getting together with a bunch of the guys for brunch. And then I'm meeting Doc; he was busy yesterday. But do you still have that Fruity Crisp cereal?"

While he ate, we chatted about my brother, Dan, who was in town from Kitchener-Waterloo for a few days.

"You'll be around this evening to come for dinner at Grandma's?" I asked.

"Yeah, for sure, I'm looking forward to it. Haven't seen Uncle Dan for a while—since last year, I guess. He's got the best laugh!"

The last time Dan had been in town was when Tristan was at Westgate and they'd had sports day. I reminded Tristan how much we'd cheered and laughed watching him on obstacle courses and playing soccer while inside huge plastic bubbles.

"That was such a fun day." I smiled at the memories.

"Yeah, it was," he said, looking away. "A lot's happened since then."

"Yes, it has," I said. "Lots of good things, though. Just think back to where you were barely more than a year ago. You've come a long way, put in a lot of work. Made a lot of good friends."

"True, true," he said, nodding.

"So, what's your plan for tonight? Have you got a place to stay?"

"Yeah, a few friends said I could stay with them until I figure out what I'm doing. You're right, I do have some kick-ass friends. But I gotta talk to Doc before I nail down a plan. Hopefully, I'll know more tonight when I see you." Tristan finished his cereal, rinsed his bowl and spoon, and put on his shoes. Then he came over to where I was pouring myself another cup of tea. "Thanks for letting me stay the night, Mom. I really appreciate it. And please don't worry about me," he said. "I love you."

He wrapped his arms around me in a big hug, holding me close, his cheek against my head. I felt his heart beating, felt his love for me.

I hugged my sweet boy goodbye, breathing him in. "I love you too, Tristan."

That was the last time I saw him.

I GOT the phone call three days later, just before six o'clock on Wednesday evening, August 23. I was sitting on a lawn chair on Mom's patio, enjoying a glass of wine and the warm summer evening with her and Betty, a family friend. We had decided to order Indian food and were debating the merits of chicken tikka masala versus lamb korma.

It didn't happen the way I thought it would.

I always figured I'd be the first to know. Perhaps a phone call, but more likely a knock on the door. I'd open it and see two police officers, a man and a woman, concerned but unflinching. I imagined my legs would give out and I'd collapse. Then I'd collect myself because I'd need to tell my daughters and his dad and be strong for them.

As it turned out, his dad called me, and he was hysterical.

I heard his words, but couldn't take them in.

"He's dead, Kathy," Brad cried. "Our son is dead. He's gone."

His voice continued but the words blurred. I didn't know what he was saying. I didn't know why he was talking at me.

I walked inside the house and up the stairs. Brad was still talking. I needed him to stop.

"No," I said. "No. Stop saying that. Just be quiet. Be quiet a second." But his voice went on and on, crazy sounding. He wasn't listening, he wasn't stopping, so I repeated myself louder each time, but calmly and firmly so he'd understand. Finally, I yelled. "Stop it already! You can't say this to me if it isn't true!"

Then he paused. I heard him take a deep breath. "You know I'd never lie about something like this," he said, his voice broken, barely there.

Of course, he wouldn't.

III

REWRITING
HOPE

31

I FOLDED to the floor at the top of the stairs. In one split second, eternity had collapsed and nothing made sense.

"Just hold on," I whispered into the phone. "Give me a minute." I lay on the landing, not listening, not hearing, not breathing. I shut my eyes and pretended for one glorious moment that it wasn't true. Then I breathed in and took another moment to accept the fact that it was.

"Okay," I said, finally. "What happened?"

I crawled to the spare bedroom, still talking to Tristan's dad, asking for details over and over because I couldn't hold on to them. I hung up and phoned the RCMP and the coroner's office. More details. They were comfortably business-like. Just another day at the office, just a regular day. Yes, a drug overdose, suspected fentanyl poisoning, but it would take months to get the full coroner's report. Too many deaths to wade through. They informed me of the location of his body, the timeline of events. They gave me the address of the police station where I could pick up his backpack and belongings. I wrote it all down.

They offered to send two officers to speak with me and I asked them, "What for?"

I felt oddly absent, uninvolved somehow, but had an unstoppable need to know more. I phoned the friend who'd been with him, the girl who'd found him on her couch that morning, unresponsive and cold. She cried as she told me how Tristan had helped her elderly neighbour carry groceries the night before, how they'd ordered pizza with extra cheese, how he'd seemed okay, even optimistic. She told me she didn't know he was using; she didn't recognize the signs. She said he'd talked about taking his sixty-day sobriety fob next week.

I jotted "pizza" and "60 days" on my notepad.

I phoned my girls, needing to hear them, needing them near me. They already knew. They were on their way over. Brad and one of his brothers were also on their way over. My mother's home had long been the place for family gatherings and we all felt the need to be together.

I stared at the ceiling in the spare bedroom for I don't know how long, trying to feel something, *anything*. All I felt was a terrible weight, an overpowering heaviness that made it difficult to breathe, let alone move. Eventually, with extraordinary effort, I pulled myself up and went downstairs where Mom and Betty were waiting, dinner long forgotten.

Later that night, after everyone had gone home, I messaged my cousin, Kimiko, who was a United Church minister, and told her the news. I told her I didn't know what to do—literally, logistically—and asked for her help. I was referring to making the necessary arrangements, planning a funeral. But really, I simply didn't know *how to be* anymore. I didn't know how to keep breathing without Tristan. I didn't need condolences; I needed instructions. She told me she'd be over in the morning.

Two days later I received a poem written by Doc in response to Tristan's death. It was a poem of rage, and impotence, and pain at losing yet another sensitive soul to addiction. It was raw, and real, and beautiful, and it made me furious because Tristan would feel terrible to know he'd caused Doc such pain. I wanted to protect Tristan's feelings, now, more than ever, when he seemed so vulnerable in death. He loved Doc like family and wanted to make him proud. I didn't want him to feel responsible for anybody's pain. I didn't want him to feel guilty about dying. I needed him to know we understood how hard he'd tried, and that it was okay, it wasn't his fault, we didn't blame him. We were still proud of him and we still loved him—we still loved him *so* much. I sat in the middle of my bed and wrote my own poem. And as I wrote, I cried. For the first time since his death, I let myself cry as long as the tears kept coming.

Be free, sweet boy
From the fight
From the struggle
From the shadow's calling

You did all you could
In the rooms, in recovery
For laughter and love
For the new guy
For yourself
But still not enough
Never enough
And now.

Be free, sweet boy
Weave your wings
From our prayers
Let our love raise you up
We're right here with you
We always will be
Be free, my sweet boy

As I wrote, the pain almost drowned me. I'd gulp for air and then sink back into my ocean of tears until, eventually, I had not a single tear left.

I was empty.

WE HELD Tristan's celebration of life at Centennial Lodge in Queen's Park eleven days after he died, the same park where he had flown Emily over the pig poo barely a year before.

I arrived early to set things up. Over the past week, I'd gathered Tristan's martial arts medals, cooking awards and sobriety fobs, his black belts, the first board and brick he ever broke, and a few other odds and ends that were important to him: a camel ornament made of leather, a carved wooden box. I'd collected photos for the slide show, framed a few and printed three large poster boards with others, one with photos of him with family and food, another of him doing martial arts, and a third of him with his recovery friends—the things he loved most in life. I arranged everything on tables, just so, along with the urn that held his ashes, the guest book and the framed forgiveness letter he had written to himself just weeks earlier.

I wasn't thinking, and certainly not feeling. I was simply going through the motions, arranging and rearranging things with impeccable detail. Everything had to be perfect, for Tristan.

My sister-in-law and the moms from my step group had organized the food, and women were bustling in the kitchen. Rows of chairs filled the back half of the hall, and tables with tiny vases holding white flowers were set up for family at the front. Two large bouquets of lilies bordered the massive fireplace and podium at the front of the room, and an entire wall of windows looked out onto the lush green of summer.

When there was nothing left to organize, I went outside. I needed to get away from the guests starting to arrive. I didn't want to talk, to be polite. Would they expect me to be sobbing? Would they judge me if I wasn't? It was all too much. I found a quiet rock to sit on, until it was time.

The room was packed with family and friends when I returned. It looked like most of the New Westminster recovery community was there. People overflowed through the open doorway and onto the lawn. I ignored everyone as I headed to my designated spot but was grateful for every person there.

When it was my turn to speak, I walked to the podium, wearing my new dress and black pumps and holding my carefully crafted speech in my freshly manicured hands. I hoped I looked well put-together; that seemed important to me, like it was a sign of respect for Tristan, though it felt more like armour that gave me shape and kept me from blowing away. I took a few deep breaths and then shared my love and pride in Tristan, memories of him that I'd hold forever in my heart, and my gratitude to his recovery friends. My soul was safely encased in stone, so I shed no tears and showed only a smidge of shakiness.

Afterward, people lined up to pay their respects to me. I was happy to see them but their words blended together and held little meaning. Tristan's best friend from his teenage years had come from Vancouver Island and I thought how horrible this must be for him. Tavia, the woman who'd found Tristan dead on her couch, was there and I thanked her for spending time with him the night before he died and told her to look after herself. Mary's son had come, recently sober after yet another relapse, and I gave him a deep hug and smelled his young-man scent, reminding me so much of Tristan. A young woman I didn't know told me Tristan had been a rare and beautiful spirit and she slipped a polished quartz stone into my hand, which I clutched and held for the rest of that day, and for weeks to come.

The people were never ending. Kimiko, who had presided over the ceremony, appeared at my side. "You don't need to talk with all these people," she whispered. "It's okay if you want to, but you don't have to."

"I don't want to," I said, suddenly tearing up. My armour was crumbling. She ushered me onto the balcony where my brothers were chatting and told the guests it was a family-only area.

I was grateful.

A FEW weeks after Tristan died, I drove by a bus stop where a young man stood wearing a white cook's jacket and checkered pants. He had a backpack slung over one shoulder and a cigarette in his hand. It could have been Tristan; it *should* have been Tristan. My sweaty hands gripped the steering wheel as a pain deep in my belly rumbled up and through me. I rolled down the window, hoping the air would blow it away, but it didn't. I was shaking so hard I had to pull over.

At the side of the road, under the shade of a chestnut tree, I let the tears come, great racking sobs of anger, almost hatred, toward the young cook at the bus stop. *How dare he be alive when Tristan isn't?* I was sure he'd used drugs at some point; why wasn't he dead, instead of Tristan? As I grappled with the impossible "why," it occurred to me that perhaps this man was alive because his mother had done a better job than I had. My sobs lost their anger and became confessions of guilt, tearing my heart with every racking breath.

It was true. I hadn't been the best mom.

I remembered the times I'd paid for Tristan's drugs. I remembered how I excused and accepted his lying and stealing and emotional outbursts as if they were okay; how I fixated on him and assumed his responsibilities as mine; how I didn't offer him a place to live and welcome him home; how, once, I'd told him "No" when he'd asked to crash at my place, leaving him with nowhere to go and no option other than to spend the night on the streets; how, finally, I'd told him to figure out his recovery, if not alone, exactly, then at least without me as an active participant.

And days later, he was gone.

Maybe that cook at the bus stop had a mom who didn't do those things. Maybe that's why he was alive and Tristan wasn't.

ON TRISTAN'S twenty-second birthday, two months after his death, my girls and I gathered at Mom's to plant a fiery-red Japanese maple under which we buried some of Tristan's ashes. I was fuelled by fury.

It wasn't just his death that angered me. It was the fact that people's sons and daughters continued to die in this fentanyl crisis, relentlessly, day after day after day. It was knowing that I was only one in a long line of mothers burying their children—beautiful, talented, loving children. An invisible evil had snaked its way into every corner of the country, growing fatter and fatter as it gobbled up the lives of people who used drugs, and those who mourned for loved ones lost. And nobody seemed to care.

I was mad because no mother should need to bury her son on his birthday.

Mostly, though, I was mad so I didn't need to feel the pain waiting for me on the other side of my anger.

Mom had made a gift for Tristan on that birthday. Over the past year, she'd hand-knitted blankets for me and Jenn and Tanis. She gave them to us on our birthdays, saying that each stitch was one hug, and that each blanket wrapped us in the warmth of ten thousand hugs from her to us. She'd been halfway through knitting Tristan's blanket when he died. When the tree was in the ground and the soil patted down, she draped his now-finished blue blanket over a patio chair and said, through her sobs, that it was stitched with five thousand hugs, and five thousand tears.

We stood silently, staring at the blanket hand-knitted with love and grief, and cried.

Then we set heart-shaped candles around the bottom of the tree and gazed at their tiny flames. Jenn and Tanis and I had each bought Tristan a birthday card, in which we had written all the love that we could no longer share with him. We burned the cards and let the ashes fall to the ground beneath the newly planted tree, laughing awkwardly as the plastic-coated cards refused to burn as dramatically as they had in our imaginations.

Then Mom and Jenn and Tanis went inside. I stayed in the garden a while longer, looking at the tree and wondering how I would survive. I knew I *would* survive—I'd continue to eat and sleep and breathe—I just didn't know how I'd learn to live my life again in this new land of grief. It seemed more than I could manage.

I thought about Tristan's radiant grin and how it overflowed into a goofy belly laugh. I inhaled his young-man smell, distinctive through the veil of tobacco and Axe body wash. I tasted the love in his homemade gnocchi, prepared specially for his grandma on her birthday, and felt his solid warmth as he hugged me and said, "Love you, Mom," on his way out in the morning.

I remembered Tristan's beauty, his kindness, his big heart. It occurred to me I might find clues to my survival in those memories.

When I was ready, I thought, I'd look for them there.

AS THE weeks passed, I was often angry at random young men for being alive when Tristan wasn't, and even angrier at older men for living so long. What a surplus of years they carried. I learned to brace myself for anger before leaving the house and breathe deeply to release the anger when I returned home.

Early in Tristan's recovery, when he was learning to navigate his own raw emotions, he'd told me how he'd focus on the idea that an uncomfortable feeling was not a fact. "Feelings are just feelings," he'd told me, during one of our visits at Westgate. "They're like waves. They come and they go and then another one comes. I'm learning that I don't need to react to every feeling I have like it's a forever truth. I just name them, acknowledge them and then let them go if I can, or talk them out with a buddy. But most of all, I'm not supposed to act on big feelings when I'm feeling them." He smiled. "That's the hard part."

I knew I wouldn't act on my anger, but I didn't like holding it so close. I disliked the tension in my body, the narrowness of my thoughts, the inability to see from another's perspective. I knew my feelings were skewed with grief, that I didn't really wish that all these men on the street were dead; they weren't to blame for Tristan's death, even if it felt that way to me. *These are just feelings, not facts*, I told myself. *They're not forever*. I tried to soften my anger by refocusing my thoughts on something more positive: the weather, my lunch or Emily's beautiful smile.

One afternoon, I walked to the market at the Quay to buy vegetables and stroll along the boardwalk. Thin October sunshine peeked at me, now and again, from behind the clouds, its warmth a reluctant gift. As I approached the market, my sweater wrapped tightly around me, I noticed three young men in front of me. Two of them had Westgate's branded blue lanyards hanging from their back pockets, no doubt holding the key that indicated they were Gate Boys. More than just a key to the house, it represented community, connection, recovery. At least it had to Tristan, when he had tucked it in his back pocket, lanyard hanging out in just the same way.

I was taken back to the last time I followed three Gate Boys. It was early December, less than a year before, when Tristan and two of his friends, Jack and Ryder, had come with me to do some last-minute Christmas shopping.

As we'd walked into the mall, I'd imagined we created quite the picture: a harried-looking middle-aged woman tagging along behind three tattooed guys in their twenties, branded lanyards from an addiction treatment centre dangling from their pockets. They were laughing and jostling each other like a pack of large puppies, rambunctious and unpredictable, always eager to please; I was relaxed and smiling, comfortable and happy to be around Tristan's friends. That was still such a new feeling at that time that it seemed fantastical. I felt so grateful for that moment, and for all the possibilities that came with recovery.

Passing a Winners store, we popped in to look for a scarf I wanted to get Jenn for Christmas. Ryder and Tristan wandered off through the aisles in search of who knows what. Jack, though, stayed to help me find the perfect scarf. He asked me about Jenn's taste in clothing and the jacket she wore, and then spotted a sale on Michael Kors scarf and toque sets.

"Oh, you have to get her these! All girls love Michael Kors, it doesn't even matter what it is or what it looks like—they just have to have it, seriously. This one is pretty sweet." He held up a black and gold set, hopeful. "I have a sister," he added, as if that gave him credibility. After a lively discussion, we agreed on a white and gold set; they were Jenn's favourite colours. Walking to the till, he stopped abruptly and said, "But don't get it just 'cause I said so! Like, if it's too much money or you want something different, that's totally cool." Jack looked so concerned it made my heart swell. I assured him it was perfect, and it was.

I was extra glad to have the boys along when we finally got my artificial Christmas tree, which had been the main goal, as it would have been impossible for me to carry it on my own. It was only a six-footer but came in a huge rectangular box with two handles, one on each end. Two of the guys could have easily carried it, and one in a pinch, but they found a way for all three to participate, laughing and stumbling their way to my car.

When I dropped them off at Westgate, Tristan came to the driver's side window and leaned in to hug me. "Thanks for everything, Mom," he said. "They were both having a bad day, Ryder especially. It meant a lot to them to come along."

Now, a year later, I appreciated that on a whole new level. Such good memories. Such love and hope and innocence, almost. Just a sweet day together, not a drop of grief in sight.

I realized I'd passed the vegetable market and was still following those three Gate Boys, close enough to hear their laughter but not their words. I imagined one of them was Tristan, laughing with his friends, strong in his recovery.

The tallest of the three held the door open to the main market for the other two and glanced behind him.

"Oh! Tristan's mom!" he said, catching sight of me still a dozen feet away. He let the door close and walked over. He looked familiar, but I couldn't put a name to his face. "How are you? I'm so sorry for your loss."

"Thank you. Thank you so much."

"Tristan was such a good kid, always so positive and encouraging. Such a..." he searched for words, "I don't know, he was just so easy to love, you know? He helped a lot of people. I was devastated when I heard."

"Thanks. It means a lot to hear that." I nodded and tried to refocus my mind on the present, pushing away my reverie where, moments before, I'd been imagining Tristan in this man's place.

"It's like a war zone out there right now, with that fucking fentanyl—pardon my language," he added, looking at me to see if I was offended. "We're losing so many good people. Too many." I agreed, we were. "I'm just taking two new guys out for ice cream. I better get back to them before they start scaring people or something!" he laughed. "Nice seeing you, though. Take care."

"Thank you, good seeing you too," I said.

I watched him enter the market in search of his buddies and then sat on a bench outside. That man with the Westgate lanyard wasn't Tristan. It *had* been Tristan, not long ago, but never would be again. I took a few deep breaths and closed my eyes. I felt sunshine warm my face as I fought back tears at the unfairness of it all. It seemed so arbitrary. Tristan was gone and these boys were still here. But these boys *were like* Tristan, fighting the same hellish battle, finding joy and laughter in the midst of it, and committed enough to connection to say hi to the mother of one of their own.

I wasn't angry at these Gate Boys for being alive. In fact, I found myself, once again, overwhelmed by the possibilities of recovery. I hoped those boys would make it. They deserved to live good, long lives.

32

I COULD no longer go to Parents' Group, which had been my greatest source of strength and support for over a year. It was simply no longer the right place for me. I remembered how upset I was in my first Parents' Group, hearing about Mary's son relapsing. What would new parents think when they heard about a son who died? I wouldn't do that to them and I wasn't ready to surround myself with the hope other parents still had for their sons.

The step group I shared with the other moms—the strong, brave women who had become dear friends to me—disbanded. We hadn't even completed step four, but I couldn't continue, and our step work was the glue that held us together. Tristan's death, and Mary's love for her own son, spurred her toward a forceful advocacy, a determination to do what she could to save those she could, but without our regular get-togethers, we gradually lost touch with each other.

In search of people who understood, I joined *Moms Stop the Harm*, a support and advocacy group of Canadian mothers and families who've lost loved ones to drug harms. Through their Facebook group, I poured my grief out to those women and they poured theirs back to me, and we found comfort in not being alone. We reached out to each other on difficult days. We knew the anniversaries of our children's birthdays and deaths and said their names. These people not only understood what it was like to have your child die but understood the stigma and shame of addiction and the injustice of our systems of care, or lack thereof. And they fought fiercely to make positive change.

I added my voice to their loud chorus, raising awareness, rallying for changes to laws and policy. I sent letters and photos of Tristan to the Prime Minister and my MP. I spoke with the British Columbia Minister of Mental Health and Addictions. I attended rallies and memorial events. I did interviews with the media. For months, I channelled my grief and anger into action.

But the media and *Moms Stop the Harm* had their own agendas, weighed heavily toward harm reduction: decriminalizing drug use and providing people with a safe supply of drugs so they weren't reliant on the increasingly poisoned street supply. I supported those things, absolutely; I joined marches and wrote letters to improve harm-reduction services. But I wasn't passionate about them, like I was about improving access to quality treatment and recovery, about creating systems of support to help people move from addiction to wellness and joy. In interview after interview, my enthusiasm for recovery ended up on the cutting room floor and Tristan became just another face lost to an opioid crisis that demanded more harm-reduction services. The media wanted a simple story, and harm reduction was the solution *du jour*, but addiction is complex. I wanted every means available to save lives, but I also wanted support for our children to live fully, in health and wellness. They deserved nothing less. Instead of working together to save and support lives, the harm reduction and abstinence communities fought like political rivals, tearing each other down in order to raise themselves up.

It was exhausting and discouraging.

I stepped away from advocacy. I would have gladly gone back to my old life, but there was no path back without Tristan, and I didn't want to dishonour him by creating a new life without him.

So, I ran away.

I GAVE notice to my landlord. I gave my furniture and household goods to Jenn and Tanis, who seemed grateful. Jenn was now out of treatment and setting up a small apartment for herself and Emily.

Tanis had been making do with only bare essentials in the basement suite she was renting and appreciated some extras. Mom agreed to take care of Balloo, and to store the few boxes of things I wanted to keep at her place.

I sold both my car and Jenn's, and was surprised at how easy it was. Grief had shown me that I had previously been attached to many of life's details that were, in fact, entirely unimportant. Jenn's car was not my problem at all.

I spent night after night mesmerized by the endless options on Airbnb, where I found an assortment of lodgings in a variety of places within the twelve-hundred-dollar monthly budget I'd been paying for rent. My travel plans felt like a comforting but impenetrable wall that stood between me and my day-to-day life without Tristan. And there was no reason I couldn't work, when I was ready, from anywhere in the world that had an internet connection.

In early November, I was at the Vancouver airport with plans to be gone for most of the next eight months. I'd built a detailed itinerary: Portugal, Vancouver Island, Costa Rica, and Bali.

And then, I'd see.

IN A tiny apartment on the hills of Sesimbra, Portugal, overlooking the ocean and a small fishing village, I could finally let myself fall apart. Here, nobody could see me. Here, a thousand-year-old history reminded me that death is part of life, as universal as it is painful, and that life carries on. I imagined Sesimbra's cracked cobblestones soaked with centuries of mother's tears, its steep narrow alleyways a meeting place for mourners through generations. Grief seemed more at ease here than it did back home.

During the first few mornings, I pored through Tristan's journals for hours, sometimes laughing at the memories he wrote about, but more often crying in anguish as grief tore through me. "I loved to go against my mom or do things she accused me of to prove her right," he wrote. "My thoughts were, if she thinks I'm always doing bad things, then why should I even bother doing respectable things? I hated my mom for many years just because she was worried about me and didn't know what to do to help."

In a later entry, he wrote, "If I knew it would feel this good to be sober, I would of done it a LONG TIME AGO. I am so happy to be Alive and here!"

Further on, "I believe very simply that I am just a man with a drug problem. Yes, I have hurt those around me—my family, friends, strangers—but I have also helped many people, loved many people, and helped them grow as human beings. I am human. I make mistakes and I solve them. I cause anger and I cause happiness. I could be seen as a monster, or a guy with a good heart who cares for people."

And then, "I really want a healthy relationship with a woman. This is unrealistic at this moment. I want to have a true love and be happy... but I'm obsessing over having a girlfriend. My thoughts are toxic."

When I finished his journals, I pulled out his workbooks. I remembered Tristan stumbling on step four of his twelve-step program, frustrated about taking so long to write down "all the bad shit I ever did." These were not thoughts Tristan wanted to share with me. I placed his black binder on the coffee table, loose pages poking out in all directions, and questioned myself. These were Tristan's most private thoughts, experiences and feelings. Did I want to know what was in them? Would he want me to know?

I made my morning tea in the tiny kitchen nook and considered what I should do. The answer to both of those questions was "no," but it didn't matter. I *needed* to know. I needed to know more about my boy—the good, the bad, the tragic, his whole beautiful, tormented self.

Finally, I decided to go ahead. *If you didn't want me to read it, Tristan, you shouldn't have died!* I accused him silently, angry at him for putting me in this position.

Then I sat and began reading.

There were no real surprises, at first. He wrote about his lying and cheating and stealing—money from me and his dad, food from a grocery store when he was hungry. He wrote about how he'd called me names and walked out on every job he'd loved, how his pay-cheques went to cocaine and prostitutes, and how disgusted he was with himself. He wrote about his obsessive thinking and compulsive behaviours and the damage they caused, and about how badly he wanted to be loved, and how unlovable he became in his addiction.

He wrote about his need to be there for his dad after our divorce, to make sure he was okay. Tristan was five at the time. He wrote with heart-crushing remorse of the friend who overdosed in front of him while he did nothing to help. He wrote of his heartwarming gratitude for his family and friends, who loved him when he couldn't love himself.

It was all expected, until it wasn't—until something new hit me like a taser to the gut. First in a long list of bullet points, under the heading "Shame & Guilt," he confessed to having sex with another boy as a young teenager.

I stopped reading and took a deep breath. *What in god's name?* I thought. *When? Why?*

Then I remembered. When Tristan was fourteen, just months after I took him to the emergency department for overdrinking, Brad phoned to let me know that Tristan had been going to our local pan-cake house after school and wrestling with other boys in the back room while the middle-aged manager watched. As Brad demanded details from Tristan, red flag after red flag came up. Brad decided to confront the manager directly, threatening him if he didn't stay away from our son.

I believed now that this man had not just been watching boys wrestle but getting them to perform sexual acts with each other in return for drugs. Brad had done too little too late, and I had done nothing at all. Tristan had borne the weight of the abuse and his shame like an anchor.

I heard an awful moan—coming from me, I realized—and drew into myself, a tiny ball on a lumpy couch. Through my tears, I noticed dust particles dancing worry-free in the sunlight and I envied them. *What a wonderful thing to be a dust particle,* I thought. Then I clenched my eyes and willed myself to sleep, soothed by the distant lullaby of my moans and sobs.

READING TRISTAN'S worksheets didn't get easier. I had known, vaguely, that Tristan had been bullied through elementary school and junior high. I'd known in the way a mother knows when her son comes home from school quiet and upset, when he has a hard time making friends, when he doesn't want to talk about it. I didn't know about the names he was called because he was chubby and wore his hair long. I didn't know the pranks other children played on him. I didn't know how acutely his need for belonging warred with his fear of being ridiculed and how, eventually, his fear won out, drawing him into isolation.

I *had* known about the time Tristan had been beaten up by a gang of boys in his high school, but I hadn't known about the bookend event, the coming full circle later that school year, when Tristan was still fourteen. This time, Tristan had been the assailant. He called this entry "Grade 9 – Fitting In." There had been a group of boys he wanted be part of, "cool kids" who sold him smokes. He'd hung out with them a few times, and then they told him they were going to teach another kid a lesson for offending one of them, and Tristan needed to help out. "In my head, it didn't feel right," Tristan wrote. "But I agreed." About a dozen teens, Tristan included, jumped a small guy as he came out of the woods. Apparently, this boy had been expecting a one-on-one fight, not this gang beating that Tristan became part of. They punched him and kicked him. Somebody stomped on him. Somebody peed on him. Somebody took his shoes. Tristan felt sick and disgusted. "The most brutal thing I've ever been part of," he wrote. "I felt so bad, and everything that my dad, family, and teachers have taught me I easily disregarded in order to make some new friends."

Yet after that, Tristan did not count them as friends. He avoided that gang of boys, never wanting to be part of anything like that again. Instead, he found a more welcoming, accepting and less violent group of friends in the drug crowd.

That brutality would have messed Tristan up so badly, I thought, sickened by what I'd just read. This was the boy who rescued caterpillars on the sidewalk so they wouldn't get stepped on, carefully escorting them to nearby bushes; who took in an abandoned kitten when he was in China, keeping her in his room and feeding her boiled eggs until he got to the store to buy kibble. This was Tristan, who knew only too well what it felt like to be bullied and beaten.

The year he was fourteen was tragically horrific for my sweet, sensitive boy, and I'd had no idea. It was no wonder he was in full-fledged addiction by the time he was fifteen.

Heartsick, I closed the book. I could take only so much pain in one day and I was over my limit. I crawled into bed and numbed myself by playing Candy Crush for hours and hours and hours.

THE NEXT morning, before anything else, I forced myself to eat an orange and a handful of almonds on the sunny balcony. I watched gulls soar over the crystalline ocean. I was giving myself a pause, an opportunity to opt out of what seemed inevitable. Part of me wanted to stay in the sunshine, walk to the beach, put my feet in the sand, drink lemonade. I badly wanted to listen to that part of me.

Instead, I went inside and, with masochistic determination, opened Tristan's workbook again. *Surely, I now know the worst*, I thought.

I was wrong.

I read about how Tristan had been hanging out with a woman shortly before he entered treatment. They were using cocaine and meth. Tristan wanted to have sex, but the woman didn't. "And I had sex with her anyway," he wrote, "even though she didn't want to. All I could think of was my own selfish wants and had complete disregard for what she wanted."

I saw the words on the page yet I couldn't articulate the one word that screamed inside of me. I swallowed bile and closed my eyes, aware of the bitterness in my mouth, the churn in my stomach. I stood and began to pace in brisk circles, anger and nausea fuelling me.

I remembered the only other time I'd been unable to say a word. I'd just learned of Tristan's death and, after endless phone calls and empty staring, had finally come downstairs to find my mom and Betty waiting for me, electric in their fear and expectation.

"What is it?" Mom had asked, voice shaking.

I walked past her and sat on a dining room chair. I couldn't look at her.

"Is it Tristan?" she asked.

I nodded my head.

"What happened? Is he okay?"

It felt like every cell in my body was being torn apart and scattered into oblivion. With a heroic effort I pulled enough of myself together to speak one word: "No."

"Kathy," Mom said, clearly panicked, "tell me what happened. Is he hurt? Please, just tell me."

I wanted to. I needed them to know. But the word stuck, and I couldn't find it, let alone say it. "I can't," I gasped. And then I became frantic, scared that somehow, someone would make me say the word. "I can't say it. Don't make me say it. *Please* don't make me say it!"

Mom looked at me as if I'd hit her. I shut my eyes.

Then, I heard Betty's voice, compassionate and clear. It cut through the whirlwind of my emotion and gave me something to hold on to. It gave me the word. "Is Tristan dead, Kathy?"

I covered my face with my hands. And I nodded.

TRISTAN'S WORDS were on the page in front of me. His binder was splayed open, almost jauntily, as if it didn't care what horrors it held.

I stopped pacing. Tristan had never written the word that tore through me, the word I never wanted to associate with him, or with anyone I loved. Perhaps Tristan couldn't say the word either, so he wrote around it. Yet reality was reality, no matter the words.

And rape was rape.

I couldn't say that word, even to myself. But I knew that words mattered greatly, that speaking the truth mattered even more, and that pulling painful truths from the darkness within and exposing them to the light of reflection and a compassionate listener was the only way to heal. I felt glad Tristan had not stayed silent, that he had shared this with his counsellor and his sponsor, even though I was slayed by what he had needed to share. I said a silent prayer for that woman and for all women who experience violence and disregard at the hands of men. God knows, I'd been one of them.

I tucked the loose papers carefully back into the binder, slid it and Tristan's journals into the bag that held them, and returned them to the bottom of my suitcase. I wouldn't look at them again for years. I wouldn't even let myself think about what he'd written on those pages, although the knowledge of it sat dirty within me—his secrets, his shame, now mine to carry.

33

A FEW days after arriving in Sesimbra, I walked to the market to buy swordfish fillets, vegetables and fresh bread because, somehow, I still needed to eat. I braved the crowds and ignored vendors who held out cabbages or oranges for my inspection. I sought out the quieter stalls and, not knowing the language, pointed to items I wanted, trusting the vendors to give me correct change. The market was overwhelming—too many people and glassy-eyed fish on ice—so I didn't linger. In and out, eyes down. *Just get the job done*, I told myself.

Over the next few weeks, though, I began to notice the women behind the market stalls, laughing and gossiping with each other. I envied them a little bit.

In the late afternoons, I began a ritual of going to the beach, nestling my feet in the cool white sand and letting the glistening ocean blind me. I'd hold my grief close, like a worry stone. At first, if I noticed people at all, they were simply part of the backdrop. But one day I saw two small children laughing at the shoreline, searching for pebbles and shells, screeching as the waves lapped their feet, two tiny packages of overflowing joy. They reminded me of Emily, and I suddenly missed her terribly.

Once a week, I went to a small restaurant where I could sit on the patio overlooking the ocean, eat mussels with thick slices of toast and drink sangria or sparkling water. Sometimes an orange tabby cat slept on the chair across from me, a perfect dinner companion.

The owner of the restaurant was a radiant woman about my age who spoke a bit of English. "I'm Rita," she said one day, smiling as she placed my sangria on the table. "What brings you to Portugal?"

I told her about Tristan and my need to be alone. As I spoke, I was aware I should have spun a different story, said something easy and touristy so as not to burden a stranger with my problems. But I couldn't help myself. I'd talked to so few people about Tristan's death, and it came pouring out. She listened without interruption, her brown eyes holding mine. She didn't look uncomfortable in the least. She looked as if she saw me.

"Ah, life is hard," she said, when I had run out of words. "As mothers, we grieve. I do not have your story, but my grandson has deformities. He is eighteen months now and we save for his surgeries, but he will always be different. He will always have challenges. I don't tell many people, but you understand." She brought her hand to her heart and patted it. "Our hearts are full of love, and full of grief, no?"

I smiled and nodded my head, but a lump in my throat prevented me from speaking. I was so grateful for that simple human connection.

Rita suddenly smiled. "We must find joy where we can. When you come next, I'll make you a special meal," she said, and headed back to the kitchen. "A meal that will bring joy!" she called out before disappearing through the doorway.

A few days later, as I watched the gulls squabble on the water, I realized life was all around me and I was still part of it, decades of sunrises and sunsets ahead of me. I couldn't hope for Tristan anymore, but perhaps I could hope for myself. Maybe, I could hope to laugh again with friends, like the ladies in the market, or to lose myself in the innocent joy of decorating cupcakes with Emily one more time. Just *maybe*, I could hope to feel the fullness of human connection again.

As I sat on the beach with my back against the coolness of a stone wall, centuries old, I began to feel hope for my life after Tristan's death.

I'D PROMISED Mom I'd be home for Christmas, but it was excruciating. Everything reminded me of Tristan. His absence was deafening, yet people wanted to be merry.

Emily's squishy hugs nourished me, and provided me with sparks of joy, but mostly I just walked through the motions of Christmas as best I could, screaming and suffering inside. My stress overflowed into nightmares.

A few days after Christmas, I dreamed I was searching for Tristan in a crack house, trying to find him, to bring him back to recovery, to save him. I knew if I didn't find him soon he would die. Only *I* knew where he was, so it was all on me. In my dream, the crack house looked like a party scene from *Breaking Bad*: emaciated bodies lying amidst garbage, people shooting up or half-heartedly having sex or just staring at me with vacant eyes. I walked over these bodies, desperately searching for Tristan. I stumbled from room to room, growing more panicked with every second until finally I found him. I reached out to where he lay in a corner of the room, his eyes gazing lifelessly at me, his body already cold. Pain exploded, and I woke up.

I sifted through the nightmare in search of reality, urgently, as if Tristan's life depended on it. *Oh*, I thought to myself, taking deep breaths to slow my pounding heart. *It's okay. I'm okay. He's already dead.*

And that was the worst part. Not the nightmare, itself. That wasn't so different from many of the dreams I'd had. What scared me most was the feeling of deep relief I had when I woke and remembered Tristan was dead. And then I felt anguish and guilt for being relieved.

I spent most of that day in bed, crying, feeling like a terrible mother. I thought that, somehow, I must subconsciously be relieved that Tristan was gone. Yes, some things seemed easier now than when Tristan was in the depths of his addiction; it was easier for me to manage my own pain than to watch him in pain. But that wasn't what my relief had been about. It would make sense, in a way, to be relieved that I didn't have to fear for him or try to save him anymore. But that wasn't quite right, either. All day, I wrestled with that feeling of relief until I finally understood it. I hadn't been relieved that Tristan was dead in my dream. I had been relieved, when I woke, that I didn't have to live through his death again, that I hadn't somehow been swept back to the moment of his death. Instead, I was here, months later, still in a sea of pain, but inching my way toward an unknown shore. That was a legitimate relief.

FEBRUARY FOUND me in Ladysmith, a small ocean town on Vancouver Island. It had been six months since Tristan died, and I figured it was time to get back to some sort of normal, whatever that meant. I'd just started working again and was leading a large project with a global client, but my brain wasn't cooperating. I couldn't make the connections I once had and struggled to focus. Perhaps, I thought, exercise would help.

On my first day of doing online workouts with Ivana, the trainer I'd been working with before Tristan died, I cleared the floor beside my bed in the small studio suite I was renting and positioned my laptop on the table in front of the windows showcasing an expanse of ocean. I had no weights or other equipment, but Ivana assured me we could make do for a while.

"Let's start with slow crazy jacks," she said. "You remember these. Just one side, nice and controlled, and then the other." On the screen, I watched her model a slow half-jumping-jack, minus the jumping, on one side, and then the other. After crazy jacks, we moved to torso twists and then to slow jogging on the spot.

As I started jogging, I felt a now-familiar warmth rushing between my legs. I was wearing black workout tights and wondered if I could just ignore it. I continued to jog on the spot, knees high, for a few more seconds. More wetness, running down my legs this time. I excused myself and ran to the bathroom, blood dripping on the floor as I went. This had been happening for months—since the day of Tristan's memorial service, which seemed fitting. I thought I'd been prepared, but a super-plus-sized tampon and pad was no match for my body. I couldn't work out like this. Aside from the fact I was undoubtedly anaemic and had little energy, I literally could not bounce without bloody repercussions. After quickly cleaning up as best I could, I told Ivana I was so sorry, but I had to stop. My stomach wasn't feeling well and, anyway, I wasn't ready to begin workouts again after all.

After a quick shower, I lay on the bed, curled in fetal position. I was scared I'd never be able to function again. My emotions were sketchy and erratic. Neither my brain nor my body were working properly. I could give up on the idea of exercise, but I needed to work. I supposed I'd just have to slog through my project as best I could and not worry about being smart. The project would get done, and hopefully not too many people would notice if it wasn't done well. That thought saddened me, as I'd always taken pride in my work.

Tears rolled down my cheeks as I let my gaze wander to the windows where a double rainbow stretched across the horizon. I wondered if the rainbow was somehow a message from Tristan. I tucked the logical part of my mind into bed for the night so it couldn't tell me anything different, and then watched the rainbow and its reflection on the water until it faded into the azure evening, and then indigo, and then the ink-black darkness.

TRAVELLING IN this way was an odd mix of dream come true and living nightmare. I'd always wanted to travel extensively, to immerse myself in other cultures, but not like this. Where I might have felt like a great explorer on an expedition though the Amazon, I had so far felt more like a sickly cat crawling into the woods to die without witness. By the time I made my way to central Costa Rica, I was indifferent to travel. But I wasn't ready to go home and didn't know what else to do.

Three weeks after my arrival, I watched a hummingbird flit from flower to flower in the raucous garden that flowed from my tiny *casita* down to the main house and spilled over the hillside below, a tumble of reds and oranges and greens. I was told that toucans and monkeys sometimes visited the garden but hadn't seen any. I lay on a lounge chair in the warm shade beneath a large tree, laptop closed beside me. I was thinking.

Soon I'd have to walk the twenty minutes to town to get a few groceries, and the forty minutes back uphill. I had to time my shopping excursions carefully: late enough for the sun to have lost its most scorching heat, but not so late that I'd be caught walking back after dark.

But first I needed to make a decision. I'd continued to muddle my way through project work, but the internet here had not been as stable as promised. On video calls with clients, the video or sound often froze. Even with video turned off, using only audio, it was a frustrating problem. I needed a better internet connection to maintain any degree of professionalism. Was it time to go home?

I hoisted myself out of the chair, gathered my shopping bags, put on a sun hat and headed out. Perhaps the walk to town would help me think.

Flowers scented the warm air and birdsong broke the silence. I'd miss the summery heat and riotous colours of Costa Rica, but it was April already. Vancouver wouldn't be cold and grey anymore and the cherry trees would be in blossom. I passed the gate at the bottom of the hill, nodded to the guard who kept watch over the gated community and turned toward town.

Professionally, yes, the best option would be for me to go home. But personally, I was conflicted. I wanted to go home; I was missing out on so much. Emily was growing up quickly and I worried I'd become irrelevant to her. Jenn had just got a new job and was slowly and carefully rebuilding her life without me. Tanis was buying an apartment, a major bucket-list item for her. I'd agreed to pay half of the mortgage and strata payments, so we would be co-owners; Tanis could live in the apartment and we'd both have an investment for the future. But I was missing out on the exciting part of house-hunting with her. And Mom was not getting any younger.

I approached a blue slap-dash house on the corner and listened for the yelling I often heard when passing. I didn't understand Spanish, and I was glad. It was bad enough to hear anger and pain spilling out into their yard, landing heavy amongst the children's toys strewn about. I didn't need to know what was being said. But today, it was silent as I walked briskly by.

My heart went out to those people. Home could be a scary place, I knew. Everybody's pain magnified by each other, one dysfunction fitting nicely into another like a malevolent jigsaw puzzle that doesn't provide anyone with space to heal.

As much as I wanted to go home, I was scared. I still felt numb much of the time. What if my emotions were broken and I couldn't properly love anymore? Jenn had been doing so well, but what if we both slid back into our previous roles of "relying on" and "doing for"? I wasn't sure I'd have the strength to set boundaries. What if we all were so broken that we just couldn't come together as a family? What if they resented me for leaving them alone in their pain when they needed me these past months?

I rounded the corner that heralded the beginning of town. Skinny dogs lay in the shade and the street was lined with rows of houses in various states of care and decay. All the homes had porches. Elderly folks sat on rocking chairs, many holding babies or watching toddlers playing at their feet. My attention was drawn to one home, where four women laughed loudly on one side of their porch while an older man played guitar on the other side, the obligatory grandma on a rocking chair in the middle. Near-naked children shrieked and scurried in the yard, chasing each other. Behind an old truck in their driveway, I could hear more laughter and smell barbecue. I stood staring at the happy family on the porch and let their happiness wash over me.

To really heal, I realized, I needed to go home. I'd done all I could on my own and I needed to be with family again, to feel our loving connection, even if it was different than before. I didn't know how we would be a family without Tristan but I was ready to learn. I decided to get the next reasonable flight home and cancel my trip to Bali. I'd rather miss Bali than continue to miss my family for two more months.

I took that as a hopeful sign that I could still love.

34

EVEN WITH my broken heart, the love I had for my family was strong. In fact, it now felt almost desperate. I loved them and feared for them more than I'd loved or feared for anybody since Tristan's early addiction. Like a twisted vine, I couldn't separate fear from love. I knew that anybody I loved could die without notice or warning, and my fear wasn't completely unreasonable.

Jenn was doing well in recovery now, but it was early days still and what would happen if she relapsed? Jenn's ex, Alan, was certainly capable of drinking and driving, I thought. What if Emily was in the car with him and he got in a terrible accident? My mom, who I always felt was invincible despite having high blood pressure and COPD, was almost eighty years old. Logic alone told me that any day could be her last. And then there was Tanis. Living with type 1 diabetes for the past ten years had been like living with a sleeping dragon—as long as it's under control, life is good. But if something goes wrong—and it *always* does at some point, no matter how careful one is—it can be lethal.

I'd learned to live with the risks of Tanis's diabetes. Until Tristan died.

Back home in Mom's spare bedroom, I stayed awake at night, crying, convinced that Tanis was dying, alone, in her bed. Night after night, I planned her funeral, as I'd planned Tristan's during the years of his addiction. Every muscle in my body clenched, ready to spring up to answer a middle-of-the-night knock on my door that would tell me she was gone.

One night, with my mind wrapped tightly around thoughts of her funeral, I remembered a recent conversation I'd had with Tanis. She and I had been leaving the funeral of an acquaintance she'd met through a youth program for diabetic teens. This young man had other medical complications which, together with his diabetes, had killed him. He was twenty-six years old. The week prior, Tanis had been to the funeral of a high-school friend who had passed away from complications related to drug use. We were feeling the heaviness of too many young people dead.

"At my funeral, Mom, I want something uplifting. Like an ice sculpture!" Tanis said, smiling, as we walked past the food table on the way to the exit door.

"An ice sculpture? Like one of those swan things?"

"Yeah, that's so fancy! But maybe not a swan. How about ... an oyster? A big, giant oyster with an iridescent pearl in the middle of it. That would be super fancy, wouldn't it?"

I laughed. "It would. But what about a chocolate fountain? I thought that would be more your style."

"Oh, great idea! But why not both?" she said. "Promise me you'll get me an ice sculpture of an oyster *and* a chocolate fountain for my funeral. If it's all too expensive, skip the flowers. They're gloomy, anyways."

"No, you need to promise me that you won't die until after I do. I have first dibs. Promise me."

"Okay, fine, I suppose." She sighed dramatically, then laughed.

The dark humour of this memory soothed me, but it didn't relieve my fear—my obsession—that she would die. If I sent her a text and she didn't answer quickly, I'd panic and follow up with anything I could think of to prompt a response. Some of my ideas were more effective than others: I rarely got a response when I asked her to go for a walk with me but got consistently speedy replies when I offered to bake her favourite cookies and drop them off.

Every time we got together, I tried to sleuth out how well she was managing her diabetes and how often she checked her blood glucose levels. If she was tired or unwell in any way, I'd become alarmed. "Have you checked your blood sugar?" I'd ask. "Maybe it's high. Or low. When did you last check?"

"Mom, for god's sake, I'm having my period and had hellish cramps all night, so I didn't sleep," she'd say. Or, "I have the sniffles, Mom, it's a cold. Everyone gets colds." Or, "I think there must have been gluten in those pancakes I ordered; I should sue those fuckers."

"But that could mess up your blood sugar levels, couldn't it?" No matter what her response, I was like a dog with a bone and wouldn't let go.

Finally, in the midst of one of these increasingly frequent exchanges, she stopped me cold. "Mom, just back off. It's not helpful, and I'm starting to hate our time together. I don't even want to call you anymore, you're so naggy. I've managed my diabetes for ten years already and I haven't died yet. I know more about it than you ever will. Seriously, get over it."

It felt like a slap in the face, but she was right. I apologized and promised I'd stop, but my fears continued.

Things changed, instantly, on a hot June afternoon. Jenn, Emily, Mom, Tanis and I had spent the morning at a local park, paddling in a wading pool, watching Emily clamber over the monkey bars and eating our packed picnic lunches and ice cream bars from the concession. As I drove Tanis home, I had a sudden urge to spend the rest of the afternoon with her. The feeling was vaguely obsessive and fearful, but unfocused. I didn't reflect on it, then; I simply went with it. Only later did it seem like an angel's whisper.

"What're you doing this afternoon, Tanis?" I asked. "Maybe we could do something."

"I'm pretty tired, Mom. I think I'll just go home and relax."

"Okay, well, I could come in and make the granola for you?" I'd promised to give her homemade granola earlier in the week but had not gotten around to making it. Instead, I'd brought the ingredients so she could make it herself.

"It's a pretty hot day to have the oven on, isn't it?"

"Well, I suppose, but who knows when you'll get around to making it yourself?"

"That's true," she admitted, and I followed her into her apartment.

An hour later, the granola was golden brown and the sweet scent of toasted oats and brown sugar filled the air. But Tanis was crabby.

"Oh my god, it's so hot in here. I don't know why you needed to have the oven on for the last forever," she complained. "And the smell is making me sick."

"Go lie down then," I said. She didn't want me there and with her grumpiness, I wasn't sure why I still wanted to be there. I didn't usually invite myself into her home and hang out, but I didn't want to leave yet. "I'll just wash these dishes and tidy up. You can rest."

"Mom, I don't need you to clean up. Granola is done and I'm going to have a nap, you can go home now."

"I will, sweetie. As soon as I tidy up."

Tanis lay on her couch and closed her eyes. I washed the dishes and then dusted her coffee tables. I glanced at Tanis now and again, filled with vague anxiety. I swept her floor. All of this was out of character for me. We'd had a good day. There was nothing unusual about Tanis or me that day, but I had a knot in my stomach that was not going away, a knot that somehow tied me to her. I worried I was becoming truly obsessive.

When I couldn't find another excuse to stay, I approached the couch to let Tanis know I was going and noticed one of her hands trembling.

"Tanis?" I shook her shoulder lightly.

"Mmmm, wha'?" she mumbled, not fully awake.

"Tanis!" I said, louder this time, with a firm shake to her shoulder that would have woken anyone who was passed out, drunk.

Tanis's eyelids opened to reveal unfocused eyes, rolling one way, then another, clearly not seeing, and then closed again. Her arm reached up as if to push me away, but it only rose a few inches before its trembling forced it down. She mumbled and then lay still except for a constant tremor in her hands and forearms.

My heart raced and my mouth turned dry as I realized she was hypoglycemic—her blood sugars had become dangerously low. She needed sugar and she needed it now.

I knew Tanis had some Dex4 fast-acting glucose somewhere in her house because I'd recently bought her some. It was too late to give her tablets because she could choke, I couldn't remember if I'd bought her the gel and, even if I had, I didn't know where to find it.

"Tanis, where's your Dex?" I yelled, shaking her to see if I could wake her up enough to get a response, but she only mumbled.

I hurried to the kitchen looking for pop or juice or honey. Anything sugary. Nothing. *Shit!* Then I remembered the brown sugar I'd brought for the granola. I grabbed the bag and a spoon.

"Tanis, open your mouth, eat this," I yelled. She opened her mouth a bit, like a baby bird waiting to be fed, and I emptied a small spoonful of dry sugar between her lips. Her brow furrowed and her jaw moved up and down as the brown sugar stuck in her mouth.

Bad idea. I needed a gel of some sort. I went to the kitchen and put some sugar in a glass and added enough water to form a thick liquid, then tried again.

I dripped spoonfuls of sugar water into Tanis's mouth, trying to get it under her tongue where it would absorb faster. She moved around and my hand was not steady, so much of the sugar ran down her chin and cheeks. It had been three minutes since I'd noticed her hypoglycemia, and I figured I'd give it a few more to see if the sugar could turn things around before calling 911. Tanis would be so angry if I called 911 when a bit of sugar would do the trick. She would not want to spend most of the day in the emergency room, feeling perfectly fine.

I kept dripping sugar into her mouth, talking to her, trying to wake her up. Soon, the trembling in her hands subsided and she was able to form words.

"No more, that's disgusting," she said, eyes still closed. She turned her head away from the spoon, her scrunched-up face reminding me of when she was a baby.

"Tanis, you need to eat more sugar. You're having a low."

"No, I'm not, I'm fine. I'm just tired. Lemme sleep."

"Tanis, you're having a low and you need more sugar or else I'll call 911."

She turned her head to me and opened her mouth.

After ten minutes of spoon-feeding her sugar, she was still not fully coherent. "Tanis, I'm going to call 911."

"Fine, whatever," she said, and turned over, which signalled to me how seriously out of it she still was.

By the time three paramedics arrived, Tanis was on her feet and angry with me for calling them, but her eyes still looked vacant. I felt such relief, knowing that medical help was there. Her life wasn't in my hands anymore. Angry or otherwise, Tanis would be okay.

"I'm fine!" she told the paramedics. "Really, it's just a misunderstanding. I'm all good now." She moved her hands as if brushing these people away.

"That's good to hear," said the older paramedic, a man in his early sixties. "But since we're already here, let's check your glucose levels. Lance will do that for you—you won't mind looking at his handsome face, will you?"

Lance, a young man in his late twenties, sat Tanis back on her couch and pricked her finger to get a sample of blood to measure her sugar levels. I stood back and told the third paramedic, a woman in her thirties, what had happened. Lance looked up at me and asked, "You've been giving her sugar for the past... what? Ten minutes, you said?"

"At least. More than that now. Why?"

He turned back to Tanis and spoke to her. "Tanis, you're still only at 2.3 millimoles per litre, which is really low. To be honest, I don't know how you've been standing or talking. We're going to get some more sugar into you and take you to the hospital to get your glucose stabilized." He went to his bag, retrieved a tube of Dex4 gel and gave it to her to suck on.

Tanis could walk by herself but was grumpy about it. On the elevator, the older paramedic tried to reassure her. "Tanis, it's just one day in the ER, not a big deal. You gave your mom a pretty good scare. You don't want to die on her, do you?"

My eyes instantly teared up at the thought, and the reminder of Tristan's death. I blinked them away. Tanis glanced at me. "Nope," she said, quietly. "No, I do not."

We spent five hours at the ER, where Tanis had an IV glucose drip for much of the time, and her blood sugar levels were monitored every twenty minutes. I brought her a dinner of French fries and a meat patty, the only gluten-free options in the hospital cafeteria.

"I'm sorry you're having to spend your day here, like this," I said, scooching in beside her on the hospital bed. "I hope you're not mad at me for calling them, but I didn't know what else to do."

"No, it's okay, Mom. Thanks for being there. They told me I probably would have died if you weren't, so... I guess I can forgive you for saving my life." She smiled.

"What happened, anyway? Do you have any idea what caused it?"

"I think when I started to go low, my mind was foggy, and I thought my sugars were high, instead of low, so I gave myself more insulin. Which, obviously, was not a good thing."

"Why didn't you check your levels first?" I asked, before I could help myself.

Tanis just shrugged. "I wasn't thinking properly. I don't even remember it. I remember you making granola and feeling sick at the smell of it. And next thing I knew, we were at the hospital."

That was the terrifying part—how can you protect against something that can hijack your mental faculties, like diabetes?

Or like addiction.

A thought occurred to me. "Tanis, what if this is one of those moments where everything happened for a reason. I really didn't want to leave you today, which was weird. Why didn't I go home earlier like I would have any other day? Maybe part of me somehow knew this would happen."

"Maybe it was Tristan," Tanis said, "telling you to stay."

"Yeah, maybe it was," I said, leaning deeply into that thought until it wrapped around me like truth, comforted by the idea of Tristan being Tanis's guardian angel.

TANIS'S BRUSH with death didn't change her at all. In the days and weeks that followed, she just kept doing what she always had. She couldn't live a healthy and happy life fixated on the possibility of her death. She simply needed to live her life.

Watching her, I realized I needed to do the same. As I walked along the river by Mom's house one day, I thought about that. As I thought, I walked faster and faster, as if I could outpace my world and get to a place where I didn't need to think about such things. But I couldn't outpace my thoughts.

I wished that Tanis didn't have diabetes, but nobody could change that. *Life on life's terms*, I thought. Diabetes was a term of her life, and the fact that I had a child with diabetes was a term of mine. I wished Tanis didn't live alone, but that was her choice and her right; I had no control over that. I wished she'd monitor her blood sugar levels more often, eat more healthfully and do the many things that are easy to want for other people but much harder to do for ourselves—all the things that we, as parents, wish for our adult children. But none of those issues were mine.

My worry for Tanis felt very much like my worry for Tristan in his addiction. Had I not learned anything? I knew I needed to let go again and accept the fact that Tanis was, and always would be, at risk. I cried, knowing the effort it would take to release my fear and desire to control her situation, feeling already so worn down and exhausted by grief. I was soul-sad that not one of my kids got off easy, that even the one who avoided addiction still carried risks other people did not. I cried because I was so tired of being strong, and I knew how much more strength it would take for me to change my way of thinking, my worrying and fear mongering.

But I also knew I could do it, and it would be worth it. I had done it with Tristan—learned to accept that he was at risk without letting myself be consumed by fear, to offer support and ride the waves of inevitable worry while still paying attention to myself and my needs. I'd trained myself to have thoughts and behaviours that fed hope, acceptance and gratitude rather than the fear that was always hungry for more of me. I'd learned how to enjoy spending time with Tristan without fixating on him. And to a lesser degree, I'd done that with Jenn, as well.

I'd done it before, and I'd do it again. The only other choice would be to hand myself over to fear, which would ruin my life while not doing a damned thing to improve Tanis's. And it would, quite likely, destroy my relationship with her. That was not a choice I was willing to make.

Tanis's close call with death reminded me that life, while we have it, is what's important. We all die at some point, so why obsess about it? Nobody is immune. I didn't fear death for myself—I figured I was either here with my girls or wherever Tristan was, and either was fine with me. But since I wasn't likely to die anytime soon, I needed to release my fear for other people so I could live fully. It struck me as ironic that, to let go of my fear of death, I had to accept it as inevitable and unpredictable.

I walked slowly under the canopy of trees, listening to the gurgle of the river, and felt a familiar energy pulse through me. An energy of forward movement, of being aligned with the world around me, of stepping upon that bridge that held me above life's chaos and led to my own peaceful shore. I recommitted to defining my life based on love, hope, peace and now, also, grief, but never again on fear and dysfunction. I committed to enjoying the hell out of Tanis, and all my friends and family, for whatever time I had with them.

Instead of ending in tragedy, that frightening day with Tanis had somehow brought me back to myself. I knew, once again, that my life's work was simply to live, and to live well—to feel joy with people I loved, to be grateful for the multitude of blessings that filled my life, to share my hope and happiness with others when it didn't hurt me to do so. I remembered living that way before, and it felt comforting and warm and safe. It felt like home.

35

TO FULLY focus on myself, I needed to move out of Mom's spare bedroom and set up home for myself again. But first, I had to do one thing: take Mom to England. We shared a love of nineteenth-century British literature and had a lifelong dream of visiting England together. We'd talked about this trip as a future certainty but decades had piled upon decades and we'd never made the time—there was never enough money, there were too many other priorities, and we had all the time in the world. Tristan's death had taught me that "all the time in the world" was a lie. I would find the money, make it a priority and make it happen now. Staying at Mom's for a few months, paying minimal rent, helped. Credit cards got me the rest of the way.

Early July found us in the south of England, driving along narrow country lanes, through busy villages and around endless highway roundabouts in a large rental car. We walked around a five-thousand-year-old stone circle, tied a ribbon to a wishing tree and visited a regal manor house with a world-class zoo. We visited the cottages of Thomas Hardy and Jane Austen, had more picnic lunches and high teas than we could count (including one in a village where horses roamed free) and toured Queen Victoria's summer getaway. We lit a candle for Tristan in Canterbury Cathedral. And through it all, we relished each other's company.

I enjoyed travelling with Mom so much more than living with her. At home, I felt like a child, often annoyed by her prattling and never-ending instructions about how I should do things. Here, we were friends. In these unfamiliar places, she relied on me more, which turned our parent-child relationship on its head, in a good way. Every day had been easy, a comfortable flow between us from morning to night, focusing only on each other and whatever was in front of us.

One overcast day, toward the end of our vacation, we decided to have a relaxing afternoon reading our novels, snug in our renovated Airbnb farmhouse. Floor-to-ceiling windows framed golden fields, birds flitted about, horses meandered in their paddock. Yet I felt unsettled, anxious and unfocused. By mid-afternoon I had only read a few chapters of my novel, putting it down frequently to gaze out the window.

My phone rang and I startled. I'd been using my phone to communicate with Airbnb hosts and a friend of Tristan's whom we were seeing the next day, but that was always by text. Who would phone me here?

I glanced at the screen: BC Coroners Service.

Oh god. I grabbed the phone and went to the bedroom, my heart pounding. I'd been expecting this call for months but was still surprised by it. Ten months after Tristan's death, I was desperate to hear news—*any* news—of him. I took a deep breath and answered.

A woman introduced herself as the coroner in charge of Tristan's case. "I'm so very sorry for your loss," she began, her voice warm and sincere, sounding a little heartbroken in her own right. She must have made hundreds of those calls, just this year.

I sat cross-legged in the middle of the bed, pulled a pillow onto my lap as a makeshift desk, and grabbed a notebook and pen.

The coroner told me her report confirmed what we already knew: Tristan died of an accidental overdose. He had lethal doses of both cocaine and fentanyl in his system, and a therapeutic dose of his antidepressant. It seemed to me that Tristan continuing to take his antidepressant was evidence that he wanted to live. I tucked that information away in a pocket of my brain where I could retrieve it later, when needed.

The coroner asked if I had any questions. I had many, and she patiently answered every one of them.

She told me it wasn't unusual for regular drug users to take what was technically considered a lethal dose of their drug of choice—in this case, cocaine. They built up a tolerance so that what might be lethal for others would be just fine for them. The risk was that after a period of abstinence, a person's tolerance dropped, and they could no longer handle the doses they'd used before. In this case, though, she was confident it was the fentanyl that killed him.

"Do you know if it was actually cocaine, or could it have been crack?" I asked, remembering the burnt tinfoil I'd found in his backpack. Cocaine he would have snorted, but he would have put crack on the tinfoil, heated it with a lighter and then inhaled the smoke. Tristan would have been more ashamed of using crack and I hoped, if he had to die, he was at least using cocaine. But if he hadn't been using crack, what had he used the tinfoil for?

"No," she told me. "We don't know that. They're the same thing, chemically, in the body."

I asked if she knew whether the fentanyl was cut into the cocaine (or crack) or Tristan could have deliberately used it, perhaps thinking it was heroin, taking it together with the cocaine—a speedball, it was called.

She didn't know for sure. They hadn't tested any of his paraphernalia for drug residue, but based on what they knew the street drugs were like, and on people's accounts of Tristan being a stimulant user, they were assuming it was a poisoned supply.

Well, I thought, *that's a naïve assumption.* Not the assumption that the drug supply was poisoned—that was stark reality—but that Tristan, as a stimulant user, would not have knowingly paired his drug of choice with an opioid. He'd told me that he'd used heroin during his last relapse and was ashamed of it. He had felt his addiction was pulling him lower and lower every time it took him out, and he had feared for his life if he were to relapse again.

I turned to a new page in my notebook and asked about the specifics of Tristan's death and the paramedic's report. The coroner answered from written statements made by Tavia and the other roommate, whose name could not be released to me, piecing together the last few hours of Tristan's life.

Tavia and her roommate were both in recovery, abstaining from hard drugs and alcohol, but were comfortable smoking weed, which the three of them had done that evening while watching a movie and eating pizza. Tristan had appeared low on energy, was drinking lots of water and had gone to the bathroom a few times to throw up. After going to bed around midnight, with Tristan on the couch and the others in their respective bedrooms, Tristan must have woken up periodically and continued to use drugs. He was snoring loudly through the night and, around 3 a.m., Tavia had turned on the air conditioner to drown out his snores, not knowing that deep snoring with gurgling sounds may indicate an opioid overdose. At 8 a.m., Tavia had found him on the couch, pale and unresponsive, and phoned 911. Tristan was not breathing but the paramedics found a faint pulse and began rescue efforts, which lasted until 8:58 a.m., when he was pronounced dead.

After the coroner finished explaining this to me, I listened to the silence on the other end of the phone for a few seconds. Finally, I had no more questions, not because I had all the answers I needed but because I could ask no more; I could feel myself shutting down. My emotions, thoughts and feelings were turning off like they were tucking me in at night, keeping me safe by their absence.

I glanced at the time. I'd been speaking with the coroner for forty minutes and had never felt rushed. I was so grateful to her for recognizing that, while this was her job, it was my boy. "Thank you so much," I said, setting my notebook on the side table. "I appreciate you taking this time with me."

"Of course," she said. "If you have any other questions or concerns later on, please feel free to call me back and I'll help if I can. I'm so very sorry this happened."

After I hung up, I sat on the bed for a few minutes, aware of my Mom's presence in the other room. I didn't want to answer her questions yet, but I didn't want to lie down and escape into sleep either. I wiped my eyes and got up.

"It was the coroner's office," I said, in response to Mom's inquisitive glance. "I'll tell you about it later. I'm going to walk for a while."

"Good idea," Mom said. "Take as long as you need. I'll sort out dinner."

I walked through the paths between paddocks and hayfields and forest and let myself cry. Tristan had still been alive at 3 a.m. and could have been saved. If only Tavia had checked on him instead of drowning out his death rattle with the comforting hum of the air conditioner. I didn't blame her; she didn't know, just as I wouldn't have known if he'd been staying with me. And I was so, *so* grateful this hadn't happened at my house, that I hadn't woken to find Tristan gone and learned later that I could have saved him. It was far easier for me to forgive someone else for their ignorance than it would have been to forgive myself. I was glad I had sent flowers and a heartfelt card to Tavia after Tristan's death, knowing how traumatic it must have been for her.

It just seemed so random. Tristan might have been saved. He could still be alive today. But he wasn't.

THE NEXT day, the sun was out again and Mom and I were in the small castle-town of Arundel, having yet another extravagant afternoon tea with dainty sandwiches, scrumptious cakes and, always the star of the show, tender scones spread with jam and thick cream. But this time, we were with one of Tristan's friends from China, Arash.

"Oh, he was a little shite!" Arash said with a bright smile. "He used to make waffles in his room for him and Chris, his roomie, and the dorm hallway would have this gorgeous smell of waffles. But would he share? No, the rest of us were left drooling. Except once, I had some egg tarts I traded him. That kid would do anything for egg tarts. I'll always remember those waffles, slathered in Nutella. They were brilliant. Pretty soon after that, his waffle iron blew up or something, so that was that."

I watched Arash take another tiny sandwich from the tiered tray and pop it in his mouth, his eyes still sparkling at the memory. He was in his early thirties, almost ten years older than Tristan would have been, but Tristan had been the baby in China and all his friends from that time were older.

Suddenly, Arash looked at me with concern. "Hey, Kathy, maybe you don't want to hear stories about Tristan. Do they upset you? I can talk about something else." We'd already spent the past two hours together, exploring the gardens around the thousand-year-old castle. We'd chatted comfortably about the fragrant roses, the expanse of beautiful flowers, the town and the history of the castle, and what Arash had been doing in the six years since I'd last seen him in China. Arash had been charming and attentive to Mom as we'd talked about everything *except* Tristan. And that had been okay because I'd known that when we sat down together, over tea, the real conversation would happen.

"No, I love hearing memories of Tristan, truly," I assured him and then paused. "Memories are all I have of Tristan now and finding a new memory, even if it's someone else's, or sharing an old memory with someone new—it's almost like I get to be with him again for a little while. I'm *so* happy to hear your stories of Tristan."

"Okay, good, I've got a bunch of them," Arash laughed, but immediately became serious again. "And it's good for me to talk about him. I hope you don't mind, but one of the reasons I wanted to get together was because I feel bad that I didn't do more to help him. He was my little Shaolin brother. Hardly a week went by when we didn't talk on Facebook or whatever. I should have brought him over here, knocked some sense into him, or helped him get back to China. Shifu would have straightened him out for sure. I knew what he was going through, I did, but . . ." Arash paused, and shook his head. "We all mess up, you know? He was so young. I just thought there'd be more time, that he'd be okay. I wanted to tell you in person that I'm so sorry I didn't do more."

Tears choked me; so many people carried so much guilt over Tristan's death. "Arash, there was nothing you could have done. I do understand the feeling, though. I'm his mom. If anyone should have been able to save him, it was me."

"No way, you were such a good mum. Tristan always told me that, and I saw you with him in China. He was lucky to have you."

"Thanks." I smiled at the acknowledgement. "But you were also a good friend. It wasn't my fault, and it certainly wasn't yours. I don't even believe it was Tristan's. Addiction and a poisoned drug supply are to blame." We were silent as I poured myself another cup of tea.

"Arash," Mom asked, "were you there when Tristan saved that kitten and raised it up? Kathy, I remember you sending all sorts of flea collars and deworming medicine and whatnot over for that thing. What was its name?"

"Cheeky Charlie!" Arash and I answered at the same time and laughed.

"Oh yeah," Arash said, "she became our school mascot. She's still there, as far as I know. Probably always will be; she's a survivor, that one. I have the video Tristan took of her having kittens on his bed, that second year after he came back. He was scared she wouldn't remember him after being gone so many months, but she did. Moved into his room as soon as he did, and promptly gave him kittens!"

We shared stories of Tristan and China until the teapots were empty, our stomachs were full, and the other tea-goers had long since gone home. When we said goodbye, I thanked Arash and gave him a big hug. He wrapped me in his arms and hugged me back, and I imagined I was getting a hug from Tristan.

A COUPLE hours later, we arrived at our next Airbnb, a restored dairy house on a farm in Surrey. I said goodnight to Mom and went to my room. I needed to cry—alone. There had been times since Tristan's death when I'd chided myself for not letting myself cry around others, not giving them the chance to comfort me. I had felt selfish in my grief, but I hadn't wanted to deal with other people's concern, or their trying to fix me, or watch me, or touch me, or even understand me. I just wanted to cry, in my own way, without thought of another person.

Now, I needed to feel the pain of my grief. The pain that held Tristan close to my heart. I gave into it, was comforted by it, knowing that every stabbing jolt was my love for him.

I had felt such happiness on this vacation with Mom. I'd felt joy and connection when seeing Arash, as if he was an extension of Tristan himself. I now knew that I *could* be happy again, but I didn't want happiness if it meant letting go of my son. I would rather hold him in pain than lose him in joy.

When I'd cried all I could, I got up from the bed and opened the window to breathe the fresh air, scented with hay and sheep from the pastures nearby. A black cat sat on the fence, its shadow elongated by the setting sun.

How do I live my life, allow myself to be happy and still stay close to Tristan? I asked myself. How could I still feel him, without my anger and despair? How would I remember him when his story grew old but he remained young, if not through my pain? I didn't know but I didn't want to take the chance of losing him forever by loosening the vise grip of grief.

But then, as fresh tears trickled down my cheeks and my head tilted up to a sky just beginning to sparkle with stars, I heard Tristan's voice. It wasn't like the voice of God that I'd heard when I'd had a breakdown in the bathtub, years before; that had been a tsunami that had washed over me and through me, undeniable and life changing. This voice was more like the gentle warmth of the setting sun, soft and abundant with promise of a bright new morning. This voice was Tristan's.

I'm not going anywhere, Mom. Relax, already, go have fun. You don't need to hold on to me, I'm right here with you. I always will be.

I simply needed to trust.

36

I HAD survived a full year of firsts without Tristan—his birthday and Christmas, Mother's Day and Easter, the anniversary of his death—all of them days of mourning for me, with years more of them looming ahead. Yet, if that were to be my life, it was time to make it my own.

I had begun my recovery journey, the slow process of learning who I was and how to love myself, prior to Tristan's death. It seemed imperative now to continue that journey in his honour, and I was determined to bring recovery into all aspects of my life.

My home had always been a mish-mash of hand-me-down furniture, garage sale finds and kitchen appliances I'd received as gifts but rarely used. It was the household equivalent of a baggy grey T-shirt, practical but with no personality. I wanted a home that felt like me.

In early September, one week before my fifty-third birthday, I moved into an apartment overlooking the Fraser River and New Westminster Quay, smack in the middle of good memories of Tristan in recovery. I chose mid-century modern furniture for simplicity, bought houseplants for warmth and added splashes of colour to make me smile—table chairs in multi-coloured plaid, throw blankets in teal and salmon. I made sure that there were clean lines and lots of open spaces. Since Tristan's death, I'd lost the capacity to deal with anything unnecessary, and too many things in my space overwhelmed me. I didn't mind that I moved in with a beautiful living room and dining room, and a full and fun playroom for Emily, but with bare walls, only a mattress on my bedroom floor and an office space that held nothing but potential. It would come. I would take my time to collect things I loved.

Jenn and Tanis both lived in New West, just up the hill from me. Jenn rented a cute little apartment where she had Emily half-time and was working as a marketing manager for a real estate company. Tanis lived in the older but well-maintained loft apartment that she and I had bought, using the remaining portion of her education savings for the down payment. She worked as a medical office assistant and dreamed of getting a puppy. We were each setting up homes and lives that felt right for us, even though nothing felt right without Tristan.

When I could no longer distract myself with unpacking and organizing my apartment, I began the hard work of unpacking and organizing my thoughts and feelings. "Do you think I'm... emotionally flat?" I asked my friend Tessa one day when we were on a neighbourhood walk, sipping our bubble teas: oolong milk tea for me, taro for her. She looked at me and laughed.

"No, not at all. Why do you ask?" Tessa was vibrant, with an easy charismatic smile and natural red curls I envied. She was also thoughtful and analytical and took the time to listen deeply. We'd known each other for a decade through work, but had recently become friends as well as colleagues.

"I don't know, I'm just so tired of people calling me stoic or reserved or strong. Maybe part of me is broken and I'm missing out on something," I said. "And not just that. I've always been the calming influence, the one that people lean on when they're busy freaking out. Since Tristan died, I just don't have the patience for that anymore."

"Good for you!" she said. "Maybe that's part of an earlier caregiver role that doesn't suit you anymore. You don't need to be anybody's rock when you don't want to be. That sounds exhausting." We crossed the road and headed into Queen's Park. "And no, I don't think you're emotionally flat, Kathy. I've seen you excited about things and I've seen you in pain. I've seen how much you love your family, and you're a great friend. I think you're emotionally steady, which is a good thing. Do you think you have a habit of surrounding yourself with people who are emotionally volatile?"

I thought about that. "Yeah, that's probably true. In the past at any rate."

"Something to think about. We're not meant to be in a constant state of intense emotion, it isn't healthy. But if we grow up with emotionally dysregulated people, as I did—maybe you too—then we end up either overly emotional ourselves, or emotionally repressed because we're too busy looking after everyone else. Maybe that does make us emotionally flat at times. Either way, it's not good, but our dysfunction feels normal to us because it's familiar. Or the third option is to spend years in therapy, like me, and kinda-sorta get your shit together!" She laughed and tossed her cup in a recycling bin as we passed. We continued into the rose garden, admiring the radiant summer colours that had stretched well into autumn.

That conversation with Tessa reassured me. I'd been worried that I was doing *too* well since Tristan died. Setting up my new apartment, carrying on, finding moments of happiness. Through the *Moms Stop the Harm* Facebook group, which I was again involved with, I knew people had a range of different reactions, but many moms were unable to function after the loss of their child, sometimes for years. *Maybe they loved more deeply than I did*, I wondered, though I wasn't sure how that was possible.

I'd been measuring my emotional health against other people's emotions, healthy or not. *That mom isn't doing well, so why am I?* I'd ask myself. Or, *This person is so upset the dog chewed her favourite shoes, why do I not care about such things?* I didn't even want to be like those people, so why was I comparing myself to them?

I realized I had a knee-jerk response to question the worthiness of my own emotions when confronted with people who had a different emotional reaction to a situation. Recognizing that gave me power—the power to accept my emotions, to see others' emotions more objectively, and to build relationships with emotionally healthy people. It gave me the power to heal. And that gave me hope.

One evening in mid-winter, I trudged up the hill, yoga mat strapped to my back, to have dinner with my cousin, Kimiko, before going to a deep-stretch yoga class together. We chatted as we chopped vegetables and she prepared her version of *okayu*, a hearty Japanese *congee*, adding extra vegetables and an egg. After bringing the food to the table, we sat, and Kimiko spread her hands and said grace.

"For food in a world where many walk in hunger, for faith in a world where many walk in fear, for friends in a world where many walk alone, we give You thanks." Kimiko's words and peaceful energy spread a sense of calm, which I appreciated. And then promptly disrupted.

"You know what I really hate?" I asked, surprising myself. I hadn't been consciously thinking about Tristan, or his death, but it was suddenly on my mind. Kimiko waited for me to continue. "I hate when people tell me that Tristan's death was God's will, or he was taken early because God needed him, or some other bullshit. I just cannot wrap my head around his death being part of God's plan."

As a United Church minister, Kimiko was more in tune with God's plan than anyone else I knew, and I appreciated her progressive perspectives. She often referred to God in the feminine, as Mother Creator, and understood the value of Christian stories as allegory and parable rather than preaching them as literal facts.

"I don't think it was God's will that Tristan died, Kathy," she said. "I believe it was God's will that Tristan lived and healed and became well. That's her will for all of us—to live in a state of love and connection and grace. She'll always guide us in that direction if we listen. *And* humans have been blessed with personal choice in all things, and the choices we make are not always in alignment with God's love. I'm not just talking about Tristan's choices, but all of us as a society. Tristan was trying his best. But help is limited, people are judgemental about addiction and the drug supply is poisoned. That's why Tristan died. None of that was God's will. That's the society that we, as humans, have chosen to create for ourselves."

I thought about that as we finished our meal, and later through our yoga session, and for many months to come. The idea that it was not just possible, but *right*, that Tristan should have lived and become well brought me endless comfort. As did my new-found friendship with Kimiko, whom I'd known my whole life.

One sunny Saturday the following summer, I was literally racing from one spot to the next in a most surprising manner. "Hurry up!" I called to Leigha, then glanced back at my phone. "Mewtwo's about to hatch!" We were running toward a fountain near Metrotown, but Leigha's bad knee was slowing us down.

"I'm coming as fast as I can!" she yelled, laughing. She was wearing her signature black sports pants and aquamarine T-shirt, nothing that would impede movement. "I may be a slow old bird, but I'm not letting Mewtwo get away!" she said, continuing her uneven lope with renewed effort.

We'd recently reconnected over Pokémon GO, of all things. Tanis had introduced me to the game years prior, though she no longer played and I hadn't for years. But New Westminster was teeming with the imaginary animated creatures, so I'd taken it up again and, much to my surprise, game-averse Leigha had shown an interest. Now, we got together at least once a month to have lunch, play Pokémon and laugh like teenagers. With the help of other Pokémoners, we caught the prized Mewtwo and decided to rest up over lunch at Cactus Club, where we ordered our usual: Szechuan chicken lettuce wraps and a glass of chardonnay.

As we were finishing our meal, Leigha set her fork down and looked at me. "Sometimes it just hits me that Tristan is gone, and I can't believe it. He was such a sweet, kooky little kid." She shook her head in sadness, even as she smiled at her memories of Tristan. Leigha was one of the few people who regularly spoke of Tristan to me, and I so appreciated it. "Do you remember how thoughtful he was with my Katie when she first started at your kids' school? Tristan was, what? Must have been in Grade 4. He showed her around the school, made sure she knew where everything was and checked in on her at recess. It made all the difference to her."

"Yeah." I laughed. "I remember Tanis being surprised because she'd been convinced that Tristan didn't even know his own way around the school, after four years of being there!"

"And remember when he was a teenager," Leigha said, "he was happy to visit with us and our mothers—four old women quacking away, but he'd take the time to stop and say hi. How many young guys do that? And how about that lobster risotto he made us? Oh my god, that goes down as one of the best meals of all time." She drank the last of her wine and set the glass aside. "You're lucky to have so many good memories of him. Hold on to those memories. *That's* who he was."

Leigha was right. I knew that, and yet there was that dirty burden of shame that kept whispering to me: *Tristan did bad things.*

I loved listening to other people's memories of Tristan because I had already forgotten so much. I was terrified I'd forget how he felt, or smelled, or the quality of his laugh, or that telltale glint in his eye when he was being mischievous. I spent hours upon hours poring over old photographs: Tristan as a baby, Tanis's arms wrapped around him in a loving headlock; as a toddler, living his dream as a knight-in-shining-armour for Halloween; as a five-year-old doing his Incredible Hulk impersonation in his new purple underwear; as a ten-year-old, plump and long-haired, striking a musical conductor's pose in tuxedo with tails. So many photos of him breaking bricks and doing flying sidekicks, or proudly displaying the pasta or doughnuts or cheesecakes he'd made to share with family and friends. So many photos of him laughing with his recovery friends on hikes, in parades, having brunch.

He did a lot in his short life, I thought one evening as I tucked his childhood photos back in a box. He'd lived passionately. So many people had loved him. Those thoughts comforted me, lifted me up, allowed me to breathe.

But always, the whisper would breathe into me: *He did bad things.*

I'd push those thoughts away, every cell in my body knowing of Tristan's essential goodness, holding that knowledge like a life raft. But the whispers continued in my nightmares.

MANY MONTHS later, I was at home in the evening, bored and unsettled, and I found myself drawn to the closet where I kept Tristan's things. I pulled out his journals and workbooks, carried them to the living room carefully, as if they were fragile porcelain eggs, and placed them on the coffee table. I hadn't been thinking about them and had not planned on reading them ever again. But now, for whatever reason, I knew it was time.

I made myself a pot of jasmine tea and gazed out the window while the kettle boiled, watching the tug-boats pulling log booms and admiring the golden glow of the setting sun on the river. I wiped away a tear. Then I opened Tristan's first journal and felt an immediate surge of relief—of surrender. I was no longer repressing those shameful whispers; I was inviting them forward, where we could have a proper conversation.

For the first time, I acknowledged how much trauma Tristan had experienced. From our divorce—which had not been easy on anybody and my five-year-old boy least of all—through him losing himself in his efforts to fit in, and finding comfort in the escape of using drugs. In his short life, Tristan had been bullied, assaulted and abused, and he had also bullied, assaulted and abused others.

There was so much I had not, or could not, protect him from, so much of his pain I hadn't known or understood. I'd be haunted by guilt for the rest of my life, I knew. I closed my eyes and felt the soul-deep pain of knowing I hadn't been able to save Tristan from the nightmares I had feared for him, knowing I had played a part in setting the stage for those nightmares through my own ignorance and dysfunction born of generations of family addiction.

Hurt people hurt people. The phrase came to me as a whisper in my mind.

Yes, I countered. *And healed people heal people.*

In recovery, Tristan had begun to heal and share his healing with others. Three people had approached me after he died to tell me how he had saved their lives by listening to them, encouraging them and believing in them, and by sharing his struggles and sobriety with them. His sister, Jenn, was one of those people. And who had inspired my own journey of recovery if not Tristan?

To heal, Tristan had needed to acknowledge his challenges, his actions, his trauma, to share them with others and to own them. With work and time, they might have been transformed from shameful secrets that pulled him down into strength that brought him compassion and insight to help others. Like alchemy, his pain and trauma may have been transformed, but they would never have gone away. They had been part of him.

By denying Tristan's troubled soul, I realized I'd been denying his experiences, his budding strength, his *wholeness*. I'd been denying his hard work and healing.

I remembered all those years when I had separated my son from his addiction, whether it was his gaunt face and vacant eyes, or disgusting bedroom filled with garbage and worse, or the profanities he hurled at me, I had labelled that *his addiction*, not *him*. It was true on some level. I knew, without doubt, that Tristan's soul—the essence of his being, the part that made him *Tristan*—could never be marred by addiction. We all have an impenetrable kernel inside us that shines with our brightest potential. But that's the source of our divinity, not our humanity.

Separating Tristan from his addiction had comforted me, but it was a luxury that he had not been able to afford given the reality of his human existence. Even when his addiction had hijacked his mind and taken control of his life, as I knew it had, Tristan was right there along for the ride—sometimes enthusiastically, sometimes passively, and other times as a resisting hostage fighting for his life. Whichever way, *he was there*, living those experiences, having those thoughts, taking those actions. He lived with the damage of his addiction every minute of every day, and then put in heroic efforts to stop the damage and, wherever possible, reverse it. His addiction *was* him, just as surely as he was so much more than his addiction.

Yes, Tristan had been good and loving and kind-hearted—*and* he'd done bad things. Tristan had been thoughtful and empathetic and generous—*and* he'd been abusive. It was not one or the other; it was both.

Life on life's terms, I thought. I didn't get to pick and choose the terms like I was ordering from a menu. We get what we are given.

These thoughts soothed me. I could feel a softening within, a stillness where there had previously been struggle, an acceptance. I was no longer defending Tristan, or myself. I would always have regrets, as I knew Tristan had: we had both done things we'd been ashamed of, but we'd also both done things we could be proud of. We'd done our best, and I could be okay with that.

I wondered how Tristan's life would have unfolded, had he lived. Would he have landed solid in recovery, learned to love himself and helped others to heal? I liked to think so. Or would his addiction have kept him in pain, a hurt person who continued to hurt himself and others? I knew that was also a possibility.

"Oh, Tristan," I said out loud. "How would you have shown up in this world if you'd had the chance to keep living, to keep fighting?"

Silence answered me.

On a whim, I stood and walked to my closet. Reaching to the top shelf, I pulled out the carved wooden box where I kept knick-knacks and found the green silk bag that held a deck of tarot cards I'd gotten a decade ago, when Leigha and I had had fun reading each other's futures. I hadn't used them for years. I took the cards to the living room, shuffling them as I walked, and repeated the question: "Tristan, how would you have shown up in the world, had you lived?"

I sat on the couch, drew one card from the deck and placed it face up on the coffee table. It was The Sun. I looked at the large shining sun and joyful infant riding a white horse. It was the one card that personified health and happiness, freedom and fun, optimism. I smiled, laughing at myself for feeling relieved by the flip of a card, but I was happy to take that as a message from my son. I placed the card on top of Tristan's journals and workbooks, tucked them carefully back in their bag, and returned them to the closet.

Tristan had not survived to continue his healing journey and carry his message of hope forward. But I had.

37

"OH MY god, it's happening!" Jenn shrieked in a stage whisper, not wanting to attract attention. "I need water. Is there water?" I laughed and got a bottle of tepid water from the car. She took a long swig and passed it back to me. "Am I good?" she asked, taking a deep breath to calm herself, flapping her hands to get rid of the jitters. She was strategically hidden behind my car, in the provincial park's parking lot.

I looked her over carefully, from top to bottom. Jenn was beyond beautiful with her dark hair swept up, fastened with jewelled combs and topped with a veil that whispered its way down her back. Her make-up was impeccable, happiness and hope shone through her bright green eyes, her smile was as radiant as the Okanagan sun above. And her dress was the wedding dress of her dreams: a V-neck bodice softened with embroidery and leaf appliqué above an A-line skirt made of clouds of soft tulle. Her short train fell naturally into place, a swath of white fabric swirling behind her. She wore no jewellery but held a presentation bouquet of soft pink pampas grass and dried florals she'd made herself.

I barely noticed the tattoos covering her right forearm anymore, they were so familiar to me now. In the centre of those tattoos was the Archangel Michael, the ink of which included some of Tristan's ashes. He was her angel now, protecting and guiding her, too.

"You're perfect, sweetheart. So beautiful." My voice choked with emotion.

I was thinking about how hard Jenn had worked over the past three years to build the life she deserved to have—to be the mom she wanted to be to Emily, and now the partner she wanted to be to Damyen. Like Jenn, he was in recovery. Like Jenn, he had a child, Shane, just a year older than Emily, who was a driving force in his recovery. They shared a strong sense of family, a ridiculous sense of humour that kept them, and everyone around them, laughing, a commitment to working toward their goals, and a sweetness and compassion that made my heart happy.

I supposed I'd come a long way in the three years since Tristan had died, too. I'd worked at creating my life anew, with grief as a cornerstone rather than a millstone. I deserved the joy of this day, the comfort of seeing my child at peace and in love.

The sight of Tanis leading her dad, Emily and Shane toward us pulled me back into the moment. "Okay, here they come!" I said and gave Jenn one last glance of encouragement. And then all I could see was Tanis, stunning in her elegant blush-pink gown, her hair pulled up in a soft twist, her make-up as perfect as a model's. The heart necklace she always wore, engraved with Tristan's name, was the perfect finishing touch. She had a soft, natural femininity that she often covered with sweatpants and baggy T-shirts, but today she took my breath away.

"Tanis, you look so gorgeous!" I said as she approached.

"Mom, we got dressed together, and you've seen me already," she said, laughing. "I haven't added any extra pixie dust or anything in the last twenty minutes!"

"I know, I know, but it's different seeing you walking toward me."

"Grandma," Emily said, "can I come with you? I don't want to be the flower girl." Six years old, Emily was shy and nervous about being the centre of attention.

I knelt down so I could look her in the eye. "You'll be just fine, sweet pea. Look at you!" I said, leaning back to admire her angel-like dress, cascading blond ringlets and a touch of gloss on her lips. "You're the perfect flower girl and your mama needs you with her."

"Okay," she sighed. Then, as Jenn passed her a nosegay of bunny tail grass, Emily's eyes lit up. "Oh, they're so pretty!" And she was, once again, lost in excitement.

"Hi Shane, you look very handsome!" I said, sensing his awkwardness. He was adorable with his gelled hair, button-up shirt, vest and pink bowtie like his dad's. His expression was equally solemn and sweet.

Behind me, I heard Brad, proud father of the bride, greet Jenn and rain compliments upon her. As I stood up, he turned to me. "Hi, you look really nice," he said.

"Thanks!" I felt pretty too, for the first time I could remember. I'd lost thirty pounds over the previous year, had started working out again and was eating healthfully—most of the time. If anyone looked closely, they might even see a touch of muscle tone in my shoulders, proudly on display in my floral burgundy dress.

"You look great too. Are you going to take your hat off?" I asked. Brad was wearing a smart dove-grey suit and a black ball cap with sunglasses perched on top.

"Nope," he smiled. "It's my brand."

I laughed at that; it was true. I acknowledged my knee-jerk impulse to fix something that wasn't mine to fix, something that wasn't even broken, and then I let it go. What's the point of a small, casual wedding if we couldn't each be happy being ourselves?

Tanis and I made our way to the small group gathered in the park and found our spots close to where Damyen waited, looking a bit nervous, chatting with the celebrant who would officiate the wedding. It was a picture-perfect setting: the lake behind us, dappled sunlight shining through leaves overhead, an expanse of parkland around us.

I glanced around at the nearly thirty people gathered to celebrate Jenn and Damyen, most of them standing in their own family "bubbles," appropriately distanced from others during this first summer of Covid. My brother and his family were the only extended family on our side who had joined us in person, but Mom and my oldest brother, who lived in Ontario, were joining us via Zoom. Damyen had a similar number of family members attending, with the rest being a small group of their closest friends.

A few people moved from group to group, saying hi, but nobody was shaking hands or hugging. Only a few people wore masks, but we were outside and there was a gentle breeze. I liked the idea of a Covid-style wedding: fewer people, more space and a good excuse not to hug near-strangers.

Soon, the celebrant called for our attention. "Hello, everybody! On behalf of Jenn and Damyen, welcome." Her voice carried easily over the sound of birdsong and the occasional speedboat passing by. She was a stunning woman in her sixties, with short spiky silver hair, a contagious smile, elegant clothes and a bit of a bad-ass attitude. She was, herself, in recovery, with over twenty years of sobriety. She introduced herself, asked us to form a large, well-spaced semicircle, and then told us all to place our hands over our hearts and make a vow to enjoy celebrating Jenn and Damyen, life itself and a fabulous day of love. "And now," she continued, "the moment we've all been waiting for . . . let's get these two married!"

The air filled with Justin Bieber's voice, singing "Purpose." The guests at the back of the circle, closest to the parking lot, stepped back to reveal Emily and Shane walking down the grassy slope toward us, loping quite fast and very seriously—sweet little angels, both of them. Their eyes stayed on their flowers and the ring cushion, and I was terrified they'd stumble, but they arrived with no mishaps, each giving Damyen a big hug and then standing by his side.

Then Damyen's gaze lifted from the children and I turned my head. Jenn was walking toward us holding her dad's arm. My heart stopped. She was so beautiful. Not just her gorgeous bridal outfit with all the trimmings; *she* was just so beautiful. Everything she ever was and ever would be seemed rolled into that moment. She was strength, resiliency, kindness, compassion and creativity along with a splash of the dramatic.

Jenn stood beside Damyen, her grin lighting up the world. Brad gave her a quick hug and stepped back to take his spot among the guests. Damyen seemed lost in her smile.

The celebrant began to speak again, but I was so filled with love and happiness and pride that I couldn't hold on to her words. I wanted to drown myself in the sight of Jenn and Damyen, with Emily and Shane by their sides, and all that represented.

I listened more closely as the celebrant turned to Shane and Emily, and said, "You are their greatest treasures and the magic sparkle in their relationship."

Emily beamed hearing that and looked a bit mischievous. She loved teaming up with Damyen to pull pranks on Jenn, and I imagined she thought that jumping into the woods with Damyen to hide from Jenn when they went on walks together and then bursting with laughter as Jenn searched in all the wrong places was the magic sparkle she brought to the table. She, herself, was the magic sparkle in my life.

I shifted my gaze to Tina—the woman who'd taken Tristan home with her after his first relapse, giving him food and a safe place to sleep, and then rallying the recovery troops to come up with a plan to bring him back to recovery. And it had worked. Tina had brought Tristan back not only to his recovery family, but to ours as well.

Today, she was bringing my family together in a different way, using her iPhone to stream this special celebration on Zoom. My heart hurt knowing I could never repay the kindness she'd shown my family—quietly, confidently, with nobody asking, she'd stepped forward not once, but twice, as if it were simply what she did, who she was.

I refocused my attention on the celebrant's words as she honoured friends and family not here today. "One such person," the celebrant's voice rang out, "that remains not only an important part of this day but is an inspiration of change, a guiding light of love and in fact a part of this very union is Jenn's brother, Tristan." Her voice was uplifting, not sombre, and I was lifted by thoughts of Tristan, here and now.

"Tristan was the one who brought Jenn to her first meeting and got her into recovery," she continued. "If it wasn't for him, she believes she would never have met Damyen. Tristan's ashes were released into the wind yesterday, free among the wild sage and blowing grasses of the mountain above us. His spirit is here, celebrating with us, today."

I suddenly missed Tristan so much. A tear rolled down my cheek and I let it fall. I had thought I couldn't be happier than I was today, but of course I could be. If Tristan were here, looking dapper in his suit, sharing his laughter and hugs with us ... *then* I would be infinitely happier.

And yet, I wasn't so sure. My happiness at seeing Jenn and Damyen get married, my relief in being able to participate in this wedding without being responsible for it, my pride in everything that Jenn had accomplished not just for her wedding day, but for her life—those feelings were absolute and undiluted. My grief didn't change or diminish them, it simply added another element. My feelings were more like a symphony rather than a single, pure note. And, I thought, the beautiful joyous notes rang out even more clearly with grief as their backdrop. After all our hardships, I appreciated joy so much more than I had before.

Again, I refocused on the ceremony as the celebrant, in Tristan's honour, began to read a passage that Jenn and Damyen had chosen from his favourite recovery book, *Living Clean*:

Our capacity to love grows in proportion to the effort we make to show love, and our willingness to accept it ... The harm we've done, the pain we've suffered, the loss we've experienced all deepen our compassion for others, and our understanding of their struggles. Our real value is in being ourselves, not in spite of what we have been through, but because of it.

Tristan would have liked that, I thought. For all his faults, he had an intuitive wisdom about him. Whenever he was at his best—whether training in martial arts, cooking a fine meal or finding his flow in recovery—he was following his intuition, sharing his wisdom with others. At those times, he was never alone; he was learning from others, giving to others and building relationships. Here and now, he continued to share his wisdom through those words, and I was grateful to Jenn for letting Tristan shine on her special day.

I wished that Tristan and Damyen had had a chance to get to know each other. They would have gotten along: they were both sweet, sensitive and goofy, and they both loved Jenn. Tristan would have enjoyed having an older brother; he would have been happy to know that his older sister was safe with a man who respected her and treated her well. I hoped he knew.

Then it was time for Jenn and Damyen to say their vows, and they had all my attention. In turn, they pledged their love and commitment to each other, in a way that was uniquely theirs. They vowed to take each other as partner, friend, love and lifelong companion. Damyen vowed to have the patience that love demanded, to speak when words were needed, to share in the silence when they were not—and to take out the garbage, even in the pouring rain or freezing cold. Jenn vowed to love Damyen unconditionally for exactly who he was today, who he would be tomorrow and every day, for the rest of their lives—and to never put tomatoes, onions or mushrooms in any of her cooking or to at least hide them very well. They both promised to treat each other with respect, love and loyalty through all the trials and triumphs of their lives together.

After Jenn and Damyen exchanged their rings, the celebrant asked Emily and Shane to come stand by their parents. "As this ceremony is about two people committing themselves to each other," she said, "it is equally about two families blending and committing themselves to a future. It's about honouring inclusion and the power of love in all forms."

Damyen knelt down to make his vows to Emily, and then Jenn knelt down to make her vows to Shane. They promised to love them with all their hearts, to be their allies, to learn from them, to listen to them, to protect them and to treasure their individuality and independence. And in due time, they promised to earn their love, respect and true friendship. Then they gave each child a ring, similar to the ones they gave to each other, on a neck chain, and placed it over their heads, saying, "This ring symbolizes the beginning of our family, and we hope whenever you look at it, it reminds you that you are so loved."

My heart swelled. If I had any doubts that I could ever be happier than I was in that moment, they were put to rest. Jenn and Damyen were finally married, and I was part of a clapping, cheering, socially distanced crowd of love and happiness.

I glanced at Tanis beside me and saw her happiness and pride in Jenn. I remembered how much Tanis had resented Jenn as a teenager, and later in Jenn's addiction, and for good reason. Jenn had been angry and not easy to be around, and she'd kept stealing Tanis's clothes. Even though those times were well in the past, I had never been sure the damage between Jenn and Tanis could ever fully heal—until now, when I saw nothing but generous love and connection on Tanis's face.

"That was a great ceremony, wasn't it Mom?" she said. "Very 'Jenn and Damyen.'"

"It was. *So* good. My heart almost exploded when they said their vows to their kids!"

"Oh my god, did you see how Emily's face lit up? And I thought it was so touching how they read that piece from Tristan's book." I put my arm around Tanis and gave her shoulder a squeeze. I felt so wonderfully connected to all three of my children. One beside me, laying down past resentments in favour of present-day possibilities; one in front of me, stepping bravely into her new life with another; and one above me, who brought the gifts of recovery to our family without which none of this could have happened.

Tanis moved away to talk with her dad and I stood back, catching my breath and savouring the scene before me. The circle of guests had disbanded and was now a swirl of people waiting for Covid-friendly openings to congratulate Jenn and Damyen, or not waiting and crowding around them with old-style hugs and good wishes.

Shane was running fast as lightning, leaning low with arms straight behind him, in a supersonic-superhero-something-or-other that reminded me of Tristan as a boy—pure energy.

I saw Aaron say something to Emily and point toward her little white parasol, which she had rested against a tree. This was the same Aaron who had been one of Tristan's best friends, who'd held Tristan through Jenn's thirty-day meeting when he was just coming back two days sober after relapsing, broken and ashamed, but needing to be there to show Jenn how much he loved her. Now Aaron was one of Jenn's best friends. I knew he still struggled with his own sobriety, but nothing would have prevented him from being at Jenn's wedding, clear-eyed and clear-minded. He was here for both Jenn and Tristan.

Emily passed Aaron her parasol; Aaron opened it and ran to Jenn, putting one arm around her and raising the parasol high with the other. He bent his knee and threw his head back just in time for the photographer to capture that moment, Aaron and Jenn both with smiles top models would envy.

As I made my way toward Jenn and Damyen, Anna approached me—another picture of perfection in blush-pink. Anna was Jenn's maid of honour, a role more of recognition than responsibility given the informality of the wedding. Anna was Jenn's soul sister and had been by her side since they were in treatment together. She'd been with us the evening I drove the Manor Girls to the speaker's meeting, in a car full of laughter and recovery that was the perfect antidote to my worries about Tristan relapsing again. Anna had been by Jenn's side when they'd both skipped out of treatment a month early and had stayed by Jenn's side after Tristan had died, keeping her safe and wrapped in love until Jenn could breathe on her own again. She had been with us when we'd bought Jenn's wedding dress (or, more accurately, I had been with them), and through all of Jenn's trials and celebrations over the past three years.

"Hi Mom," she said, smiling broadly. It still warmed my heart when my kids' recovery friends called me Mom. "Can you remember back three years? I bet you never thought this was possible then!" She laughed. "We were so crazy, who could have known Jenn would turn out so well?"

I laughed along with her and caught the unexpected scent of sage on a gentle breeze. "I knew she would. You *both* have done so well," I said, and meant it. There was nobody more kind-hearted and hard-working than Anna. "Even three years ago, you guys were both so committed to your recovery, doing the next right thing, always. I knew this was possible. And really," I said, looking around at all the love and friendship surrounding us, "isn't this the point of working so hard? Why you do it? Not to get married, I mean, but to have the life you always dreamed of? Maybe three years ago *you* guys didn't know you could get to where you are today, but *I* sure did."

We chatted a bit more about her own wedding coming up the following year, and then I made my way over to Jenn and Damyen and gave them each a big hug—Covid be damned.

BACK IN my hotel that night, Emily asleep by my side, I reflected on the day.

Grief had been a constant bass note. For all the ways we'd recognized Tristan and included him in the day, he had not been there in body. I couldn't hug him or smell him or hear him laugh, or say, "Yes, your tie is perfect and you look oh-so-handsome." He wasn't where he belonged, and his absence burned like phantom pain.

Fear had fluttered against me, too, in soft percussive strokes, light enough to easily brush away, but persistent enough to make itself known. *Bad things happen in life*, it whispered. Marriages fail, loved ones die, children grow up troubled and turn to drugs for comfort. My fears were not wrong, I knew. The only guarantee was that life would go on, with all its inevitable ups and downs.

Stronger, much stronger, than either of those two emotions had been the solid brassy notes of hope. My hope now expanded through future generations. Emily was not destined to live with a mother sick in addiction, hiding herself in a bottle; she would have a proud, strong, sober mom and a stepdad too, who had the bravery and resiliency to live their lives well, joyfully, connected. I knew they may need to wrestle their demons into the mud at times but, either way, my family's demons were out in the open where demons never thrive, and Emily would see that. She would learn that sometimes bad things happen, both inside and outside of us, but they can be talked about, shared and dealt with. That gave me so much hope.

And love. The overarching melody of the day was love. Love and gratitude rising to a crescendo, far above everything else. That day, love for Jenn and Damyen brought us together, but it was love for each other, for all our family and friends, that held us. Every heart that gathered was filled with love, the sun shone love's light on us and the breeze blew love around like confetti until my heart and soul and eyes and ears were swollen with it. These were my people, my loves, and they were perfect.

The magic sparkle, though, the high note of my day, was joy. Where love stretched my soul, expanding me forever, joy simply chimed in, playful, light and easy. There was nothing significant in my joy other than the fact that it existed. Light and airy, joy was a visitor come knocking on the breeze, here, then gone, then back again, sometimes in surprising ways and places.

Through it all was Tristan. Ever-present in my day, not just through all I was feeling, but *in* all I felt. Tristan was my grief, and an inseparable part of my fear, hope, love and joy. He was with me, that day, as always, in everything I did and in everything I felt.

I turned to Emily, peaceful and innocent beside me, tucked the sheets under her chin and kissed her forehead.

"That's from Uncle Tristan, sweet pea," I whispered. "Sleep well. Live well."

IN TRISTAN'S
WORDS

FORGIVENESS LETTER to himself, July 24, 2017—written one month before he died.

Dear Tristan,

I know you have been through a lot and have had some tough times. And this past year has not been easy for you. Firstly, I just wanted to say I love you. And I am so proud of you for coming back again and again and not giving up before the miracle happens. You have been living in depression and fear of failure for far too long. Shame and guilt doesn't have to be your life story. You are young still at 21 years old with your whole life ahead of you. You have accomplished so much in life already and I am so proud of you. Martial arts competitions, traveling, living on your own for years in another country where they don't speak English, culinary school, working in some of the best restaurants in Canada, and going through the process of recovery. Today you're clean and not using. You have stopped the damage and stopped digging. The past doesn't define who you are, it's what you do today that matters. I know you have family and friends that love you and are there for you. Whenever times get tough remember you are not alone. You are a caring person with an exciting and rewarding life ahead of you. I love you, man. And if I can forgive you, so can you.

Love, Tristan.

ACKNOWLEDGEMENTS

OVER THE past five years I've learned that while writing may be a solitary activity, writing a *book* requires a community. And I'm so grateful for mine.

First, and always, I'm eternally grateful to my family. To Jenn and Tanis: thank you for generously giving me free rein to tell my story, my way, even when it meant telling an incomplete version of yours. You are so much more than I conveyed on these pages, and you mean more to me than I can ever say. To Mom: thank you for being my number one cheerleader and for teaching, by example, unconditional love. And to "Emily" (you know who you are!): you will always be the magic sparkle in my life.

I want to acknowledge family and friends who have been essential in my life and Tristan's but do not appear in this book or appear only briefly. Dave, Mike, Laura, Alex, Julia, and Zach, your absence here was an editorial decision and fails to reflect your huge presence in our lives and the unquestionable impact you had on Tristan and me during the years I wrote about. You were, are and always will be incredibly important to us both.

I'm very grateful to have found such a supportive network through my writing. To my weekly writing partners, Annie Newman and Mary-Jo Campbell, who've been by my side from the beginning: thank you for your encouragement, laughter and thoughtful critiques, which have held me and kept me moving forward even when I didn't know where forward was. To my writing coaches from The Narrative Project, Cami Ostman and Anneliese Kamola: thank you for your support and wisdom through an emotionally difficult writing process. You were an important part of my healing and this book would not be here if not for you. I'm grateful to the Banff Centre for Arts and Creativity for providing me with an invaluable writing retreat under the mentorship of the brilliant Matthew J. Trafford. Thanks to the writers in the Facebook group Canada Writes for being available whenever I needed a jolt of encouragement or rapid feedback, and to my beta readers, Lisa Dailey, Jessica Stewart, Dana Tye Rally, Laurie Mueller, Diane Wood, Diedre Hammons and Cynthia Machamer. You showed me how an early version of this book was terribly broken while still managing to provide enough encouragement to make me want to fix it. Thanks to my early editors, Laurel Leigh and Anneliese Kamola, who managed the perfect blend of ruthlessness, warmth and professionalism in helping me get my manuscript ready for agents and publishers.

I won the lottery when I landed with Douglas & McIntyre. Anna Comfort O'Keeffe, thank you for believing in my story and being a true partner in bringing my book to life. Rachel Rose, your artful insights and encouragement have not only made this a better book but have brought me greater peace and acceptance. Lynne Melcombe, thank you for your attention to detail as you smoothed the many remaining rough edges, large and small.

To all my other writing mentors, reviewers and cheerleaders along the way: thank you! And to you, dear readers: thank you for hearing my story. I wish you love, hope and peace throughout your journey. You are not alone.

I also want to thank one special person who absolutely gave it her all—and that's me. In keeping with my ongoing commitment to self-love and acknowledgement, I want to say how freakin' proud I am of myself for doing this! It was heart-wrenching, healing work. I put more of myself on the page than I ever thought possible, and more of my son than I ever expected. I had to wrestle with words in a way that felt beyond my skills and ability. I wanted to give up numerous times, but I didn't. None of it was comfortable. All of it was hard. Every bit of it was worth it and I'm so glad I persevered.

And always, Tristan: thank you for continuing to inspire me and for being my son. This Hoʻoponopono prayer is my message to you, echoed in every beat of my heart, every minute of every day:

I am sorry. Please forgive me. Thank you. I love you.